EDWIN VINCENT O'HARA

Bishop Edwin Vincent O'Hara conducting an informal confraternity class in the Church of St. Mary of Tears, Rome, August 30, 1948.

Edwin Vincent O'Hara

AMERICAN PRELATE

By J. G. Shaw

FOREWORD BY
MATTHEW F. BRADY
Bishop of Manchester

FARRAR, STRAUS AND CUDAHY

NEW YORK

Nihil obstat
  John A. Goodwine, J.C.D.
    Censor Librorum

Imprimatur
  ✠ Francis Cardinal Spellman
    Archbishop of New York

The nihil obstat and imprimatur are official declara
tions that a book or pamphlet is free of doctrinal or
moral error. No implication is contained therein that
those who have granted the nihil obstat and the imprimatur agree with the contents, opinions or statements expressed.

Published simultaneously in Canada by Ambassador Books, Ltd.,
Toronto. Manufactured in the U. S. A.
American Book–Stratford Press, Inc., New York

To

MRS. ANNA DANIELS

a gracious lady who gave
her brother his first schooling
and shared his years of achievement
this book is dedicated in
admiration, friendship and respect.

Foreword

FROM THESE PAGES there emerges the life-like figure of a priest and prelate of whom a discerning American Cardinal said short years ago, "Under the inspiration of St. Pius X, he has been and is the great catechist in the Church in the United States." That title alone justifies the recording of the simple but significant life of Edwin Vincent O'Hara, who was the father and organizing spirit of the Confraternity of Christian Doctrine in this country.

Every age in progress has its distinguishing marks and the first half of this century has witnessed in the Church the great surge of Catholic Action, that "participation of the laity in the salvation of souls under the direction of the hierarchy." The apostolate of the laity is on the march and coming to its own. Both the Holy See and the Apostolic Delegate have called the Confraternity of Christian Doctrine the finest form of Catholic Action.

God's wisdom moves in mysterious ways and God's finger touched the soul of a farm boy in Minnesota, endowed him with a keen analytical mind, a flair for organization, and encompassed him with circumstances of life and early assignments in the priesthood, to fashion an instrument that was to play an important role in a great crusade. To all this He added a gentleness of spirit, a calm of manner and a deceptive hesitancy of approach that were but a cloak for dynamic activity.

There were two motives, "lamps to his feet," that drove and directed Archbishop O'Hara's activity: a profound realization of the teaching responsibility of a priest; and a simple wholehearted acceptance of the directives of the Holy See. The wisdom of Leo XIII guided his thinking on the Minimum Wage Law and the Oregon School Question; the judgment of Saint Pius X inspired his teaching in Catholic Rural Life and in the Confraternity of Christian Doctrine. "We are forced to agree with those who hold that the chief cause of the present indifference and as it were infirmity of soul, and the serious evils that result from it, is to be found above all in ignorance of things divine" (Acerbo nimis). Once he anxiously asked the present Holy Father how long it would take for the canonization of Pius X. "The answer," His Holiness replied, "is prayer. Prayer will bring miracles and miracles will bring the approbation of the Church." That was enough to start a great crusade of prayer and none more humbly happy and thankful than our prelate when he stood in the throng that witnessed the solemn ceremony of canonization.

The Confraternity of Christian Doctrine is the monument of Archbishop O'Hara. Other activities that occupied his energy, the revision of the Catechism, the new English translation of the Bible, the use of English in the ritual, were but corollaries of the all-consuming interest in teaching eternal truth. This was the fulfillment of Our Blessed Lord's mission, "I have come to cast fire on the earth and what will I but that it be enkindled" (Luke XII, 49). The Confraternity is a movement, still in lusty infancy, but growing apace toward maturity. It is reaching toward the stars and beyond—to the Eternal Kingdom of God.

Along the way a vast legion of co-workers from all ranks of life, a legion that finds new recruits daily, labored valiantly in the work. They heard no intense exhortation and felt no compulsion but somehow or other at the humble almost hesitant approach of the leader found themselves swept along with a crusader's spirit in a new but divine undertaking. The good Archbishop was as unconscious of his own effulgence as is the candlelight that burns bravely in the surrounding darkness.

We commend this volume to the thoughtful reading of prelate, priest, and layman that all may find added inspiration to enkindle divine fire, to be grateful for the spark already struck by Archbishop O'Hara and bring it to all-consuming flame.

✠ Matthew F. Brady
Bishop of Manchester
February 8, 1957

Contents

INTRODUCTORY NOTE

EDWIN VINCENT O'HARA was born on a farm and things kept growing up around him all his life. They didn't grow unassisted and they weren't just any old things. They grew from planning, plowing, sowing, and knowledgeable care. They were good things, healthy things, things basically necessary—wheatlike things. Things like the first minimum wage law to stand the test of the United States Supreme Court, or the national Catholic Rural Life Conference, or America's Confraternity of Christian Doctrine, or a new translation of the Bible, or a revision of the catechism, or the first use of English in the Roman Catholic ritual.

It is not that Edwin O'Hara was the seed from which all these sprang. Nor did he even plant all the seed himself or harvest it alone. But he was the good farmer who knew what crops were needed, what ground was suited to them and how much work it would take to make that ground bear most of that crop. He also knew how to work, and, a rarer quality still, how to inspire those around him with some of his own quiet satisfaction in the dignity of doing things well.

So in telling the story, as the present writer first set out to do, of the Confraternity of Christian Doctrine in the United States, we must go back to a farm boy in Minnesota whose habits took form from his daily chores and whose ideals were rooted in his Catholic faith. In tracing that story we find that a little redheaded Minnesota farm boy grew up to be the Roman Catholic bishop of Kansas City, Mo.

We also find that in Kansas City, as in all four cities in which he spent the fifty-one years of his priesthood, the same man was regarded by people of all faiths as a model citizen, one of the "leaders in our town."

He stands, therefore, by the unadorned recitation of the facts of his life and work, as living refutation of the error that loyal Catholicism and loyal Americanism are incompatible.

The simple record also stands as a striking demonstration of the spreading influence of the work done by a good pastor going quietly and purposefully about his immediate tasks as a priest among men. Within the twenty-six years of Archbishop O'Hara's episcopacy, it reveals something that is not always obvious to the layman—the primary importance of a bishop, and of the body of bishops, to the contemporary strength and the future welfare of the Church in a region and in a nation.

Although Edwin Vincent O'Hara's particular set of accomplishments is unique, as is the total achievement of any individual's lifetime, there is an essential sense in which his story is the story of virtually every bishop in the American hierarchy. Starting from any one work set on foot by any one bishop, one could place it as an inevitable link in the chain forged by that man working out of his own background with his given talents in a given set of circumstances. In that essential sense, Archbishop Edwin O'Hara's story is the story of every bishop.

These considerations drew the writer away from the purpose for which he was first given access to Archbishop O'Hara's archives. He had found a much more interesting story, but one that became progressively impossible to write as he would like.

Things at a distance of fifty years can be viewed by the outsider with some objectivity. But as we come closer to contemporary events shared by other living people, the narrative must suffer from lack of that freedom of expression which common decency yet permits only to those who took part. All the observer can hope is to keep the record straight.

It has been the author's wish to make this book as undemonstrative and as genuine as was the man it is about. It is a record of achievement rather than the portrait of a man. Yet that record is itself a portrait, the kind of a portrait the subject would have liked most.

CHAPTER I

A Farm in Minnesota

OUR FATHERS did not speak of "book learning" merely because they were unfamiliar with the word "education." They did so because, unlike many of us to whom the word "education" is very familiar, they understood the thing the word stands for, and that understanding let them see with simple clarity that book learning was only part of it.

Education is a continuing process. It goes on from morning to night, from the cradle to the grave, from generation to generation. Someone has defined it as "being with" and there are few better definitions.

Nowhere is this process of fuller education more thoroughly realized than on a farm. The child's responsibility is not limited to paying attention during his hours in the schoolroom. He has things to learn and work to do before he goes there and after he comes home. Even earlier, from the time he can walk, he has been learning a dozen jobs and experiencing the pride and the responsibility of doing them. He is not very old when he senses the significance of being his father's son, the knowledge that what his father does to the farm will make a difference to him; and he grows naturally into the feeling that what he himself does is important both to his father and to those who will come after him. This comes from "being with" his father and his brothers in a very complete way, laboring physically beside them, sharing their worries about this season's crop, their memories of what a similar condition brought about five years ago, and their plans about what they should do next year with the back forty acres.

Things were very much that way on the O'Hara farm in the township of Amherst, eight miles outside the little town of Lanesboro in southern Minnesota. Edwin was born on that farm on September 6, 1881, the youngest of a family of eight. Three of his five brothers and his two sisters had been born on the same farm. The two oldest brothers, Peter and Robert, had come overland with the parents from Laporte, Ind., to take possession of the 320 acres with a stone house which had become home to the O'Haras.

The first experimental years of establishing a working formula for successful mixed farming had been passed and things now moved in a disciplined routine. The father, Owen O'Hara, with his feet firmly planted in the present had already fixed his eye on the future. Himself a working man of limited schooling, he had the respect of the Irish for formal education. When he had moved west from Pennsylvania to Indiana, the aristocratic-looking girl he had courted and married had been Margaret Nugent, the schoolteacher at Elkhart who taught catechism for Father Sorin, C.S.C., Missionary and founder of Notre Dame University. (She cherished all her life a prayerbook given her by Father Sorin for this service.)

One of Owen O'Hara's earliest concerns after settling in Minnesota had been to pick out a piece of land just down the road from his farm and see to the building of a school. For the twenty-five years he was clerk of the township, he made a principle of "no teachers but the best" in that country schoolhouse.

Long before Edwin was ready for school, he formed part of the family group around the big kitchen table going over the day's lessons by the light of an oil lamp. Mother and father were also in the group, mother still a teacher. Owen O'Hara, from youth addicted to reading, educated himself along with his sons. He got to love the roll of good verse and he had pages of Alexander Pope's *Essay on Man* committed to memory. His sons were to carry through life the delightfully mingled sensations of jolting rides to town atop a wagonload of bulging sacks with the sound of their father's voice reciting Pope's smooth-flowing and thought-laden measures. The comforting warmth of the autumn sun bringing a pleasant lassitude to muscles tired from the labor of loading, the prospect of a day in town teasing the mind, the clop-clop of the horses' hooves as they kicked up dust whose dry odor mingled with the freshness of new grain, all formed a strange American accompaniment to Owen O'Hara's Irish voice rounding out the measured philosophy of the eighteenth-century English poet.

It was such evenings and such days that gave life in the O'Hara family the peculiar individuality which is the mark of every well lived-in household, that self-created ambience of living which makes every true family a world within a world and distinguishes it from every other family no matter how similar their outward activities may appear. The O'Haras were good farmers and they were proud of it. But they were something more. They were the O'Haras. And they were proud of that too.

If the pride had its immediate origin in the preserved personal integrity of the present, it also drew from living contact with the past. They grew up with the native Ireland of their parents close to them. When the O'Hara grandparents moved into town after five years, the elder Nugents took their place in family life on the farm. There were nearly a hundred years and a lot of history between Edwin and his grandmother Nugent. She had been born Anne Doyle in Ireland during the historic year 1798. When she was three

months old, her father had been killed in battle during the
'98 rebellion. Her mother's brother, Dennis Tyrrell, was
killed in the same uprising and her mother never recovered
from the double shock.

Although Mrs. Nugent died when Edwin was six, her
memory remained very much alive in the family. The girls
particularly were fascinated by the fact that she had made
her own linen sheets from flax she had spun and woven herself. They loved to look at and touch the goodness of the
things and to admire the fine workmanship of articles of
clothing made as far back as 1820 and still clearly marked
with hand-sewn labels bearing the name Anne Doyle. One
of them could say sixty years later that she "had never yet
seen anything like her clothes."

This talent had been passed on to her daughter along with
the industry to put it to use. For Mrs. O'Hara made all the
clothes for her large family. This did not seem too strange
in that place and time when the farm family prided itself on
the extent to which it could be self-sustaining and independ-
ent of bought goods.

There was another demonstration of this in the big smoke-
house always plentifully hung with meat the O'Haras had
raised, butchered, dressed, and cured themselves.

It was a full life the O'Haras lived on that farm, comprehensive enough to absorb the outer world wherever it seeped
in, intense enough to preserve its integrity and impinge itself upon that outer world as one by one the children grew
up and went into it.

When the children left to build their own lives, they did
so in dignity and with justifiable pride in the home they
were leaving. Owen O'Hara had done well. He had increased
his acreage, extended and improved the stone house and given
the area its first herd of pure-bred Shorthorn cattle. All his
sons knew what one of them said proudly as bishop of Kansas

City more than half a century later, "My father was a farmer. He was a *good* farmer."

Robert O'Hara was one of the first boys from the district to be sent away for higher education. He went first to St. Thomas' College in St. Paul, and then to Notre Dame University. He set a pattern which saw all eight of the O'Hara children go to college and several of them carry on to post-graduate degrees.

Robert became a lawyer and pioneer builder of Hamilton, Mont., where he died in 1954 at the age of eighty-seven. Peter went into business and farm management in North Dakota. James was his father's successor on the family farm and he kept the O'Hara tradition alive in more ways than one. He had six children and, like his father and mother before him, he gave one son and one daughter to the Church— Father Robert and Sister Edwin Marie of the Sisters of the Holy Names, both stationed in Portland, Ore.

The oldest girl, Mary, taught the first school in Hamilton, Mont., where her brother Robert had sold the first city lots. She continued her career until she found her spiritual home in the convent of the Poor Clares, Omaha, Nebr. Cast in the same mould as her youngest brother, she was an ornament to her Order for forty-six years and served many years as Abbess before her death at the age of seventy-six in 1946.

The next girl, Anna, was also a qualified teacher who taught as Mary had in the little school in Amherst and then succeeded her in Montana. Through the years Anna was to enrich the lives of all the other members of the family by lending them in turn the strength, the dignity and the lady-like graciousness of her presence and aid. She worked with Robert in Hamilton, was widowed after a brief married life of four months, helped Peter conduct his affairs in North Dakota, spent winters with John or Edwin in Oregon, stayed by the side of Frank's wife through a prolonged and critical illness, came to look after her priest brother when he was bishop of Great Falls and, at the age of eighty-five, was still housekeeper and hostess at the archbishop's house in Kansas City. For some forty years, the life of Mrs. Daniels cannot be separated from that of her brother Edwin and no little part in the calm accomplishment of his may be credited to the intelligent loyalty of hers.

The two boys closest to his own age, Frank and John, we shall meet again in this story as the three form a remarkable trio in working for God and the Church, each in his own way.

Edwin was just a toddler when Robert went off to college. By the time he was ready to start school, his sister Anna, eight years younger than Robert, was already a qualified teacher in their little schoolhouse.

It was a public school. The majority of the children were Norwegian and Lutheran. There had been other Irish Catholic families on the farms around them, but most of them moved back to the city to be near the church.

Outside of their home, the religious training of the O'Hara family was rather scanty. The children got to Mass only every second Sunday since the buggy could not take all of them at once. There was a somewhat haphazard twenty minutes of Sunday school after Mass. When Edwin rode into town on a load of grain one Saturday and stayed over to be confirmed by Bishop Cotter, his formal preparation had consisted of exactly one instruction. His boyhood was so far removed from any ecclesiastical atmosphere that he still remembers his utter bewilderment when he heard that his Sunday school teacher, Honora Leahy, had "gone to be a nun." He had never in his life seen a nun and he could not at all associate nuns with real people he knew, like the Leahys.

But the home atmosphere of that family was such that they did not suffer from the lack of outside religious instruction. Every night the O'Haras gathered for family prayers around a picture of the Sacred Heart. Through October and during Lent they recited the family rosary every evening, the father leading. The well-thumbed books on the unusually adequate farm bookshelves were predominantly on religious topics. The youngsters all cut their teeth on some very stiff nineteenth-century apologetics and became familiar with the pointed paragraphs of the Imitation of Christ.

The non-Catholic surroundings brought Edwin an experience he was to recall with telling effect in later life. At the time, his father had taken over a hardware store in Lanesboro. As many of his customers were Norwegians, he decided it would be a good idea if some of his boys learned that language. The Lutherans had a flourishing system of religious vacation schools which their children attended daily for a month every summer. The Norwegian neighbors of the O'Haras conducted one in their own language. So the future Roman Catholic bishop of Kansas City learned Norwegian by studying the Lutheran catechism and the scriptures in that tongue!

In 1895, Edwin started at Lanesboro High School and moved into town to board with a friend of the family. It was during this period that he began to direct his mind to the priesthood. There was no road-to-Damascus decision about it. It was a gradual, apparently inevitable development. People around him, and he himself, began taking it for granted that "Edwin was going to be a priest."

Residence in Lanesboro brought Edwin into more frequent contact with the pastor, Father James Coyne. This brilliant but unpredictable Irish priest with a biting sense of irony was a Maynooth man who had formerly taught mathematics in an Irish college. He had come to Minnesota via New York in answer to Archbishop Ireland's appeal for help in his priest-poor diocese.

Edwin's relations with him were always most cordial. But it wasn't everyone who could say the same. Many of the parishioners had no great liking for the short plain remarks that would occasionally flash in their direction, though they retained a decent and patient respect for the lengthy erudite sermons which soared innocuously over their heads.

The private lessons in Greek he intermittently gave young Edwin—and the conversation that went with them—were sparks that helped kindle the flame of intellectual curiosity in the fifteen-year-old mind. But it can never be said that this parish priest rushed the boy into the seminary. When Edwin came to him at the end of college and asked about his vocation, the extent of the encouragement he received was a terse, "I know of no obstacle to your studying for the priesthood."

Living in town did not free the boy from his farm duties. He was back at work every weekend and any evening he was needed. On days when harvest time or spring preparation demanded everybody's effort, there was no school for him at all. The twelve-year-old who had been shucking corn when a passing wagon brought word of Grover Cleveland's election in 1893 was still a working farm boy when he heard of William McKinley's election in 1897. But by the time McKinley's assassination in 1901 brought Theodore Roosevelt to the White House, Edwin was a seminarian whose farm work was limited to summer vacations.

In January of 1898, Edwin O'Hara became a boarder at St. Thomas' College in St. Paul. The school had been founded thirteen years previously by Archbishop Ireland with the principal aim of preparing young men for the priesthood. Although at first called a seminary, it had always served, as Quebec seminaries, for example, still do, as a liberal arts college for Catholics aiming at other professions. In 1895 Archbishop Ireland's friend, the railway magnate, James J. Hill, a non-Catholic, donated the funds for St. Paul's Seminary. From then on, aspirants for the priesthood did not become seminarians until they went there, put on the cassock, and began to study philosophy.

Edwin already knew the routine at the college. His brother Robert, by this time married and practicing law, had been a co-student with the school's first graduates. John, just two and a half years older than Edwin, was still there to lend support and break the feeling of strangeness. But a country boy still feels lost when he first comes to the city. And any boy enters a new world when he goes to boarding school.

There is the feeling of being cut off from the close circle which previously limited your activities and governed your decisions, the sense of being your own man with a choice to make among a totally new offering of companions and activities. It is a lonely moment when you find yourself standing in an empty world stripped of the familiar trappings and under the immediate necessity of establishing yourself as Edwin O'Hara, not just Owen O'Hara's son.

It is also an exhilarating moment, the moment of freedom. And, youth being what it is, the exhilaration triumphs.

On his half-holidays, Edwin would work off his homesickness by going down to the railway yards to watch the cattle unloading. His critical eye would size up the animals, comparing them unfavorably with his father's pure-bred herd. But most of his free time went in the delight of long hours of reading. He discovered the poets and explored them to his heart's content. The recreation periods that sent others to the playing fields would find Edwin seated beneath one of the large shade trees that bordered Lake Mennona on the college grounds. His mind, which had previously been inclined to mathematics and the physical sciences, took a distinct literary bent. When the students decided that it was time the college had a paper, Edwin O'Hara was one of the names that were signed at the end to preserve the anonymity of the fifteen hand-duplicated pages. Though most of the work was done by seniors, among whom his brother John was a leading light, the content of Volume One, Number One of *The Sybil* gives a good picture of the atmosphere in which the St. Thomas days were passed. In the little paper the breeze of college gaiety carries the scent of blossoming learning.

Young men, particularly the young writers who speak for them, are like mettlesome horses. They toss their heads, stamp their feet, tug at the reins, and don't care which direction they take as long as they go. The St. Thomas group was no exception. Prose or poetry, borrowed wit or wild humor, facetious accounts of school events, wise *obiter dicta* on the world of letters or weighty pronouncements on the most profound questions of the day were all grist to the mill.

The senior cheer was recorded:

> Who are, who are, who are we?
> Sumus, sumus populi,
> Per deos immortales,
> Class of '99!

This Latinized version of the typical American college cheer is quite characteristic of the rather odd combination of refined classical teaching and crude pioneering conditions at St. Thomas' College in this period.

To understand the place, one has to know something of the powerful personality who brought it into being and under whose influence Edwin O'Hara was formed to the priesthood. Archbishop John Ireland was a dominating figure physically as well as intellectually and morally. He stood six feet two but had shoulders of such breadth that he seemed stocky. His strong features, surmounted by a striking shock of gray hair, added to the dramatic effect of oratorical powers that never failed to sway crowds or make him the central figure in any group.

Although Irish of the Irish and an unabashed flag-waving American, he was still, by training and outlook, a cosmopolitan. He was completely at home among the Italian cardinals in Rome and there was accuracy as well as oratory in the

statement that France was "the land of his youth and the
school of his soul."

There was nothing indecisive about the stand he took on
any question. As a temperance leader, he wore Father Matthew's mantle in triumph even back in Ireland. In politics, he
was Republican to the core and vocal about it. As a churchman, he championed his favorite causes in high ecclesiastical
councils against no matter what opposition. He was in the
thick of three great controversies that almost split the Church
in America during the last half of the nineteenth century:
Cahenslyism, the Public School Question, and the furore in
France and at Rome over Father Isaac Hecker and "Americanism."

When this strong man decided to found his own college
and seminary, he had to put something of his own stamp
upon both. One of the ways this showed was in a sprinkling
of professors from backgrounds rather unexpected in this
"cow college" of the American West. Father Cornelius Clifford, for example, who taught Edwin O'Hara *Virgil* had
been a tutor at Oxford. He later went east, became respected
as a man of letters, taught scholastic philosophy at Columbia
University, grew to be an intimate friend of Alexis Carrel
and one of those to whom *Man the Unknown* was dedicated.
He remained in Archbishop O'Hara's memory as a devout
priest and a fine example of combined scholarship and faith.

The president of St. Thomas' when Edwin arrived was
Father James J. Byrnes, later a monsignor and vicar general
of the diocese of St. Paul. He taught religion in a most interesting manner using the technique, unusual in that period, of
encouraging discussion in class. Though the discussion was
on no superficial level, it smacked of childhood to the farm
boy who had done his early reading in the O'Hara home library which included Milner's *End of Controversy*, Archbishop Purcell's debates, Bishop Spaulding's apologetics,
Brother Azarius on Education and Hay's *The Sincere Chris-*

tian. By the same token, the boy was an eager student in the equally stimulating English classes also conducted by Father Byrnes.

A fatherly influence at the college was the vice-president, Father Fitzgerald. White-haired, genial and kindly, he traveled around the state recruiting students for St. Thomas and had visited the O'Hara home at Amherst in this capacity. It was his mediation that settled an incipient student rebellion in Edwin's graduating year which might easily have taken the young student away from St. Paul's for the next stage of his studies.

The incident smoothed over, however, without causing a ripple outside the college walls. Edwin went back for a summer of work on the farm where he was joined by John, home for the holidays from Notre Dame, and Frank, who had just taken his B.A. with honors in economics and history at the University of Minnesota. That summer saw a lot of the good talk and the unspoken communion of ideals and interests that bound these three brothers in one mind throughout their lives. They would go together into Lanesboro and surrounding towns to attend the lectures and Fair Day speeches that provided much of the intellectual stimulus of that time and place. Though the family was staunchly Democratic, national politics as such were not a major interest with the O'Haras. But they were very much interested in the large social, economic, and religious questions of the day. The great Populist orators were traveling the country. One Fair Day, they heard the golden voice of Ignatius Donnelly and thrilled to his demand for the people's rights. They were even more interested in the fact that he was the author of *The Great Cryptogram* in which he set forth all the clues that had led him to believe that Shakespeare was Bacon's pen name. They heard Dan Lawlor, candidate for governor, exhort them, "Be no man's man and wear no man's collar." They discussed the ideas of Theodore Roosevelt and the philosophy of William Jennings Bryan whom Edwin, clinging to the rafters of a crowded St. Paul auditorium, had heard expounding the sentiments of his "Cross of Gold" speech: "You shall not press down upon the brow of labor this crown of thorns. You shall not crucify mankind upon a cross of gold."

In that autumn of 1900, Edwin O'Hara began the new century with a new life. He entered St. Paul's Seminary and put on the black cassock of a student preparing for priesthood.

CHAPTER II

The Seminary Years

LIFE IN THE SEMINARY is a very special sort of thing. It is one of the few places in which the ancient tradition of spending years shut off from the world, entirely dedicated to learning and the formation of character, still survives. It is a combination of the intense intellectual activity that goes on within the group of sensitive young minds who form the core of any good university and the spiritual "first fervor" of early years in monastic life. Seminaries, like universities, are hothouses specializing in close cultivation and forced growth before the graduate is transplanted into the colder earth of the outside world.

Edwin O'Hara's life at St. Paul's followed its own line through the same path followed by all young men with similar endowments in similar circumstances. There is nothing out of the ordinary in a seminarian noting down resolutions of perfection, finding himself near moral failure because he takes vain satisfaction in a high mark, a successful debate, a nod of recognition from a professor. It is by no means unique for an active undergraduate mind to take issue with the men who wrote the textbooks, to undertake their annihilation by quotations from original sources which the student, having himself just come upon them, is quite certain no one else has ever seen, or to live in ill-contained rebellion against the vague but omnipresent barrier which a generation excellently good in its own old-fashioned way is perpetually placing between him and the great accomplishments for which the world can ill afford to wait.

Such thoughts are common to youth wherever it is blessed with the twin gifts of a keen mind and a sensitive soul. They have struck sparks at one time or other in the breasts of most of us. In some the spark, for want of tending, no more than flickered and was gone, leaving only the sometimes painful recollection of its brief brightness. Others, having coaxed it to fire for a while, grow careless of the effort and content themselves thereafter either with the intermittent light and warmth of a smoky flame or with the minimum heat of barely living embers. The tempered breath of a happy few fans the promise to the lasting warmth of openness of mind and receptivity of soul.

Edwin O'Hara belonged in the last group. But he was more than touched by the torment and the triumph of yet another category. There are always some who catch the first sparks in a tinder box, feed fuel to it fervently and are caught up in the rage of its consuming fire. Out of this few come the great successes and the great failures. They are life's poets and to them the gods do not grant mediocrity. They are the catalytic agents of historical action, drawing to themselves as much as they can of contact with the past and fusing it to a significant moment of the present. Such men have the timeless function of a natural priesthood. They are mediators between an awful certainty of the Absolute upon which their vision is fixed and uncertain awe of the contingency within which they live. They stand at the altar of man's knowledge, attainment, and desire, offering to the Perfectly Good, the Perfectly Beautiful, and the Perfectly True, the holocaust of their own imperfection. They join themselves and all Others to the One and, in the same act, keep the nature and existence of the One clear and living in the minds of the Others.

In the natural order, these men become as much "priests for ever" as their supernatural counterparts. Once they have walked up to that altar, Time and Space withdraw and leave them alone on the island of their dedication. If they step away, they step into nothingness and nothing surrounds them in all else they do. They have seen a vision and "He who has dreamed a dream knoweth no more of doubting." Since they know, they can find no lasting refuge in pretended doubt. They may bury their vision under the drive of an ambition incompatible with it, they may try to blot it out with the flippancy of guilt-ridden cynicism, they may attempt to drown it in lusts of despair or in seas of defiance— but it stands there still, an untended altar waiting for its priest.

Many of the men called to the priesthood of Christ are also sharers in this natural priesthood and Edwin O'Hara, in a controlled, feet-on-the-ground way, was one.

He differed from the zealots not so much in the intensity of his feeling or the urgency of his thinking as in a hard-won control that harnessed ambition to action and ideals to a practical application. Contrary to the perfectionists who perpetually postpone action on the grounds that they are not yet ready to act perfectly, he seems to have believed that the best way to learn how to do a thing is to do it.

The result was a small but imposing list of achievements during these years specifically devoted to preparation rather than to accomplishment. These follow a pattern that was to become familiar in Edwin O'Hara's life: that of making systematic use of available means toward an ultimate goal. To the young man shut off in a seminary, the available means was writing. The goal, as befitting a young philosopher and theologian, was nothing less than correction of the dominant error in contemporary world thought.

The ogre that pawed and snarled against Catholic belief fifty years ago as Communism does today was Darwinism.

t of his own notebook. He was also worrying
ial worry of the conscientious student, "How
earn all this stuff before exam time?"

point, there really had not been very much to
dwin O'Hara from thousands of other young
reparing for their careers. The nation's future
e at West Point worrying about *their* examina-
en who would make its laws and write its books,
ustry and commerce, defend it or betray it, bring
ring it shame, give it strength or give it weakness
world wars and a great depression were being
their futures in the thousands of institutions dedi-
at purpose. The individuals differed in their ca-
d in their specific aims; the institutions in their at-
, their methods and their areas of activity. But,
as the individuals were serious-minded and work-
d the fulfilment of an effective desire, they were
arts of an organic unity; they were cells in the
Young America.

Americanism was something they breathed in and
granted as much as the air around them. They did
the immediate goal of their education as becoming
mericans any more than they saw it as becoming
en. Their education would make them good scientists,
ldiers, good teachers, good businessmen—and then,
ey were already good Americans, they would, by the
fact that they were more complete and more able
be better and more useful Americans.

y would take different paths according to the different
that took shape in each heart. One wanted to storm
San Juan hill, another would hide himself in a labora-
nd emerge with some great discovery, a third would
roads and rails across deserts and raise buildings to the
yet another would walk among the suffering and the
to lead them to better lives. But it never occurred t

So the David who had just come upon a weapon in the ordered methodology of Thomistic philosophy at once started
peppering the giant with his sling shot.

He did not start the battle without ammunition. A natural
bent for philosophy was encouraged by the fact that the
seminary's best teachers were in just the right subjects at the
right time to provide him the stimulus he needed.

For logic, epistemology, metaphysics, and history of philosophy, he had Father William Turner, the future bishop of
Buffalo, later to become Professor at Catholic University of
America, author of a standard history of philosophy and a
principal collaborator in the *Catholic Encyclopedia*. Father
Turner was also librarian and Edwin O'Hara, as student librarian, was in very close association with him throughout
his five years at St. Paul's.

In psychology, he had Father John Seliskar, just back with
a Louvain doctorate, a most stimulating teacher who became
a lifelong friend.

His Professor of English during philosophy was Father
William H. Sheran, an Oxford-trained scholar who taught
his class from texts that also served the study of scripture
and apologetics. Here Edwin was introduced to the writings
of Wilfrid Ward and, in his biographies of W. G. Ward and
Cardinal Wiseman, thrilled to one of those jolting experiences that open the young mind to new horizons. The rest
of Edwin O'Hara's life was so deeply affected by these readings that he said fifty years later, "They opened my mind to
Europe and gave me whatever I have in Catholic Literature."

The benefits of this class were carried over into theology
where the brilliant Father Humphrey Moynihan, later president of St. Thomas College and literary secretary to Archbishop Ireland, taught apologetics in such a way that it made
an excellent course in English literature and expression. Arriv-
ing in almost every class with an armful of "good reading,"
he introduced the students to the best of contemporary books

and to such periodicals as the *Edinburgh Review, The Dublin Review* and the *Fortnightly Review.*

All these teachers encouraged Edwin O'Hara in his literary tilting at the errors of the day. His by-line began to appear over articles in the *Catholic World,* the *Catholic University Bulletin,* and in various newspapers. While still in the seminary, he was providing an editorial a week for the *Catholic Sentinel* which his brother John was then editing for the archdiocese of Oregon City.

It was this sort of thing that set Edwin O'Hara off from his fellow seminarians. Others shared his enthusiasm. But they were content to leave action for an indefinite future. He had classmates and friends more brilliant than himself (even if they did not surpass his average of 97 per cent). But he was the one who wrestled with learning until he had made it the ready servant of the things he wanted to do.

A good example was the translation from German of Dennert's book, *At the Deathbed of Darwinism,* which the young seminarian's intensive reading on the subject had led him to regard as an excellent refutation of the false philosophy that had risen from the great biologist's work.

Under any circumstances, the translation and rewriting of a philosophical study on such a topic might well be enough to make anyone pause. Any seminarian with a full program and the load of extracurricular activities which Edwin O'Hara was carrying might reasonably have asked to be excused even if a publisher had contracted with him for the job. This particular seminarian, who had no mandate to translate the work and no least promise of having his translation published, might well have rested on his laurels as far as sheer intellectual labor on the subject was concerned. He might have contented himself, for example, with the typical assignment he was to receive from Father Moynihan—to follow and "examine" a series of articles by W. H. Mallock currently appearing in the *Fortnightly Review* under the

title "Strictures of
meant spending se
refutation which ap
Bulletin simultaneou
attack.

But Edwin O'Hara
be made available to
thor about American
Herder and Scribner.
called upon his frien
Crookston.

While he worked the
young writer heard from
written to Germany for
nert's book. So it was und
offshoot of an exercise in
seminary reached the Ame
two future bishops as co-tr

Edwin O'Hara wrote an
read proof on it at the far
1904. But that wasn't all he
notebook kept that summer l
"Threshed, baled, and drove a

Getting the book out was
dizzying accomplishment in it
and comments might easily h
narian's humility. One in partic
gleeful chuckling around St. Pau
an eminent critic, the Reveren
University, bestowed hearty pr
long preface—not too long—by
Seminary will repay careful study

By the time these reviews reache
back at St. Paul's Seminary bent ov
bling notes as fast as one of his les

read them ou
the immemor
will I ever l

Up to this
distinguish
Americans
generals we
tions. The
build its in
it glory or
during two
formed to
cated to t
pacities an
mospheres
inasmuch
ing towa
integral
body of

Their
took for
not see
good A
good m
good s
since th
simple
people

The
dream
some
tory
throw
sky,
lowl

any one of them to say the others were less American because they were not following his particular path.

Edwin O'Hara's road lay along a way that has been honored by all peoples, a life of dedication to the service of his fellow man. Whether they watch a Jane Addams walking the slums of an American city, an Albert Schweitzer expending his genius in an African jungle, or a St. Francis walking the hills of Umbria, civilized men have always been moved, and slightly awed, at the sight of one of their fellows sacrificing pleasure, comfort and gain to an ideal. For they have all heard within themselves the call of the higher aim and, at some time in some way, responded to it. They also know too well the compelling drag of immediate necessity or desire which consistently prevails against it. And they know their common humanity to be ennobled, their own failures compensated, in the man who answers without reserve. So they lift their hats to him—even when they wish he would expend himself in some other cause.

The dedicated man's decision is seldom a simple one. There are the great exceptions in which the fire of enthusiasm burns away every particle of doubt. But for the ordinary young man considering the consecrated life, the normal problems of decision are intensified by the nature of the choice and, in the case of the priest, by the irrevocability of the step he is about to take.

Fears and doubts are bound to assail him. Is it not presumptuous of him to think of such a life? What if he fails?

And the subtle appeals of self-gratification start rationalizing its desires. Couldn't he do more good by being a teacher? a writer? a prosperous member of the community who could reach people who would never come near a priest? Wouldn't it be better if he reached for some goal he was more certain of attaining? A place where failure would reflect only on himself and not on the whole ideal for which he stands?

When the vocation truly exists, however, these doubts, no

matter how annoying, are merely pinpricks against a vast certainty. They serve only to make the individual more aware of the unassailable truth that God is at once the cause, the meaning and the end of our lives; that every ambition we could possibly have is fulfilled in union with Him; that the best good we can bring our fellow man is God. Such knowledge of God brings love of Him and trust in Him. And in this trust is found strength for decision to spend a life in His service.

There remains the human element. At the age when a young man usually makes this decision, the whole world lies before him. His renunciation is an immeasurable thing. He is giving up, not the actual position, wealth, and prestige he would otherwise have, but all the splendid desirable things he at that moment feels quite certain he *could* have. The whole world is at his feet and that, no less, is what he really and truly gives up.

He has human help in his decision. Around him are men who have followed the same path. They have taught him, they have talked with him, he has met some of them who were great names to him when his ideal was forming. At the seminary, Edwin O'Hara had listened to Archbishop Spaulding and found that his talk was a summary of those first books he had read by lamplight back in Amherst township. He had been delighted to hear him reaffirm that "the only real life is that of the soul." He had treasured his advice to the students, "Education is mainly a matter of acquiring a love for study." One of his retreats at St. Paul's had been given by the English Benedictine scholar Dom Gasquet. This contact with the ancient monastic tradition of the Old World was a notable spiritual and intellectual experience for the young seminarian. In a private talk with the historian and writer, he felt a great sense of the continuity of Christian effort as he listened to the monk's account of the team of scripture scholars then working on a study of the Latin biblical texts and let his mind wander to their predecessors preserving the sacred Word on parchment all through the ages before Gutenberg.

The succession of notable men Archbishop Ireland brought to meet his seminarians widened their horizon and extended beyond the warmth of their immediate little circle their sense of security in the Faith.

Then there was that extra dimension which lifts seminary training out of comparison with other universities, no matter how good in their own fields: the annual retreats where the soul communes for eight days in silence with God, the monthly days of recollection, the spiritual conferences, the regular confession and communion, daily Mass and meditation, and the personal outpourings of incidents in the innermost struggle sympathetically heard and wisely analyzed by an experienced spiritual director.

The outward preparation of the classroom is carried along on a strong, deep tide of spiritual preparation fully known only to one soul and God. Before the seminarian comes to answer the questions on his final examination in theology, he has already given his answer to a much more important question by the daily conduct of several years of his life. He has also resolved any serious doubt that may have existed. He is able to survive isolated spasms of nervous hesitation and recognize them for the butterfly flutterings they are.

Edwin O'Hara, beginning his second year of theology in the fall of 1903, was a young man who knew where he was going. And he had the added satisfaction of knowing that he had never for a moment really wanted to go anywhere else. He would serve his God and his country as a priest and he could not imagine anything else he might do that would render better service to the One or to the other.

If his strong social instinct needed any additional proof that an American priest could serve all his fellow Americans no matter what their creed, it was at hand in the man who taught him moral theology for two years. This man was

Father John A. Ryan. Already famous for his pioneering work on the living wage, Father Ryan was to become a professor at the Catholic University, a monsignor and a national leader in the improvement of social and industrial conditions in the United States. He had an immediate and continuing influence on Edwin O'Hara. Their personal and professional relationship was to remain very close right up to the monsignor's death.

As the time for taking Holy Orders draws near, any seminarians who are not already committed must seek a bishop who will authorize their ordination for his diocese. The Church doesn't just ordain priests and turn them loose. They must always be subject to some particular authority in the religious hierarchy.

The archdiocese of Portland-in-Oregon (then known as the archdiocese of Oregon City) had attracted Edwin O'Hara for several reasons. It was badly in need of priests. His friend George Thompson was being ordained for it. His brother John was there, teaching history and editing the diocesan paper. So he had been accepted by Archbishop Christie and taken Minor Orders as his subject.

The beginning of Lent, 1905, found the seminarian making resolutions that he would intensify his study of theology during the rest of this year and all through the following year that remained before ordination. But before the penitential season had lasted a week, he received word from Father George Thompson in Portland that Archbishop Christie had decided to advance his ordination. It would take place within three months.

He had mixed feelings about this. Natural pleasure at getting out into active life a year ahead was tinged with a student's regret over the loss of a year of important study. He was given the hope that he would be allowed to go back sometime and make up the year, but on the eve of his Golden

Jubilee, he would still be remarking with a quiet smile, "I never did get back for that last year of theology."

Father Edwin Vincent O'Hara was ordained to the priesthood by Archbishop John Ireland in the new chapel of St. Paul's Seminary on June 10, 1905. For his first Mass he went home to St. Patrick's parish in Lanesboro, Minnesota. Among the priests assisting were his close seminary friends, Fathers Timothy Crowley, Frank McCarthy and John Peschges.

Death had already claimed, on April 4, 1904, the man who would have been most proud that day. Owen O'Hara was not by his wife's side as she watched the last of the eight children they had sent out from the one-room school in Amherst Township bring honor to the training they had all been given.

There was undoubtedly much emotion around Father Coyne's church when young Ed came back as Father O'Hara. But none of it showed in the new priest's notebook entries for that day: "Fr. Coyne turns humeral veil inside out to make it red for Crowley. Everything smooth except my singing. After ceremony I give blessings—hard time with big hats. I drive three-seated rig with clergy out to farm."

The weeks following ordination were spent around home. Their casual activity was sufficient to reveal something of the direction the new priest's work would take. His first sermon was on the Institution of the Church. Another was on Pope Pius X's newly issued *Acerbo Nimis*, an encyclical on catechism and the need of instructing children in the Faith. He was invited to talk at the various institutes and debating societies in the neighboring towns where he and his brothers used to find their intellectual recreation during summers on the farm. At Harmony, all their Scots neighbors gathered to hear him expound the rule of Faith in a lecture entitled, "Why I am a Catholic." The Methodist minister, the Reverend Thompson, was slightly embarrassed in the discussion following when he could not explain just how he knew his bible was inspired. At Canton Town Hall, the venerable preacher of the old Scotland Church was in the front row to hear him talk on "The Catholic Church and the American Citizen."

Altogether, this was an eventful summer for the three youngest members of the O'Hara family. Edwin was ordained. Frank arrived back with a Ph.D. in economics from the University of Berlin. John left shortly after for France and the Sorbonne to do the postgraduate work in history which preceded his volume on the history of the United States. Before autumn was over, Frank was on the faculty of the University of Notre Dame, John was married and Father Edwin was running the editorial page of the Portland *Catholic Sentinel,* a job Frank had intended to carry on while John was away.

CHAPTER III

At the Cathedral in Portland

IN PORTLAND, Father O'Hara was assigned as assistant to the cathedral parish and became part of the household of Archbishop Alexander Christie who had his residence there.

This meant that the first fifteen years of his priesthood were spent in immediate contact with a prelate of no little strength and distinction both as an administrator and as a man. In later years, Father O'Hara was to pay tribute to his archbishop in one of his historical writings. He was to write that Archbishop Christie's time "will be known as the building era of the Archdiocese . . . parishes were multiplied, churches, schools, hospitals, homes for dependent children and old were built, the number of diocesan clergy was increased, and a large number of religious communities both of men and women were called into the services of the Archdiocese." And he summed up his estimate of the man by endorsing the funeral eulogy preached by Bishop Carroll of Helena: "His commanding, kingly figure, to which the episcopal robes added comeliness and splendor, made him the cynosure of all eyes, while his stirring yet simple speech like the language of Holy Writ with which it was impregnated, was living and effectual and reached the very souls of his hearers. . . . He was the ideal archbishop. He ruled by love and not by fear. . . ."

From his first year of priesthood the deceptive calm of

the young Minnesota priest's manner proved a cloak for what can honestly be called dynamic activity. It is a general truth that the ordinary layman gets a good case of shudders the first time he sits down to analyze the schedule of the average young priest in a city parish. Mass and meditation, confessions, sick calls, christenings, weddings, funerals are only the skeleton of his working program. He probably runs at least one organization, has to be at meetings of a couple of others, teaches catechism, counsels an indefinite number of individuals, must be at the service of anyone who drops in or calls him to the telephone. He has to be as regular as a teacher, as available as a doctor and as versatile as a mother with a houseful of children. All this is expected of him and he wins no special adjectives by doing it. But Father O'Hara went a bit further. He did a few extra things and put a little extra into all of them.

The writer's problem of having to put one word down after another makes it rather difficult to give a fair impression of the curate's early Oregon activities. An artist might come closer by painting each of them on a plate and then showing a man juggling ten plates.

To start quietly, there was the Altar Society, which had been having a difficult time financially and otherwise. It started that first year $150 in debt and ending by reporting that it was $100 ahead and "we have the work systematized." There may not seem to be anything world-shaking in that, but any executive (or anyone who knows Altar Societies) will agree that whole books have been written about less.

Then there were the boys and girls who did not have any organizations at all. This, under the rules of the Old Army Game, should have meant a little free time. But that game, like the adage about fools rushing in, was never meant for young redheaded priests. What the absence of organizations meant was that the new curate would have to start some to fill the gap—and then keep them going.

By January, the McLoughlin Boys Club was organized and meeting on Mondays for study and on Wednesdays for games and the maneuvers of the McLoughlin Cadets. It is possibly of some historical interest that the Reverend Edwin Vincent O'Hara's first fund-raising venture resulted in a donation of $75 which bought sixteen caps and sixteen pairs of pants for the cadets . . . one of whom was Frank Folsom, future president of RCA.

By midsummer the boys were providing the choir at Mass and the girls were in an active unit of the Children of Mary. Contrary to current custom, each group was encouraged to realize that the other existed, instead of pretending they were inhabitants of parallel planets. The boys put on shows for the girls and the girls for the boys, and it was not long till they were staging operettas together.

The Children of Mary was one link in a chain of women's groups in whose direction the new curate took an active part. He organized a center where working girls were provided with luncheons and offered classes in sewing, dressmaking and various other subjects. The women who sponsored this and other charitable activities were gathered into the Catholic Women's League (a title hit upon locally with no reference to the international organization).

The help of these women was needed for support of an institution that had long been planned by Archbishop Christie and was finally opened in 1907, the Christie Home for Orphan Girls. A typical example of the O'Hara touch was his guidance of a well-to-do woman who responded favorably to his appeal for assistance. He pointed out to her that they were incurring daily bills for milk for the orphans when they had lots of land to feed their own cows. The lady was impressed. She donated $500 and Father O'Hara's methodical way of putting the money to use must have impressed her even more than the logic of his appeal. He did not just go out and order some cows. Nor did he content himself with

trusting his own experience as a dairy farmer or with handing the job over to some competent person. He did exactly
what he would have done had he been starting a herd for
himself. He managed the job personally but with the most
expert assistance he could find. He went to the head of the
dairy department at the State Agricultural College in Corvallis. This man was Paul V. Maris and he turned out to be
another of Father O'Hara's lifetime friends. He had records
of all the high-grade herds in the state. Together the priest
and the professor went from farm to farm over a hundred-
mile radius and picked out a starting herd of twelve good
Jersey cows. That herd, like so many things Edwin O'Hara
started, is in flourishing condition today.

Among the men of the parish, Father O'Hara was extending the experience with disparate societies going their own
ways that was to make him such an apostle of unified and
harmonized Catholic Action. He joined the Ancient Order
of Hibernians and the Knights of Columbus. As a Knight, he
was the only priest to attend meetings regularly and he was
soon appointed council chaplain. In the A.O.H. he found
himself surrounded by arguments about such things as local
politics, temperance leagues and unemployment.

As a priest the temperance question was one that concerned him. Always strong-willed and abstemious himself,
he had never been quite convinced that mass pledges of total
abstinence were an adequate answer to the alcohol problem.
After consultation with many men, he decided to launch an
anti-treating campaign and formed the Cathedral Men's Club
to conduct it. In spite of a favorable response and excellent
cooperation from a number of non-Catholic leaders, the
movement (and the Cathedral Men's Club) subsided as
quickly as it had arisen. Its father wrote its epitaph: "It had
unquestioned merit. But it would take a large part of a man's
time to keep the propaganda alive. I have made no attempt

to revive it and my conviction is increased that a society to live must have active work outlined for it."

His priestly interest in the dilemma of men caught in the unemployment crisis led him to organize a men's reading room where the unemployed could not only gather for constructive recreation but also devise means of self-employment and make use of a free employment agency. This brought Father O'Hara into closer touch with the politicians whose party differences he was leaving alone and brought him appointment to the Portland Unemployment Commission.

His activities as a priest, though above party politics, were already winning him recognition as a useful citizen.

Such things as these, and there were several more of them, were merely a matter of thoroughness in his ordinary pastoral routine. What might be called his special interests developed in other phases of that same priestly work.

This multitude of simultaneous activities was only possible because one of Edwin O'Hara's special abilities was that of being simultaneously economical in his use of time and lavish in the amount of it he consistently gave to the immediate duties he saw before him.

Conditions in the cathedral rectory at Portland were not conducive to the habit of regular hours of work. The rectory was centrally located and it housed an archbishop. Laymen from the surrounding commercial district and priests from all over the diocese were frequent visitors. Virtually all of them had to pass by Father O'Hara's door and too many of them dropped in. He learned to appreciate another grain of Bishop Spaulding's wisdom, "He who knocks is my friend. He who passes by is my benefactor."

Not that the visits were without interest of their own. Father McDevitt, the cathedral administrator, liked to bring to dinner notables who visited Portland. During his years at that dinner table Father O'Hara met John McCormack, who left a donation for his Shamrock Fund for the Boys' Home,

John L. Sullivan, who jovially proved his familiarity with things ecclesiastical by informing the archbishop in his rich Irish brogue that "we have a new coagitator bishop now in Philadelphia," and de Valera who caused consternation by having something good to say about the Russian Revolution.

With one thing and another, it would have been no great disgrace for the young priest to have excused himself from the resolution he had brought to Portland—that he would "keep up his theology, make a thorough study of the books of the Old Testament and familiarize himself with the Fathers of the Church." The percentage of young priests who have taken similar resolutions is probably somewhere around 99.1. But the proportion who managed to keep them would read more like a pitcher's batting average.

It is likely that Father O'Hara did smile rather ruefully when he thought of his seminary thesis on "The Metaphysical Basis of Epistemology in the Greek Philosophy" or came across notes like, "I have in mind to work out a line of philosophy which will harmonize Catholic philosophy with the Evolutionary concept of things. I conceive at present two fundamental centers of harmony between them: 1. The doctrine of potency and act—the process by which things come to act is the process of Evolution; 2. The doctrine of the Immanence of God. . . ."

On the other hand, the stuff of several of his published articles, like "Religion as a Credible Doctrine" in the *Catholic University Bulletin*, his studies on "Harris on Education," "St. Augustine," and "W. G. Ward" and others, was all ready material for cutting to the present pattern.

He used it with industry. A reading and study group he formed first of Catholic public school teachers grew to include many non-Catholics and became known as the Dante Club. The first year of the club's bi-weekly meetings was given to reading through *The Divine Comedy*. The next year's program was an exposition of Dante's philosophy through comparison with others. These meetings which had become accepted as a civic rather than as a specifically Catholic venture proved increasingly popular and the public library in which they were heard was taxed to capacity for talks on "Dante and . . . Aristotle, Homer, St. Augustine, St. Thomas Aquinas, Machiavelli, Shakespeare, Milton, Goethe, Kant and Newman." Best of all, each lecture was reported generously in the secular press, particularly in the daily *Oregonian* whose vigorous agnostic editorial writer, A. C. Chapman, was the actual target for the successive points Father O'Hara was making under the seductive sound of his rather ambitious titles.

This technique of using the public press to carry Catholic thought and Catholic viewpoints to non-Catholics was exercised with great skill and effect in a predominantly non-Catholic and strongly anti-Catholic city. As his activities brought him into contact with a constantly expanding circle, Father O'Hara's personal mildness, understanding and willingness to cooperate in any effort for the common good made him more and more acceptable to people of all faiths. When they saw his name in the paper, they read what he had to say and respected rather than resented the intransigent Catholicism of his uncompromising words.

He found several ways of getting into the secular press on topical Catholic issues. He was a frequent contributor to the Sunday paper on religious topics. The letters-to-the-editor column printed his reply to any public anti-Catholic statement. And, as his lectures and sermons were regularly reported, he chose his topics in church and on the platform with an eye to the wider audience he would have the next day.

It is a rather interesting commentary on the American scene to look back over forty years and more to find the same replies being given to the same objections we meet today.

When the United States was debating entry into World

War I, there was an upsurge of the sort of thing Blanshard wrought out of the atmosphere of World War II. Portland had its local Blanshard in the Reverend Dr. Brougher. Father O'Hara countered his inflammatory accusations with a series of public lectures at the public library on "Church and State." Interest was so great that a largely Protestant audience overflowed Library Hall for every meeting. The press reached the rest of the city. Its quotation of Father O'Hara's opening words is not without interest today:

> Among many whose acquaintance with the Church is superficial and whose positions are hostile to her as a religious body, the question has arisen as to the relation of this Catholic Church and the American Republic. Suspicion has been sown broadcast that the Catholic Church is a danger to our free institutions; that her members are wanting in loyalty to our government; that her clergy constitute a political organ of a foreign ruler; that her institutions are in need of public supervision; and that in a word her growth must be forthwith checked if she is not to undermine the very fabric of our American life and shatter the foundations of our most cherished liberties.
>
> The purpose of the course of lectures which we inaugurate tonight is to show how unfounded are these suspicions and what a menace to our country and its progress is the spirit of distrust which breeds them.
>
> . . . as a Catholic I recognize that the Pope is the spiritual head of the Church of which I am a member, but I acknowledge no civil authority but that of this republic . . .

In a similar vein, the *Sunday Oregonian* for November 13, 1919, carried a lengthy report of one of his cathedral sermons. The prominent headline read, ORIGIN, NATURE AND EXTENT OF CIVIL ALLEGIANCE IS DISCUSSED. The subhead said, FATHER O'HARA WARNS CONGREGATION OF DANGER RESULTING FROM ARROGANCE OF SOVEREIGN GOVERNMENTS AS DEMONSTRATED BY NUMBERLESS HISTORICAL EXAMPLES.

That these statements were given such major attention in the secular press was due largely to the fact that Father O'Hara was mentioned frequently in the newspapers as a leader in various community enterprises. On the Unemployment Commission, for example, he was a prime mover behind the municipal lodging house for unemployed men. He also represented the Consumers' League (apart from the matter of the following chapter) in things like seeking changes in the building code that would condemn the disgraceful tenements of the poor. The *Morning Oregonian* quoted him as naming "neglect, ignorance and greed" as the causes of bad housing, in a speech on "Housing the Multitude." He had become so accepted as the Catholic spokesman in civic affairs that, when a local political figure seemed to be using the A.O.H. (or the diocesan paper) to deliver the Catholic vote, the newspapers frontpaged his name in an interview which began: "In response to inquiry from members of the civic authority, the following statement was made by Father O'Hara: 'The Catholic Church is not in politics. . . .' "

But, odd as it may sound after all the above, we have to move to yet other fields to find the activities that may have taken up most of Father O'Hara's time during his Portland years.

Every priest is in principle an educator. From the first year of his priesthood, Edwin Vincent O'Hara was one in hard-working reality as teacher, professor, supervisor, administrator and articulate promoter of a Christian philosophy of education.

He started by teaching religion and apologetics at St. Mary's Academy, taking two classes on scripture at the Christian Brothers' Blanchet Institute, conducting a class for Sunday school teachers, teaching catechism in the parochial school and giving private lessons in theology to a candidate for the priesthood. Before the first year was over, he was well into his lifelong avocation of teaching teachers.

During the summer of his arrival, the Catholic Education Club had been organized to prepare an exhibit for the Portland World Fair of 1905. At that time there was no official Archdiocesan Office of Education but, on appointment by Archbishop Christie, Father O'Hara virtually assumed the functions of such an office. Using as a nucleus the Education Club that had been formed specifically to prepare the exhibit, he was able by the summer of 1907 to found a Summer Institute for Teachers and organize the Catholic Education Association of Oregon of which the archbishop named him president. He was officially appointed Diocesan Superintendent of Schools in July 1912, the year after he had been raised to the pastorate of St. Mary's cathedral parish.

One of the activities of those crowded early years was a fund-raising campaign which led to a breakdown and a trip to Europe which finished up in a course at the Catholic University of America.

The fund-raising was the institution of a Shamrock Day Fund on March 17 to put aid for the Christie Home on some kind of permanent basis. Father O'Hara's way of seeing this safely started involved spending a bitterly cold damp Pacific Coast March day walking around the city from corner to corner encouraging the Girls' Club members who were selling shamrocks (and incidentally checking on their safety). This resulted in a severe attack of bronchitis which the overworked priest was in no condition to withstand. He was ordered to rest and took the opportunity to make his first voyage to Europe.

He sailed from Quebec with his sister Anna on August 13, 1910. They saw the Passion Play at Oberammergau, had an audience with Pope Pius X, watched the liquefaction of the blood of St. Januarius at Naples and spent a week at Lourdes. He was back in Washington by October and received permission to stay there and follow a course at the Catholic University until Christmas.

Over that same period, the young priest's serious study and writing included doing the *Catholic Encyclopedia* articles on *Oregon, Archbishop Christie* and the *Poor Clares.* But his most important writing project was a book that appeared in 1911, *The Pioneer Catholic History of Oregon.*

This book was written with a double purpose: to correct in the popular mind an anti-Catholic myth which historians had already discredited, the Whitman-saved-Oregon legend, and to restore to his due place as the "father of Oregon" a Catholic layman, Dr. John McLoughlin. It was also important as a regional contribution to the total study of the influence of Catholics on the history of the United States.

Father O'Hara's work was well received by historians. As late as 1931, George W. Fuller, of the University of Chicago, could say in his *History of the Pacific Northwest,* "The best history for the general reader is O'Hara, E. V., *Catholic History of Oregon.*" But Father O'Hara did not content himself with reaching the readers of history books. He wrote newspaper stories, magazine articles and historical monographs on Dr. McLoughlin. He gave the pioneer's name to his Boys' Club. He made him the subject of sermons like one the *Morning Oregonian* reported as beginning, "An intelligent and devoted body of laymen has ever been one of the chief glories of the Catholic Church."

In his work on the history of Oregon, as in so many other things, Edwin O'Hara was first of all the priest, the good shepherd who gathers the solid food of truth and sees that it is made available to his flock.

CHAPTER IV

America's First Successful
Minimum Wage Law

O N THE EVENING of Thanksgiving Day, 1912, Father O'Hara, his coat collar turned up against a typical West Coast mist, was walking along Washington Street on his way back to the cathedral rectory when he came upon a crowd gathered around a vigorous soapbox orator. The speaker paused in his tirade against "religion, the enemy of the working man," and challenged any clergyman to stand up and contradict him.

Tom Burns, a nationally known Socialist agitator, was probably more surprised than anyone else when the quiet-mannered, soft-spoken young priest raised his hand and asked if he might take him at his word.

For twenty minutes Father O'Hara held the rostrum and drew the applause—and fire—of the audience of two hundred as he expounded the social teaching of the Church as set down by Pope Leo XIII and implemented by Catholic social leaders.

If it was a new kind of audience for the priest, the message of the Church as the friend of the working man was also startlingly new to most of his listeners. Every week for some time after that, Father O'Hara returned to share Tom Burns' soapbox and stand up to his attacks on the Church. It was an early example in the United States of the sort of street corner apologetic which the English Catholic Evidence Guild was later to evolve into a standard apostolic technique and which was to become an integral part of missionary work in non-Catholic areas of the United States.

In his talks, Father O'Hara brought the papal teachings down to specific application to the local situation. He used the occasions to arouse interest in a minimum wage law he was then in process of drafting.

The newspapers had been quick to seize upon the news value of the priest's soapbox duels with the agitator. They carried full reports of his talks and thus gave him a much larger audience than the group gathered on the street.

This publicity was a most useful thing at that moment. Those were the days when labor, seething restlessly under the denial of common rights, was turning for leadership to anarchistic and bolshevistic activists whose aim was the revolution they were to attain in Russia a few years later. Because of his insistent campaigning for social reform, Father O'Hara had become suspect as a radical in the eyes of the more conservative. The accounts of his vigorous opposition to Tom Burns did much to clarify his position and put such doubts at rest. They also set minds thinking about the necessity for social reform within the established framework of Church and State.

These street corner debates were a local dramatization of the general position at that critical moment in the social history of the United States. They also afford a simple vivid picture of the pioneer role of practical initiative Father O'Hara was taking in a great movement of national significance. For the minimum wage law of which Father O'Hara spoke on those evenings in Portland was to become the first compulsory minimum wage legislation to stand the test of the United States Supreme Court. The case which upheld the Oregon law went into American labor history as *Stettler vs. O'Hara* and its tenable provisions laid the basis for future federal laws on a basic living wage.

The social situation of those times has been summarized by Charles A. and Mary Beard in their *Basic History of the United States*. In a chapter entitled "Realizations in Social Improvement" they write:

> Older than the political insurgency that went by the name of Progressive, related to it, and yet in many respects fundamentally independent of political partisanship were efforts of humanitarians to realize ideals social in nature that transcended personal desires for self-perfection, wealth, prestige and power . . . The humanitarians were more than students, theorists, and writers, though some of them were all those persons; they were primarily activists anxious to get reforms established. They made minute surveys of blighted areas in national life and searched for ways and means of integrating social theory and social practice.

With Father O'Hara his social theory was, of course, that of Pope Leo XIII. His particular function as a leader among the above-mentioned "humanitarians" was that of finding ways and means to apply that theory to his American milieu.

Almost everything said in this chapter of a book which represents the distillation of forty years of thinking by two of the outstanding interpreters of United States history has such an uncannily direct relationship with this phase of Father O'Hara's work, that we cannot forbear one further quotation.

Speaking of the effects of the movement, the Beards say:

> The Humanitarians not only broke down the resistance of private interests and legislatures. They also compelled a reconstruction or re-education of the United States Supreme Court which for more than forty years had been reading into the Constitution, as Justice Oliver Wendell Holmes remarked, the laissez faire doctrines of Mr. Herbert Spencer, English individualist.

Active participation in the "humanitarian" causes came as a natural extension of the pastoral activities of Father O'Hara's early years in Portland. First came contact with the workers, in their homes and particularly at the Girls' Club, with their firsthand descriptions of life, working for ten hours a day in unsanitary conditions at $3.00 a week. Then there was association with like-minded people of all classes and many faiths who were attracted by the orderly mind evident in the crusading vigor of the priest's speeches and writings.

Two prominent non-Catholic citizens, W. B. Ayers, a leading and farsighted industrialist, and George Cornwall, editor of *The Timberman*, found Father O'Hara a sympathetic ally in their attempts to better the workman's position in the then scandalous matter of industrial accidents. Active interest in this cause drew Father O'Hara into the heart of Portland's turbulent labor situation. For several reasons, the city was then one of the focal points of reform effort. The seasonal nature of work in logging camps brought large concentrations of vigorous men into the city during the off-season to provide ideal material for the agitating tactics of the I.W.W. Work at the canneries was also seasonal and grossly underpaid. On the other hand, the state of Oregon had given hope to those pressing for reform by legislation in passing a maximum hours law which had withstood testing in the U. S. Supreme Court where similar measures previously had failed to hold. So such organizations as the National Consumers' League and the Association for Labor Legislation were also keeping watch on the Portland situation.

The real life business of bringing about these early social changes was a long way removed from the academic dignity of setting ideas down on paper. It meant walking among crowds organized by committeemen with flaming red badges whose speeches had inflamed beyond all reasoning the very people you were trying to help. Your reward for trying to better the condition of the workers was too often their abuse.

On the other side you had the implacable opposition of the entrenched employers who attributed to your cause every excess of the radicals and turned it into an argument against you.

When Father O'Hara faced Tom Burns from the soapbox, he was pointing the difference between himself and the atheistic materialist revolutionaries who were making no little progress toward convincing the laboring classes that they, and only they, were the hope of the worker. This attitude was voiced in a wordy but evidently heartfelt letter which appeared in the Portland *Oregonian*. The letter demanded greater allegiance to the *Communist Manifesto* on the part of reformers. It recommended abolition of marriage, sterilization of the unfit and systematic breeding by the fit. It concluded with a condemnation of people like Father O'Hara and made an interesting coupling of his name with the famous British "Sins of Society" preacher:

> Joined with us in our demand are many who never suffered as we proletarians have, are those who feel themselves dominated by morals, religion, eternal truths, freedom, justice. At the extreme verge of these are Father Vaughan, Father O'Hara and such. . . . These latter call themselves idealists, and they are creating an avalanche of reforms to submerge us true Socialists.

This was the Portland scene when Father O'Hara moved from a supporting role in the industrial accident campaign to the center of the stage in the critical Oregon phase of the American workers' fight for a basic living wage.

In the spring of 1912, Mrs. Florence Kelley, then secretary of the National Consumers' League, instigated the Oregon branch of the league to appoint a special committee to study the minimum wage problem in Oregon. Father O'Hara was asked to become chairman of the committee which also included Mrs. Millie Trumbull, W. L. Brewster and C. H.

Chapman, the agnostic editorial writer of the *Oregonian* with whom Father O'Hara had so often crossed swords.

This committee was in itself no more than a group of citizens gathered to discuss a national problem on the local level. As such it did not differ from the multitude of committees that are formed in many places year after year with similar aims. It would have been no disgrace had this committee investigated, discussed and disbanded after placing the facts at issue before the attention of the public. That it did more must, from the record, be attributed largely to the perseverance and thoroughness of its chairman.

Beginning with the formation of this committee and following through to the upholding by the United States Supreme Court of the law it drafted, we find Father O'Hara as a prime mover, a balancing element between extremes that might have wrecked the effort and a steadily working central figure to whom all interested parties could, and did, turn. In this first large-scale test of his organizational ability, the future bishop displayed several characteristics that were to mark his later work in other fields: a sense of values which allowed him to concentrate on the important thing; the ability to form a good team and win their confidence by respecting their authority in their own assignments; an awareness of the process of growth which prevented him from demanding that the seed produce its full blossom *now;* a habit of wide consultation with authoritative opinion at the highest available level; and the strength of mind not to be panicked into a single opinion, however eminent its source, when sound judgment could point a course which would balance that opinion against another and derive benefit from both.

Added to these organizational talents was the courage to adhere to papal teachings still thought radical by many of his clerical colleagues, and a firm conviction that in the American non-Catholic milieu, the function of the priest was to bring Christ out among men even—or, perhaps, especially—

when it meant working for a common good alongside men of other faiths or of none at all.

When Father O'Hara undertook the chairmanship of this committee, he was unknown outside Portland. Before he had finished the work it set on foot, he was a nationally known figure in the field of urban sociology. The eminent priest-sociologist, Dr. J. C. McGinn of Notre Dame University, could write of the satisfaction it gave him to tell his labor audiences "that the first great movement in modern times for the just remuneration of the laborer was started by a Pope; that the first great theoretical exposition of a living wage was made by a Catholic priest [Father John A. Ryan]; that the first practical demonstration of the theory of the living wage was the work of another Catholic priest [Father O'Hara]."

A future Justice of the Supreme Court of the United States, Felix Frankfurter, could send Father O'Hara a personal letter from his post at Harvard Law School saying, "It is a distinct privilege to me to have been associated, as I feel I have been, with the pioneers in Oregon in their effort to establish those minimal standards of life on which alone a healthy society can be founded." And some of the greatest names in the field of American social reform, including F. W. Taussig, head of Harvard's Department of Economics, and Henry R. Seager, of Columbia University, could send congratulatory letters to a thirty-two-year-old priest in Oregon whom, in the space of two years, they had come to look upon as a colleague in the large battle for due recognition of human values.

The Oregon Consumers' League "Social Survey Committee to study wage, hour and working conditions of women and minors in Oregon" held its first meetings in July, 1912. Its members had in common a general knowledge of the situation and a desire to remedy it. Its chairman had the advantage of having studied under the man who had made the first thorough study of the question of a basic minimum wage. He was aware that their mandate to study the facts and make recommendations would be carried out effectively only if the facts were solid enough to give unassailable reason for supporting the recommendations.

His first move was to support authorization of a competent survey, beg contributions to enable an inquiry by a professional social worker, and secure the services of Miss Caroline Gleason.

Miss Gleason, who is now Sister Miriam Theresa of the Sisters of the Holy Names of Jesus and Mary, Marylhurst, Oregon, was excellently fitted for the job. Born in Minneapolis, she had graduated from the University of Minnesota in 1908, taught for two years at St. Mary's Academy, Portland, and then gone for a year of graduate study at the Chicago School of Civics and Philanthropy. While in Chicago, she had lived at Chicago Commons, a famous settlement house. On her return to Portland she had been field secretary for Father O'Hara's Catholic Women's League in charge of evening classes and the employment bureau. In 1912 she had spent three months visiting factories in large eastern cities and conferring with people engaged in the type of work she was now called upon to do. The competence and the zeal with which she accomplished her task had much to do with the success of the whole effort.

The survey was conducted by means of interviews with workers and employers. At times the employers were uncooperative and Miss Gleason got some of her information by taking work in several different establishments. While the survey was going on, the committee continued to meet during the summer months. Their first discussions concerned the general form their proposed recommendations should take. They began to aim at drafting a proposed state law fixing a compulsory minimum wage with penalties for violation.

The question was a difficult one, particularly from the con-

stitutional point of view. Early in the process Father O'Hara
saw that the law must be framed in such a way that it could
not be set aside as a violation of freedom of contract under
the Constitution of the United States. This meant avoidance
of any elements which had invalidated previous attempts at
welfare laws in the United States. It meant seeking a basis
which had already won support in findings of appellate
courts.

He had his firm basis of argument in Pope Leo XIII's now
famous conclusion: "Let it be granted then that as a rule,
workman and employer should make free agreements and in
particular should freely agree as to wages; nevertheless, there
is a dictate of nature more imperious and more ancient than
any bargain between man and man, that the remuneration
must be enough to support the wage earner in reasonable and
frugal comfort."

But this was not enough at that stage of American socio-
legal development. Although New Zealand, Australia and
Britain had allowed general minimum wage legislation (beginning three years after Pope Leo XIII's *Rerum Novarum*)
including both men and women, the best legal precedent the
United States could then offer was the United States Supreme Court decision upholding Oregon's ten-hour law for
women. This famous decision, in the case of *Muller vs. Oregon*, was notable for turning aside from consideration of
mere legal precedence to take "legal cognizance" of the "facts
of common knowledge." It recognized that "What we know
as men we cannot pretend to be ignorant of as judges."

It laid down the grounds on which welfare legislation for
women would be upheld by the courts when similar legislation would not be sustained for men, ". . . having in view not
merely her own health, but the well-being of the race. . . ."
This consideration led Father O'Hara and his committee to
design their law only for women and minors. Once any
compulsory minimum wage law was found constitutional, the

opening wedge would be entered for further advance.

When Miss Gleason completed her survey it offered statistical evidence for two things: the prevailing wages for women in Oregon; the minimum wage on which a single woman could live "in reasonable and frugal comfort." The wages were found to start at less than $3.00 a week; $3.50 to $5.00 was quite common and $6.00 considered good. Well-paid women office workers were getting about $10.00 a week. The figures on lodging, food and clothing placed the acceptable minimum at about $8.00 weekly.

In its first draft of the proposed law, the committee made several mistakes from the constitutional point of view. One was the fixing of a definite sum as the minimum weekly wage for all occupations.

Then Father O'Hara took the next step which gave the final law its solidity. He sent out copies of the proposed Act for criticism by outstanding authorities in the United States and abroad. Comment came from people like Taussig, Seager and Father Ryan as well as from the powerful influences grouped in the National Consumers' League and the American Association for Labor Legislation. The last-named organization, having worked itself out of existence by successful campaigning for a labor strong enough to handle its own problems, is rarely remembered now as the powerful organization it then was. The letterhead on which John B. Andrews, secretary of the association, carried on a correspondence with Father O'Hara which warmed into personal friendship, bore names which read like a roll call of social reformers in the United States of fifty years ago: Jane Addams, Louis D. Brandeis, Richard T. Ely, Samuel Gompers, Frederick N. Judson, Woodrow Wilson, Felix Adler, Edward A. Filene, John A. Ryan, Henry L. Stimson, Ernst Freund, Samuel McCune Lindsay and Morton D. Hull.

It was, however, from the National Consumers' League that most aid came. Mrs. Florence Kelley, the brilliant Goldmark sisters, Pauline and Josephine, who were the league's legal advisors, Louis D. Brandeis and Felix Frankfurter all made their contributions to the law through the league.

It is interesting to note that this array of talent did not awe the Oregon committee. While the revised draft of the law incorporated several of the National Consumers' League suggestions, it rejected others including an insistent appeal to make the law apply also to men. On this point, Father O'Hara was subjected to additional pressure from his teacher and friend, Father Ryan. But he stuck to his judgment in favor of the safer counsel, like that of Henry R. Seager— "Your plan of dealing with the problem of the minimum wage is the most simple and direct that has come to my attention. . . . It would certainly present the constitutional issue in a most clear-cut fashion."

In the year the committee was meeting, Massachusetts passed the nation's first minimum wage legislation of any kind. But the law was not compulsory. As it had no more sanction than the force of public opinion, there was no hope of it providing a test of constitutionality or a basis for future laws. Although signed in 1912, it did not take effect until July 1, 1913. By that time, so steadily had Father O'Hara's committee advanced in its work, the Oregon law had been passed, made effective and put into practice.

The first draft of the proposed legislation had gone out for criticism before the end of September. The revision was sent out at the beginning of November and the completed text was in the hands of the Oregon legislature for the opening of the January, 1913, session.

The president of the Senate, Dan J. Malarkey, undertook to sponsor the bill. But before it reached the floor, Father O'Hara and other members of the committee had attended upon as many members of the legislature as they could reach to explain its provisions and win their support. It passed in both houses with scarcely a dissenting vote, was signed by

Governor Oswald West and went into effective operation on June 3, 1913.

The measure was entitled "An Act to protect the lives and health and morals of women and minor workers, and to establish an Industrial Welfare Commission and define its powers and duties, and to provide for the fixing of minimum wages and maximum hours and standard conditions of labor for such workers, and to provide penalties for violations of this Act."

Its provisions avoided the constitutional difficulty of setting arbitrary standards. Section One was worded in this way:

> It shall be unlawful to employ women or minors . . . for unreasonably long hours . . . under such surroundings or con- ditions—sanitary or otherwise—as may be detrimental to their health or morals . . . to employ women for wages which are inadequate to supply the necessary cost of living and to main- tain them in health . . . to employ minors . . . for unreason- ably low wages.

Sections Two to Five set up an Industrial Welfare Com- mission to "ascertain and declare" fit standards of hours, con- ditions and wages as called for by the Act. Section Nine em- powered the Commission to make orders which after sixty days would have the effect of law and whose violation would incur penalties of fine or imprisonment laid down in Section Seventeen.

An important step forward in American social legislation had been taken. The old notion that what went on in indus- try was the personal concern of each industrialist had been overthrown. The State had effectively claimed the right to protect the common good in the basic matters of wages, hours and working conditions.

To hold the ground gained and put the future on a firm footing, two questions had to be answered: Would the Act work and bring good results? Would it stand up to appeals against its constitutionality?

CHAPTER V

Putting the New Law to the Test

THE WORKING of the Act began with the appointment of the Commission it required. This was to consist of three people, one representing the point of view of the employers, one that of the workers and the third that of the public. Mr. Amedee Smith, a prominent businessman, was appointed in the first role, Miss Bertha Moores, a self-supporting working woman, in the second and Father O'Hara, who was also made chairman of the Commission, was appointed by Governor Oswald West to represent the general public. The Commission was authorized to employ a secretary. The post was given to Miss Caroline Gleason.

An initial attempt to gather together the employers and seek a general agreement, without investigation and debate, proved fruitless. So the Commission proceeded to the next step in its appointed procedure.

It started separate hearings for the various industries in which women and minors were employed. The hearings, open to the public, began with a conference in which three representatives for each group presented the views of employers, employees and the public. Their findings were taken into consideration by the Commission which had full authority to accept or reject them. There was little opportunity for evasion. The Act had empowered the Commission "to examine and inspect any and all books and payrolls and other records of any employer of women and minors that in any way appertain to or have a bearing upon the question of wages or hours of labor or conditions of labor." In addition it granted the Commission authority to subpoena any witnesses it desired. It also contained a heavy penalty clause against any employer discriminating against an employee who gave evidence before the Commission.

There were a number of employers who welcomed the law. They recognized the injustice of the wages paid but had previously felt unable to increase them because of competitors who would continue to underpay. They saw in the binding decisions of the Commission their protection from sweat-shop practices of other employers.

But there were enough employers of the other kind to make things really difficult for the Commission. This put Father O'Hara squarely in the middle of two pressure groups, as a contemporary newspaper description of the situation foresaw when it spoke of "Father O'Hara, chairman of the Commission, and, by reason of his being the representative of the general public, the man who probably will hold the balance of power in its deliberations. . . ."

In point of fact there was little difficulty within the Commission itself. Due to the broad understanding of both Mr. Smith and Miss Moores, the three commissioners were able to report a unanimous decision in virtually every case brought before them.

The pincers attack on the chairman came from certain influential employers and from two different elements in the ranks of labor.

The employers who wished to guard their "constitutional right" to treat labor as a commodity to be purchased in the cheapest market and to manipulate hours and working conditions to suit a tough competitive struggle, did all in their power to label the priest-chairman as a radical. Some of these were connected with leading department stores. There was a particular bitterness when the Commission found it necessary to regulate their practices on all three counts of wages, hours and conditions, and proposed, among other things, that all women and minors be released from employment at six o'clock on Saturdays. This in effect meant the accomplishment of an early closing law for which Father O'Hara had been waging a separate Consumers' League campaign supported by all the trade union bodies.

Again the main body of the employers approved the justice of the Commission's action. In a letter to Father O'Hara, the Portland Grocers' and Merchants' Association wrote: "Your work is as important to the social welfare of the community as it is pertinent to all employers, the majority of whom would readily concede the requests of your Commission were it not for the intense competition which regulates the wage, hours and conditions of our employees."

The regulations were passed and made law. But the adamant ill feeling of the disgruntled and powerful few gave promise of the test case to which the Commission was looking forward.

On the labor side, the opposition was twofold. The revolutionaries did not want improved social conditions under the present regime. For them that meant a lessening of discontent and a postponement of the revolution. Many trade unionists, on the other hand, appreciated the gains but wanted them brought about by other means.

Opposition from the extreme Left of the labor group came with a spectacular bang within weeks of the Commission's appointment. It took the form of a riot-filled strike, well organized and militantly led by the I.W.W. The target was well chosen—the Oregon Packing Plant, about which Miss Gleason's survey had uncovered enough information to make it a primary object of the Commission's own attention. Some of the girls were working ten hours for as little as forty cents a day.

The strikers were demanding $1.50 a day and would brook no compromise. They had thrown around the plant a picket line which the *Oregonian* described as "a howling mob of 1,000 strike agitators." On the day of a meeting in which Father O'Hara participated, two people were arrested for inciting to riot and a watchman was jailed for kicking a striker. The paper said, "It was the wildest time Portland had had in a long time."

Governor Oswald West had come from the capitol at Salem to make an on-the-spot inquiry. He called a conference of the strike leaders, the company and the Commission. By this time, the two principal agitators, Mrs. Marie Schwab and Tom Burns, had the strikers so worked up that they were in no mood to listen to reason. Smart organization had packed the council chamber of the City Hall with longshoremen, loggers and strikers before the meeting got under way. A semicircle of the youngest girl strikers had been drawn up around the conference table to which Father O'Hara and his colleagues could hardly squeeze their way. The Governor sat at one end of the long table and Tom Burns at the other.

The bedlam that followed could hardly be called a conference. But it is a good sample of one element involved in Father O'Hara's fight for a minimum wage.

When Governor West tried to tell the strikers to stay away from the plant till he could attempt to get them $1.50 a day, he was howled down by the crowd. Father O'Hara met the same fate and came in for additional criticism "because of articles he had written." The Governor came warmly to his defense and the session turned into a shouting match between the head of the state and the strikers.

"Mrs. Schwab," says the account, "kept hectoring the Governor in a high-pitched voice. Father O'Hara also came in for his share of the attention from the Joan of Arc of the strikers, and she kept either the Governor or the clergyman denying her allegations, which she put in the form of questions, a large part of the time. Dr. Marie Equi attempted to make a speech from a chair, and added to the din by her vociferous protestations of sympathy for the strikers, even to the point of shedding her life-blood or being 'burned on a cross.' "

At one point Mrs. Schwab screamed that she had recently been arrested four times in one day.

While Tom Burns was holding forth with some blunt accusations of dishonesty on the part of the Commission, Governor West's remaining patience snapped. He took the only path open to get near Burns, jumped up on the conference table and ran its whole length to stand over him shaking a finger and shouting, "You know that isn't true!" until Burns subsided. But the strike leader had the last word in the exchange. As the gallery cheered him on, Tom told the Governor that he couldn't be rattled because he was cool; he was "the man who put the iceberg before the *Titanic*."

When the Governor called the canning company people, he found they had beaten a retreat under cover of the confusion.

An appeal to the strikers to wait for the decision of the Commission was met with loud derision: "So you would feed the horse after it's dead?" "What's the use of waiting for the Commission? By that time the berry crop will be gone and there'll be no work."

This last was in fact the cause of the dilemma on which the Commission was impaled. If it could not find a solution to which management would immediately agree, about three months would pass before it could complete its investigation, enact its findings into law and allow the sixty-day period before they became enforceable. Examination of the company's books revealed the truth of the claim that they could not pay $1.50 and sell the current crop in the available market.

The Commission did arrive at the distinct gain of an immediate increase to $1.00 a day minimum with an advance in piecework from ten to fifteen cents a basket which would enable capable workers to earn more.

But it had been a baptism of fire—and a salutary lesson. The Commission's mandate gave it no authority to arbitrate strikes. It was out of its proper domain. The riotous meeting, with no possibility of offering an immediately satisfactory solution to the aroused crowd, was a situation the I.W.W. loved. They had exploited it to the full.

Opposition from some of the trade unionists was quieter, though at first quite insistent. It included leaders like California's Father Yorke. These people were suspicious, with some reason in previous experience, of "boards" apparently set up for their welfare but in reality tools of the employers. They appreciated the groundwork being done and the real betterment brought about. But they wanted this accomplished, though they were not yet strong enough to do it, through their own organization. They did not see that legislative curbing of the unlimited authority of industry over labor was the necessary first step to their goal. These leaders quoted Father O'Hara's speeches freely and approvingly, while disagreeing with him on the question of means.

That all labor was not opposed to the minimum wage bill is evident from newspaper reports of the introduction of the Oregon Act for legislative approval in the state of Washington. Senator George U. Piper, who was to sponsor the bill in that state, had invited Father O'Hara and C. H. Chapman to appear before the labor and statistics committees of the Washington House and Senate at Olympia. After the Oregonians had explained the bill, those who spoke in favor of it included C. O. Young, an organizer for the Federation of Labor, and Paul K. Mohr, of Seattle, representing eighty labor unions.

The Oregon Minimum Wage Act, unchanged, was passed

and became law in the state of Washington about the same time as in Oregon. Shortly afterward, the identical law was passed in the state of California. During the same year, 1913, five other states followed suit and enacted minimum wage legislation.

All during this campaign, Father O'Hara was engaged in a steady round of writing and speaking on the conditions revealed by his committee's social survey and on the remedies proposed by the law. The tenor of these talks did much to keep labor looking upon him as a friend while arousing capital to a sense of its social obligations. One theme is found repeatedly in the reports of his talks at that time. He was very much opposed to the argument that low wages forced girls into immorality. He considered this a slur on the working woman as well as an evasion of the points at issue. "It is far more to the point to show," he told a Seattle audience, "that underpaid girls are not only preserving their virtue but are living on two meals a day and are forced to practice other pitiable economies which undermine their health and unfit them for the duties of wife and mother and thus sap the foundations of society."

He also attacked the "pin money" argument against decent wages for women, labeling it "an ancient weapon . . . sufficiently curious to be laid away in the museum of antiquated armament." He asked, "Are those who live at home and who do not need to work (supposing that they constituted a considerable number) to be allowed by competition to cut the wages of their self-supporting sisters below the cost of decent subsistence?"

The satisfaction of the benefited employees and the increasing cooperation of employers was demonstrating the workability of the law and its good effects before the Commission had ended its first year. But even before that, the diehard capitalist opposition had brought suit against Father O'Hara and his fellow commissioners on the grounds that their rulings were a violation of the Fourteenth Amendment of the United States Constitution, which ordains that "No State shall make or enforce any law which shall abridge the privileges or immunities of citizens of the United States; nor shall any State deprive any person of life, liberty, or property, without due process of law."

The man who led the attack for the dissatisfied employers was Frank C. Stettler, a paper-box manufacturer. He bore a particular grudge because his establishment had been one of those in which Miss Gleason went to work personally in order to obtain her information. It was also quite obviously the place referred to by Father O'Hara in his "Welfare Legislation for Women and Minors" when he wrote: "Suppose our friend goes to a paper-box factory and is engaged on piece work. She will stand for ten hours a day over a nauseating pot of glue and as she goes to her humble lodging at night, trying to get some fresh air into her lungs on the way, she will figure up her profits at from sixty-five to eighty cents."

The ruling against which Mr. Stettler was appealing had compelled him to reduce the hours to nine a day, provide a forty-five-minute lunch hour and pay a minimum of $8.64 a week for not more than fifty-four hours.

The appeal was denied by the Circuit Court in February, 1914, and taken to the State Supreme Court. In a judgment rendered on March 17 of the same year, this court again upheld the constitutionality of the law, maintaining that the arguments in favor of the constitutional validity of the ten-hour law for women workers also held for the minimum wage.

The case was then taken to the United States Supreme Court and argued there on December 17, 1914.

Here, as at the Oregon Supreme Court, the Consumers' League had brought brilliant legal representation to the support of the law. A brief which included a world view of the

position of women in labor was prepared by Miss Josephine
Goldmark and Louis N. Brandeis and presented by the latter
before the nation's highest court of appeal.

Four basically important legal points were at issue:

First, did it lie within the competence of the State to inter-
fere with the right of private contract to the extent of fixing
minimum wage rates for women workers?

Second, had the legislature in creating the Industrial Welfare Commission attempted to delegate its own legislative
power?

Third, did not the establishment of different occupations
amount to class legislation?

Fourth, had not the legislature, in denying the right of
appeal to the courts from the Commission in matters of fact,
infringed upon the constitutional right of citizens to a due
process of law in defense of their property?

By the time the case came up for decision, rendered April
9, 1917, Mr. Brandeis had been appointed to the Supreme
Court and Mr. Felix Frankfurter had taken his place to plead
the O'Hara side of *Stettler vs. O'Hara.*

Justice Brandeis, because of his previous activity in the
case, could not participate in the decision. The makeup of
the Court at the time was such that the proponents of the
law were not overoptimistic about the outcome. A personal
letter to Father O'Hara, from a prominent person in social
work, gives a rather sad picture that foreshadows the later
unkindness of the pungent phrase, "Nine Old Men":

> On May 12 . . . I was present. It was an amazing spectacle.
> Justice Lamar was dead and his chair was vacant. Justice
> Day was away ill, and had been for many months. His chair
> stood vacant. Mr. Brandeis' confirmation was pending. Jus-
> tice White was noticeably deaf. Justice McKenna, sitting
> next, was nearly blind. For years he has not seen the features
> of counsel addressing the Court. He wears a strange brown

portico over his eyes. Justice Holmes keen, alert, and fully up-to-date in mind and in writing of his decisions, is past 73. Justice Hughes was then deciding to go. This leaves the three reactionaries, Justices Pitney and Van Devanter (appointed by Mr. Taft) and Mr. McReynolds.

. . . in view of the power to delay needed changes that is reposed in these nine men, it is incredible that thinking people take so little part in selecting and recommending them.

That letter was written in 1916. When the decision was handed down a year later, the Court had its full complement of nine judges. With Mr. Brandeis unable to participate, it sustained the law on a divided decision. Minimum wage legislation was accepted as constitutional. This was indeed the crowning of achievement.

The local improvements Father O'Hara had set out to obtain for the working women under his pastoral care in Portland, Ore., had culminated in enabling legislation which brought about a new and more humane interpretation of the Constitution of the United States which, in turn, opened the door to a new status for the working people of industrial America. An American priest had virtually written an opinion of Pope Leo XIII's into the law of this land.

The future history of minimum wage legislation at the United States Supreme Court is interesting. Twice the Court receded from its position; once by invalidating a New York law and once by deciding against one sponsored by Father John A. Ryan in Washington, D.C. When the constitutionality of minimum wage legislation was finally revalidated in a resounding judgment which stands as today's interpretation of the Constitution with regard to the relative rights of employer and worker, the case was *West Coast Hotel vs. Parrish* (1937), the issue was whether or not the state of Washington had the right to pass minimum wage legislation, and the legislation upon which decision was rendered was that taken verbatim by Washington from the law Father O'Hara guided to enactment in Oregon.

Of that 1937 decision, Richard D. Heffner in his *A Documentary History of the United States* says, "The Supreme Court's voluntary about-face was historic—some called it 'the stitch in time that saves nine.'" It was rendered sometime before the "liberals," Hugo Black, Felix Frankfurter, William O. Douglas, Frank Murphy and Robert Jackson, were appointed to the Court.

Tribute came to Father O'Hara from many directions in testimony to the real importance of his role in the prolonged, delicate and difficult battle. The most valuable of it is that which came from the men closest to him in the legislative and practical aspects of the fight. They were in a position to know the part he had played. The congratulations received from people like Felix Frankfurter, Henry R. Seager and Father Ryan were of that order. So was the solid mass of compliment that surrounded him in Oregon from those who had watched at first hand his conduct of the Industrial Welfare Commission. This found succinct expression in Governor Withycombe's acknowledgment of Father O'Hara's resignation from the Commission in June, 1917, after the law had been upheld in the United States Supreme Court: ". . . I desire to express my high appreciation of the splendid public service you have rendered in the four years you have devoted to the activities of this commission. That Oregon has blazed the way of industrial legislation which is being followed throughout the United States, is, I am sure, in a large measure due to your own earnest efforts."

Perhaps the most surprising of these tributes to his work in Oregon came from the official West Coast publication of the Ku Klux Klan. In its leading editorial, under the heading NOT FOR SELF, BUT FOR OTHERS, *The Western American* wrote a denunciation of one of Father O'Hara's successors "the Rt. Rev. Walter Taylor Sumner, D.D., Bishop of Oregon, of the Protestant Episcopal Church" in which it said: "In contrast with Dr. Sumner, who represents a Protestant denomination, the Rev. Edwin V. O'Hara of the Roman Catholic Church, serving as the first chairman of the Minimum Wage Commission, proved himself the staunch and consistent advocate of a living wage for these downtrodden workers. He was the leading figure in the fight for higher wages for them and for decent conditions of servitude. He scourged the advocates of a niggardly pittance of five or six dollars a week and did his best to arouse public opinion in behalf of women and girls. . . . It is the pleasure of the Klansmen to give the Reverend O'Hara his due, in reference to this subject, which cannot be handled honestly without giving him credit."

Most pleasing, perhaps, was the conferring of an honorary LL.D. degree by Notre Dame on the occasion of the university's Golden Jubilee in 1917. The citation read that the degree of Doctor of Laws was conferred . . . "On a learned and zealous priest, author of the 'Minimum Wage Law in the State of Oregon,' a vindicator of popular rights and a vigorous champion of the Church: The Rev. Edwin Vincent O'Hara, of Portland, Oregon."

The Notre Dame honor must have been particularly satisfying because it came from people who fully understood the deeper significance of the work that had been done and the motivation that lay beneath it.

Not only had Father O'Hara been putting papal teaching into national practice, but he had been seizing every opportunity to broadcast those teachings to people who had never heard of them. His recognition as an authority on minimum wage legislation led to many invitations to publish his thought and experience in speeches, pamphlets and articles, not only in the Catholic field but also in media of wide general influence among people who were forming the social thought of the nation. The state of Oregon published his summary and documentation of its law in a substantial brochure which became a standard reference, *A Living Wage by Legislation: the Oregon Experience*. This official work established its basic principles by ample quotation from Pope Leo XIII. Papal teaching as a guide to progressive social thinking was also stressed in articles for *The Outlook*, a liberal review which had Theodore Roosevelt as a contributing editor, *The Annals* of the American Academy of Political and Social Science, and other influential media.

In all his work for the minimum wage, Father O'Hara was the priest-educator doing his duty as a citizen by giving his fellow citizens the benefit of Catholic social teaching. Only accidentally to the carrying out of this substantial purpose was he the sociologist who won national respect for sound theory and painstaking practice.

He was simply living the advice he gave in an article, "The Pastor and the Workingmen of His Parish":

"In fulfilling these papal injunctions the pastor will find that his activities in behalf of his workingmen will fall into three general channels, the currents of which flow largely in the same direction and frequently converge. These channels are education, organization, and legislation."

CHAPTER VI

A Study of Catholic Rural Life

A CAREFUL WRITER learns to be suspicious of words like "basic," "essential" and "national." It is too easy to fall into an inexact use of them to indicate something somewhat more important or wider in scope than the ordinary individual effort. But there is no avoiding them in their exact meaning when speaking of the major activities in which Edwin O'Hara took pioneer roles during his fifty-one years as a priest. An instinct for the important drew his interest to essential things and an awareness of the need for extension and continuity directed his industry toward permanent organization on a national basis.

The activity which brought to a close his fifteen years in the cathedral parish at Portland is a good example. How he got into it is one more demonstration of the far-reaching effects of a good priest going about his appointed duties in a thorough manner.

Father O'Hara had spent from June until December of the year 1918 as a Knights of Columbus chaplain in France. He had seen front-line service with Mobile Hospital Unit Number Five attached to the 79th Battalion during the offensive of the Argonne. After the Armistice he had attended lectures at L'Institut Catholique in Paris and visited people like Sydney and Beatrice Webb and Father Bernard Vaughan in England.

On his way back from service in France, he had followed his custom of making travel profitable to his work at home. This time it led him into a first-hand study of how others were meeting the parochial, institutional and educational problems he had to face in Portland. While in the East that summer, he found that there were some fields in which he could not get much help. The result of his questioning on one point was a request that he set down his thinking on the subject in a paper on Catholic rural education for the 1920 convention of the National Catholic Educational Association.

When he returned to Portland, he had no notion that because of this assignment he was about to enter on a whole new phase of his life work. It was, in his mind, a very simple, straightforward matter. He was a priest in charge of education for a diocese that had a lot of rural schools. These schools created special problems. In the course of his duties, he had already given those problems some thought. Now he was going to analyze the situation, order his thinking and set down some conclusions.

His farm background, combined with his interest in history, gave him a practical and factual approach to the problem and the knowledge that there had been some effort to do something about it. He was not prepared, however, for the revelation that broke upon him as he started his study.

His method was typical of his simplicity, directness and thoroughness. He first took the latest United States Census Report, that of 1910, and surveyed the general rural position in the nation. Then he turned to the *Catholic Directory* for national statistics on Catholics in rural areas. The significance of the combined figures leaped to his mind and joined his concrete knowledge of farm living to form certain immediate conclusions. He drew up a questionnaire designed to test them and sent it out to one thousand rural pastors.

From his study of the Census Report, he reached a conclusion later scientifically verified by studies like that of
Harvard's Sorokin and Zimmerman in their *Principles of
Rural-Urban Sociology* (Henry Holt, 1930) and by specially directed inquiries of the Bureau of Census. He found
that the make-up of the countryside today determines the
make-up of the city and of the whole nation tomorrow. In
proportion as the rural areas are Catholic or Protestant or
pagan today, the cities and the nation will tend to become
Catholic or Protestant or pagan tomorrow. No city of over
100,000 population perpetuates itself. If you built a wall
around it against immigration from the outside, it would
gradually die away. This remains normally true even when
we allow for immigration from outside the nation. The city
has to draw on the country. The first generation from the
country has a proportionally larger effect than native city
dwellers on population increase.

Out of this was born a conclusion that was to become a
slogan with Father O'Hara: "The primary product of the
farm is not wheat or potatoes or cattle, it is people."

Turning to the Catholic statistics, he found a situation
that was truly distressing in the light of this fact. Whereas
53.7 per cent of the total population of the United States was
rural, only 6.1 per cent of the Catholic population fell into
the same classification. At the same time, Catholics formed
30 per cent of the urban population of the nation. This meant
that the natural rural-urban population trend would work
greatly to the disadvantage of Catholic increase. In fact, the
religious census of 1916 showed this trend at work. In fifteen
rural states in which the Catholic Church was not the leading denomination, the figures showed a decreased Catholic
population over a ten-year period. There was a note of im-
mediacy in the priest's simple sentence: "The future will be
with the Church that ministers to the rural population."

This was the situation. The next step was to inquire into

what had been done about it and what more could be done.

Father O'Hara was familiar with the two principal early Catholic land movements: the Irish Catholic colonization efforts and the German groups who had coalesced in the Centraal Verein. He also knew quite well the work of the Catholic Church Extension Society.

But up to the time he wrote his paper for the National Catholic Education Association, there had been nothing done in the way of presenting the whole national rural situation from a Catholic point of view. The report he finally drew up made a rather forceful impact on the thoughtful Catholic leaders who gave it study.

If there was a certain vehemence in its statement, this may have been due to the fact that the Superintendent of Catholic Schools for the archdiocese of Portland had become keenly aware that he himself had been smugly guilty of abetting the betrayal of the Catholic cause in the United States.

He had just finished building a new school and had been quite proud of the number of country families who had moved into the city to gain their children the benefit of a good Catholic education in the cathedral parish. He now saw that this amounted to draining the nation's Catholic resources. It was also collusion in social decay inasmuch as it took men who were skilled professionals on the farm away from the dignity of their position to menial jobs in the city.

Out of this realization came one of the principal points he had to make with Catholic educators: help keep good farmers on the farm by providing their children with adequate Catholic education.

A farmer himself, Father O'Hara never for a moment thought of "Back to the Land" as a slogan of the rural movement. That, even on the rare occasions it finds practical implementation, is a solution for urban problems, not rural. His watchword would rather be "Stay on the Land." His effort would go toward supplying the farmer with the religious, cultural, social and material advantages necessary to make country living attractive.

He knew that the constant flow from farm to city was necessary and good. But he wanted rural conditions to be altered so that more of the most intelligent farm children would want to stay in the country.

Today the question of country living versus city living occupies the minds of many Americans. Three decades of material progress have brought considerable improvement to life on the farm. But the sound statement made by Father O'Hara in New York back in 1920 still merits consideration.

Section One of the paper read at the Education Convention established the fact that there *was* a rural problem: "Fundamentally the rural problem in the past has been one of isolation and drudgery."

Section Two dealt with the religious bearing of the problem: "A religious center in the country, consequently, is a fountain bubbling up like Jacob's well a blessing for future generations." In this section, Father O'Hara made a point beyond statistics when he said: "But the importance of the rural religious problem is not to be measured by counting heads. The country is the nursery of individualism; it is God's own training school in self-reliance. . . . In the country we are thrown upon our own resources and learn a self-reliance in meeting problems of life that is of the essence of leadership. If we lose the country population we lose not merely numbers but leaders of future generations both in country and in city life."

In Section Three, he proposed a program: "The first element in a Catholic rural program is the rural religious leader." He insisted upon recognition of the importance of a rural pastorate as opposed to regarding it as a stepping stone to a post in the city.

Father O'Hara went on to speak of the need for rural schools, of the advantage of religious vacation schools where

Catholic schools were not practicable, of the use of lay cate- chists, of a rural Catholic press, of religious instruction by mail which "will require national organization working through convents in every diocese which will set aside capa- ble teachers to supervise the papers of the rural pupils."

The paper ended with an appeal: "I submit to the members of this Association the desirability of entering upon a study of the rural Catholic school problem in the United States, and in the words of a zealous correspondent, 'urgently re- quest that steps be taken to formulate a national rural school policy to replace the haphazard way in which this vast field is left to the initiative of individuals, enormously handicapped by rural poverty and lack of appreciation of the work on the part of Catholics.'"

This study was presented at the NCEA New York con- vention on June 30, 1920. Earlier, as soon as he saw the shape his study was taking, Father O'Hara had decided to sow the seed of remedial action on a national scale. He had placed a memorandum summarizing the facts and his con- clusions before both the Department of Education and the Department of Social Action of the newly formed National Catholic Welfare Council. The two last items of the memo- randum expressed his opinion that the work should be taken up under the direction of both departments:

5. There should be organized a section of rural Catholic edu- cation to study the rural Catholic problem, to suggest remedies and to enlist the active cooperation of all forces necessary to apply these remedies.
6. Such a section might well be in closest cooperation with a rural section of the Social Action Department engaged in rural Catholic Social problems.

From the NCWC department of education, Father O'Hara heard nothing further. But the memorandum aroused the in- terest of some members of the social action department and he was invited to a committee meeting being held in Chicago in preparation for the meeting of the bishops. Under the chairmanship of Bishop Peter J. Muldoon, of Rockford, Ill., the proposals were favorably discussed.

Attendance at this meeting was Father O'Hara's formal introduction to an organization through which he was to exert a nationwide influence as priest and bishop for the next thirty-six years, an organization with which, in his capacity as chaplain, he had already cooperated in its emergency wartime form.

The National Catholic Welfare Council, as it was then called, is a voluntary association of the bishops of the United States for the purpose of organizing and coordinating Catholic effort in activities of a national nature.

It functions through a general meeting of all the cooperating bishops which elects an administrative board of archbishops and bishops. The cardinals of the nation are ex-officio members of this board. Each department (there are now eight of them—Executive, Education, Press, Social Action, Legal, Immigration, Youth and Lay Apostolate) is under a member of the administrative board who has the right to choose another bishop as assistant. Special committees of bishops are also appointed to coordinate national activity in a particular field.

When Bishop Muldoon, as episcopal head of the Social Action Department, became infected with Father O'Hara's urgency about the rural life situation, he immediately saw that the work fell legitimately within his scope. He asked, "What specifically do you want us to do?" The answer was ready: "Set up within your department an office for research, education and organization on Catholic rural life."

"All right," said the bishop, "I'll do it if you will be the office."

Father O'Hara replied that he could not accept anything that meant leaving a diocese already short of priests. Asked if he could do the job from where he was, he answered that he thought he could, provided his archbishop would allow him to transfer to a country parish.

Bishop Muldoon obtained approval of his action, Father O'Hara got his transfer, and the Rural Life Bureau of the Social Action Department of the National Catholic Welfare Council was born.

It took about a month to arrange the transfer to a rural parish. While awaiting the archbishop's appointment, Father O'Hara went about his duties and made parish plans for the future without saying a word to his parishioners about the change. When the announcement was made, on May 29, 1920, that Father O'Hara would be leaving Portland on June 1 it was such a shock to the city in general that the leading daily used its largest headlines to shout at the top of the front page, FATHER O'HARA TRANSFERRED BY ARCHBISHOP. A two-column portrait was set off by a boxed announcement in bold-face twelve-point type. The subheads told the gist of the news: PASTOR OF ST. MARY'S CATHEDRAL HERE AND LEADER IN MANY PUBLIC ACTIVITIES WILL BECOME PASTOR AT EUGENE NEXT WEEK. The story which reflected some bewilderment at the suddenness of the change, gave a résumé of the priest's activities and said: "The removal of Father O'Hara from Portland will be a matter of deep and sincere regret not only among the Catholic people of the city, by all of whom he is loved, but among hundreds of people outside the church, whose admiration he has won by his broad cultural attainments, his high-minded ideals and his intelligent interest and active participation in educational, social welfare and civic matters."

The next day's paper, the *Sunday Oregonian*, was able to add an interview with Father O'Hara and give the pastor's reasons for the change. After stating the principal aim of the rural work, Father O'Hara added, "In the second place, I hope to broaden the scope and interest of the Newman Club, composed of university students at Eugene [the seat of the University of Oregon]."

But the paper was not content with such prosaic reasons. The reporter contrived to titillate his readers with a suggestion of "inside knowledge." He wrote: "There are prominent Catholic laymen in Portland who venture a guess as to the reason for Father O'Hara's leaving that is not admitted by the pastor at St. Mary's. There may be possibilities, they say, of the establishment of another bishopric in Oregon with Eugene as the seat. And who would be a more logical nominee for bishop than Father O'Hara?"

Of more practical value for the record is the final sentence of a paragraph dealing with Father O'Hara's part in the minimum wage law: "The law was written mostly by Father O'Hara and has been the model for similar laws in twelve other states."

CHAPTER VII

Eugene and the Rural Life Bureau

WHEN FATHER O'HARA went to take over his duties in Eugene, Ore., he was not going to the rural parish of his first choice. He would have preferred the tiny but historically interesting parish of St. Paul where the faith was first firmly planted in the state. But Eugene had decided advantages for his purposes. Though the city had a population of over ten thousand, the parish was rural enough for anyone. It embraced fifty miles north and south along the Pacific Coast, extending back 175 miles to the Cascade Mountains. There were only five other incorporated towns in the whole area plus more than thirty distinct small communities. The parish church in Eugene served 125 families of which one-half were farmers. Three missions at Cottage Grove, Springfield and Junction City served thirty, twenty and fifteen families respectively. Twenty other rural centers had from one to five Catholic families each. The varied conditions in a single county covering such a large area provided a most suitable laboratory for a survey of rural conditions and the testing of remedial measures.

Like any new pastor, Father O'Hara had first to familiarize himself with his routine duties and the means at his disposal to carry them out. In Eugene he had a church, an elementary school conducted by the Holy Names Sisters and a hospital under the care of the Sisters of Mercy. In the country there were two mission chapels. He had no assistant. A chaplain resident at the hospital was unable to take much active duty.

The former pastor had been in ill health and there were some immediate tasks awaiting his successor's attention. The church and four rooms of the school had to be moved bodily across the tracks and four blocks down the road to a new location. A job like that generally means work, shirtsleeves work, for the country pastor and Dr. O'Hara was no exception. He had vivid memories of one night in particular.

The buildings were shored up and ready for moving. Crossing the tracks had to be done during the small hours when no cars were running. The pastor was superintendent and mechanic. His crew was one man, a fine strapping specimen of the Oregon pioneer. Around one in the morning, the big one-inch cable hauling the building snapped. The pastor-superintendent held a lantern while the man gave an impromptu demonstration of the strength of two good working hands. He took the stiff unwieldy cable and forced it into a knot that held the strain till the ninety-foot by forty-foot building was pulled over to the other side of the street.

In addition to the special needs of the parish and his regular duties, Father O'Hara was reappointed archdiocesan Superintendent of Schools, and the approach of the academic year was drawing his attention to proper provision for Catholic students at the University of Oregon.

But all these were merely the Eugene-Father O'Hara edition of the normal religious, educational, social and cultural aspects of caring for a rural parish. In attending to them he would be putting to the test of practical experience his ideas about the solution of the Catholic rural problem.

So the remarkably rapid launching of the Rural Life Bureau of the NCWC was not so much accomplished in addition to running a parish or at the expense of that work as *by* running it and by giving intensive attention to that first work of a parish priest.

It is illuminating to notice how often the beginnings of important undertakings consist of ordinary things done well and done consistently. Every new pastor takes the same three steps. He finds out what people and what situations he has in his parish, he estimates what the church can do about it, and he does it. That is exactly how Father O'Hara proceeded. But he made his investigation thoroughly, formed his estimate of what could be done according to an informed philosophy of what should be done, and set activities in motion according to sound principles of organization.

His finding out became "A Religious Survey of Lane County, Oregon" which was published, along with the things he had started to do about it, as *A Program of Catholic Rural Action*.

The question of what the Church could do involved—in Lane County as everywhere else—a union of theory with the available means. In a statement on the influence of the Church on farm home conditions, the report put the general situation this way: "No agency comes in closer contact with the rural home than does the Church, and none can more appropriately or successfully bring influence to bear to mitigate the hard and unfair conditions of life in which so many farm women live and rear their families, or which cause so many others to desert the farm for the conveniences of city life. The Church by endeavoring to improve farm home conditions will take an effective step both towards the solution of the rural problem and towards approving its own ministry to the farmer."

By the time the report was issued, Father O'Hara had already taken some of those steps. Within two months of his arrival in Eugene, he had organized the Lane County Catholic Agricultural Union. The form taken by this first organizational effort and the method of launching it are worthy of notice.

The fact that it was an agricultural union showed that the pastor was aware of the needs of his people and interested in helping them to help themselves. The men were first brought together at a luncheon held during the County Fair in August, 1920. Out of the group that attended, nine men were chosen to represent different sections of the community. Meetings were held regularly during the year for practical, pointed discussion of the facts revealed by the survey. The discussions were aimed at action under Father O'Hara's ingrained principle, "Organization without activity is useless."

Better farming was never an end with the founder of the Catholic Rural Life Bureau. It was always a means to better people. More of the best people staying on the farms meant more better people in the cities and in the nation as a whole. There were to be moments down the years when the Catholic Rural Life Movement would be in danger of confusing means with ends. But there was no confusion in Father O'Hara's mind.

This does not mean that he did not see the importance of the means or neglect to take them. On the contrary, his interest in the end made him particularly thorough about seeing to the means. As his study of rural conditions widened, he became familiar with every type of agency working for the benefit of the farmer. He took active part in several of them, brought his people to a greater use of their benefits, used their studies to increase his own knowledge, and took advantage of their nationwide memberships to spread his Catholic teaching on rural life.

The published report of the survey with its *Program of Catholic Rural Action*, which is both an account of that first year in Father O'Hara's rural parish-laboratory and the foundation stone of the National Catholic Rural Life Movement in the United States, reflects these large interests in all the forces available to help the farmer. At that time too few farmers were making use of governmental and other agencies now a generally accepted part of rural living. So the report included a listing of all the Lane County agencies engaged in promoting the economic welfare of the farmer with regard to production, credit, marketing and general promotion.

Special emphasis was placed on cooperatives. A complete list of existing statewide and local groups was given with a strong encouragement to participate in them.

The program, however, bore directly on its formal purpose in the sections which dealt with the Church's rural health program, the Church and rural social life, the Church and rural culture, and religion and rural life. Under these four headings, Father O'Hara set down, in terms of his own parish, the working philosophy for Church activity in rural life which remains as the basis of the Catholic Rural Life Movement in the United States.

In the last two sections, on rural culture and religion, the priest-educator was dealing with subjects closest to his own heart. It is among the works reported under these headings that we find the first Catholic foundation in the United States of the religious vacation school for children attending public schools.

From his own boyhood experience, Father O'Hara knew the inadequacy of the Sunday school when not bolstered by adequate religious teaching in the home. He also knew from his survey that very few homes had anything approaching the reading facilities or the sound doctrinal background his own had provided. And he saw one remedy for this in the emptiness of long winter evenings on the farm. So he established religious correspondence courses as a means of reaching the whole family through the children. With the aid of his brother John in drawing up the lessons, he was able to launch the first two courses on the First Sunday of Advent, five months after his arrival in Eugene. These courses reached beyond Lane County and may be considered, apart from the survey, as the first formal activity of the National Catholic Rural Life Bureau which at that moment was completely identified with the person of Father Edwin O'Hara.

The report was able to show that the first two courses, which offered one lesson weekly in each course over a six-month period, had enrolled students in 180 families, forty of them in Lane County. In fifteen of the forty Lane County families, the mother acted as correspondent. The father did the writing in nine others.

But the Sunday schools and the correspondence courses were still not enough. The Lutheran religious vacation school of his boyhood had taught Father O'Hara that it was not only possible but also fairly easy to get children to come to such a school over a period of one month during summer vacation. By the time his first school year in Eugene ended, he had everything arranged to put into operation the first Catholic religious vacation school to function in the United States. And he had had the good fortune to find exactly the right collaborator. Sister Mary Basilla, then Superior at Eugene and now Superior of St. Mary's Academy, Portland, became as important to the pioneer stage of the religious vacation schools as her sister in the Sisters of the Holy Names of Jesus and Mary, the former Caroline Gleason, had been to the minimum wage fight.

With another sister and Father O'Hara, Sister Basilla held that summer the first Catholic religious vacation school. While Father O'Hara indoctrinated the adults in the parlor of the Tuhy home in the nearby Lane County hamlet of Springfield and the other sister held class for the girls in the kitchen, Sister Basilla taught the boys out in the yard.

The 1922 report and program describes the first Catholic religious vacation schools thus:

"During the month of June the Sisters from the parish school at Eugene divided into three groups and undertook the daily instruction of the children of three rural communities in Lane County. At Cottage Grove thirty pupils were enrolled; at Junction City, fifteen, and at Springfield, eighteen children (of Polish extraction) were enrolled. The entire day was given over to religious instruction; periods were devoted to Bible history, the lives of the Saints, public and private prayer, the history of the Church, Catholic missions and sacred music; thus the day was spent without monotony, but every period enforcing its religious lesson. In a month as much matter was presented to the pupils as would ordinarily occupy the time allotted to religious instruction during the year in the parish school.

"The teachers were enthusiastic over the results of their work and the pupils and parents look forward to the return of the Sisters next summer."

The program concluded with a general summary which may be regarded as an epitome of the conclusions arrived at from testing theory by practice during the first laboratory year.

When the survey, report and program were printed and published, the eager response of zealous rural priests looking for just such guidance brought a final grass-roots confirmation that Father O'Hara's Catholic Rural Life Bureau was the fulfillment of an urgent national need.

The first such confirmation had come in the replies to the questionnaire sent out at the beginning of 1920; the second was the general episcopal approval of the Bureau's formation. This third came in the form of letters of commendation and requests for further direction and more literature after the 1922 distribution of the program.

A comparison between the answers to the questionnaire and the later letters reveals a major element in the success of the first thorough Catholic analysis of the rural problem. For it shows that the general directives and specific recommendations of the published program were largely based on the information and advice supplied in the questionnaire replies of pastors experienced in the rural field.

Under date of April 14, 1920, Father Francis C. Kelley had written to Father O'Hara his approval of sisterhoods specially trained for rural work, of correspondence courses and of the idea of copying the Lutheran religious vacation schools. In answer to a question about other agencies that might be made subservient to rural religious education, he wrote: "The only agency that I would suggest at the present time, would be a central organization to produce a series of what might be called 'Mail Order' instructions. I am convinced that even non-Catholics would receive a series of short instructions on Catholic truth with great pleasure."

By December of the same year, this suggestion out of the founder's fifteen years' experience with *Extension* had been put into practice. This prompt action must have justified Father Kelley in his judgment of the man who sent out the questionnaire and caused regret that he had been unable to accept an invitation, appended to the same reply, which would have started America's Catholic Rural Life Movement under the auspices of the Church Extension Society:

"The Extension Society has plans, but no men to carry them out. If we could secure the services of a priest who would devote all his time to this, I am sure of success. . . . I am confident that the Catholic Church Extension Society would put enough money back of this to test it thoroughly if we could get a man competent to handle it. . . . Here is a field for the Rev. Edwin V. O'Hara, of Portland, Oregon. If he can detach himself from the Far West and come to Chicago, I think we can give him an opportunity to exercise his boundless zeal and intelligence."

On the other hand, the questionnaire replies included a large number which acknowledged the reality of the problem but vetoed the specific suggestions as impractical and took a rather negative and defeatist view of the entire situation. One of these ended with the flat statement, "Generally speaking I would advise a young man working on a farm to migrate to an industrial or commercial center."

The formation of the program and the founding of the Bureau called for a judgment sound enough to balance against accusations of impracticality the weight of statements like the future Bishop Kelley's and the encouragement of good minds like that of the future Monsignor Matthew J. W. Smith (then a twenty-nine-year-old layman editing the Denver *Catholic Register*) who published the entire questionnaire in his paper to give it greater attention.

The pessimism of some of the 1920 replies gives place to optimism and new hope in the 1922 letters that followed publication of the report.

The rapidity with which Father O'Hara, a new man in the field, found himself the target for queries on Catholic rural affairs from all over the nation, would have been disconcerting to a less evenly balanced man. Within three years of his arrival in Eugene, Father O'Hara had the Rural Life Bureau established to the point it needed auxiliary aid covering the whole nation, had organized that aid in the form of the National Catholic Rural Life Conference, had vacation schools and correspondence schools flourishing, had started and was editing alone a Catholic rural life publication, had started forming Catholic cells in the nation's agricultural colleges, was promoting the formation of rural life departments in every diocese of the country, and was in active contact with virtually all America's outstanding rural life leaders. There had been no one person to represent Catholic thought on rural life. Now that someone had appeared, the rush toward him put the little rectory in Eugene at the center of a circle of national attention.

In those same three years, he had reorganized the Newman Club at the University of Oregon and opened a women's residence and clubhouse, Newman House; his activity in the affairs of his mercy hospital had brought him appointment to the Permanent Committee for Ethics and Code of the Catholic Hospital Association; his post as archdiocesan superintendent of schools had drawn him into the thick of the battle over the Oregon School Bill; his thriving parish had set him to work on plans for a new church; the continuation of his Portland civic activities had made him a prominent Eugene figure, the city's favorite Rotarian speaker, and a combination of interests had led him into close cooperation with the faculty of the University of Oregon.

That these things did not degenerate into the confusion of multiple incomplete efforts was due first of all to Father O'Hara's personality and background and secondly to his natural administrative capacities.

He was no more confused at the thought of many things crying to be done at once than any good farmer is at the sight of all his seeds sprouting at the same time while his stock bellows for attention. When you sow seed you expect growth. You know there is a lot of work to be done by way of cultivation before the crop ripens for the further work of harvest. You have your plans made accordingly, at least in general outline. The specific details are fitted into that outline according to the immediate need and the relative necessity. Chores come first in their regular place day by day while the seasonal work is being done as it arises. The cows must be milked and the stock watered even when the land is just right for the cultivator or when the hay is exactly ripe for cutting. Then there is the executive task of seeing what you can do yourself and what you had better have done by others; of finding the right man for the right job at the time you need him, and of making sure that his job is done without interfering with the authority he needs to carry out the responsibility you have given him. Finally there is the administrative duty of providing available and fit means, of correlating activities, of keeping the multiple operation moving harmoniously toward its single end.

Father O'Hara had all these qualities by temperament and training. His Portland years had added experience in putting them to use as a priest working for the benefit of the general community.

To him, the many activities of his first years in Eugene were not separate tasks any more than the farmer's multiple duties add up to more than one occupation. He was a priest engaged in priestly work. His Mass, his office, confessions, parish calls and the daily administration of a growing parish went on as steadily and as regularly as the farmer's chores. They were his basic life. The work of planting and cultivating the new field of the Rural Life Bureau was a matter of attending to a major crop. Its success would strengthen the farm just as much as it would feed everyone who ate bread from the wheat.

But he needed help, and it had to be within his reach and his means. From Bishop Muldoon's social action committee of the NCWC, he had received a small sum of money, enough to engage Miss Bertha McGuire as part-time secretary-assistant for one year—and their blessing. He was on his own to make something of the Bureau or to let it collapse into just another good idea that didn't work.

The sort of help he really needed at this moment came from his brothers John and Frank. They shared his ideals, had abilities similar to his, were in positions to help and were willing to do anything they could. John was a writer, highly educated, trained in Catholic journalism, an able apologete and on the Oregon scene as editor of the diocesan paper. Frank, after a brilliant scholastic record, was teaching economics at Catholic University, was in active contact with the School of Social Service and the NCWC department of social action as well as with the leading national sociological organizations. They were obvious and excellent lieutenants for the work Father Edwin had in hand. So the three boys who had been companions in the little country schoolhouse built by their Irish father in Minnesota worked together laying the foundations of a movement that was to benefit the Church and the nation.

As we have already seen, it was John who provided the necessary help in drawing up, correcting and analyzing the first religious correspondence courses. Frank's influence helped bring Father Edwin a trained social worker to conduct the survey on which the program was based. (She was Miss Jessimin McGloin, a native of Lanesboro who had just taken a degree in social work from the Catholic University.) And the initial cooperation continued in effective teamwork at whatever point it was needed.

This collaboration at the origins of the Catholic Rural Life Movement is only one instance of what may be truthfully called a lifelong partnership of the three brothers. All three were active intellectuals, public-spirited citizens and zealous apostles. All three published books and taught in universities. They shared the same interests: education, sociology, the spreading of religious truth. In addition to their teaching and writing, John became the leading Catholic bookseller of the Pacific Northwest, Frank and his wife (the former Linda Maley, of the faculty of the University of Minnesota, a lady whose years of tutoring future priests have made her with her husband part of the legend of Catholic University) were in at the beginnings of the Catholic Evidence Guild in this country, and Father Edwin was to win papal recognition for the way he carried out a priest's ex-professo duty of teaching religion. And they shared one more rare quality. Each of them in his personal contact with others gathered around him a large circle of people who esteemed the kindly, dependable and generous personality of the man even more highly than his accomplishment.

It is no exaggeration to say that a book could be written

around either John or Frank O'Hara which would show them to have been as laymen what their younger brother was as a priest.

But Frank and John had their separate fields. The Rural Life Bureau was Father Edwin's responsibility and he had to reach out for very much wider cooperation to attain the goal he envisioned. He set out, by letter and by frequent traveling for meetings and talks, to attract the cooperation of those already interested, to win influential support and to join them in combined effort to arouse the inactive. The questionnaire he had sent out to a thousand pastors had carried no more authority than his own signature. He now wrote as director of the Catholic Rural Life Bureau and his letterhead showed him to be part of the American hierarchy's organization, the NCWC. The signature itself had already begun to acquire authority in the rural field, not only because of the published program but also from articles in various publications.

One of the early moves was to draw upon the practical experience of Catholics who had already been active in the field. Mr. Frederick Kenkel, head of the Centraal Verein, proved to be a real mainstay in the first extension of Father O'Hara's work. Two priests who had been doing outstanding work for rural Catholics, individually and in their own ways, were Father George Hildner and Father George Nell. Both became cooperators with the Rural Life Bureau and good friends of its director.

Father (later Monsignor) Hildner was a man who believed in the apostolate of personal, direct action. Although born and bred in the city, with no farm background whatsoever, he was no sooner assigned to the farm parish of Claryville, Missouri, than he saw that the best way he could really help his people was by sharing their problems and becoming a farmer himself. He had quickly arrived at the important truth that better farms make better people and its corollary that his work for helping people could be done most directly through improving farming. A firm believer in teaching by example, he went to the Missouri State Agricultural College and sought expert advice on how a beginner should start. The first building he erected on his property was a chicken house built to the specifications he received. He stocked it with the best chickens the college could give him and followed instructions on methods to the letter. Soon he was winning blue ribbons and his parishioners were following his scientific approach. As he extended his work, he became a real community leader showing the way to better farm living. His initiative and zeal carried over into every aspect of parochial life, his reputation spread beyond the village and outside the state till today Monsignor George Hildner is nationally known as an outstanding example of the rural parish priest.

Father George Nell is another who built a national reputation out of zealous and intelligent application to the needs of a country parish. He is perhaps best known for his talent in instigating, fostering and organizing parish social activities, for his inventive genius in devising aids to organizational and educational method and technique, and for his central cooperative services for supplying isolated parishes with such things as playscripts and visual material for teaching or recreation. But his work, too, extended to the whole field of rural pastoral activity, including the encouragement of better farming.

These men were already well along in their work. The Rural Life Bureau was a means of giving it national influence.

CHAPTER VIII

The First National Catholic
Rural Life Conference

THE BUREAU was essentially a clearing-house for plans and information. A really effective Catholic rural movement required something more. It needed a nationwide chain of leaders using its facts and converting its plans into action. It needed an organization which would bring men like Mr. Kenkel, Father Hildner and Father Nell into direct contact with those who could benefit from their knowledge and zeal.

Father O'Hara was quietly but assiduously working toward this from the beginning. While establishing contact with rural life leaders all over the country, he was building up the cooperation of individuals who might form the basis of state, diocesan or local organizations.

Again he threw a wide net. He kept asking the Knights of Columbus to encourage rural life committees in country areas. He obtained lasting results from his constant approaches to individual members of the hierarchy and to Catholics in leading agricultural colleges.

Colleges with which he had no personal connection were reached by the industrious use of a simple technique. He wrote to the nearest pastor asking for a list of Catholic members of the faculty. If he got even one name he suggested that

that person invite other Catholics to meet him for an informal discussion.

This obvious, direct approach is something we notice about Father O'Hara's methods time after time. It is in the nature of things that it should result in a lot of "wasted" letters. (One short reply came from a pastor who said, "Father X is dead . . . there are no Catholics teaching at the university as far as I know." Some of the replies came from football coaches obviously a little bewildered at the invitation.) But it is again the approach of the good farmer who does not expect, or even wish, that every single seed he sows should bear fruit.

There was enough response to take him for talks to twelve of the nation's leading agricultural schools. At each place he made new friends among Catholics and non-Catholics alike while spreading his philosophy of Catholic rural life. His specific aim was the erection of state advisory councils to the Rural Life Bureau. As usual, he had already done what he was now asking others to do. He had established such a council at the Oregon Agricultural College in Corvallis where he enjoyed the enthusiastic collaboration of men like Dr. Hector MacPherson, head of the department of economics and sociology, Mr. Paul V. Maris, his companion of the cattle search and now head of the extension department, and the future bishop, Father Francis Leipzig, then pastor at Corvallis.

His reception was such that non-Catholics were soon looking to him as a leading exponent of a sound rural philosophy. One important group in which the director of the infant Rural Life Bureau won warm acceptance was the American Country Life Association. This association had grown out of the Commission on Country Life appointed by President Theodore Roosevelt in 1909 with the objective of establishing agriculture as a permanently satisfying institution. The association was, at least in theory, interdenominational. But when Father O'Hara joined it in 1922 there was not a single recognized Catholic leader on the roster of members. In two years, Father O'Hara had become a member of its editorial council and was receiving letters from the executive secretary, Henry Israel, in New York City, with statements like this of October 3, 1924: "You do not know how often I think of you and wish you were near to our door, for your counsel I should regard as golden on many things." And this, of November 10, after the national conference of the association at Columbus, Ohio:

"You do not know how much spiritual blessing came to our Conference on Sunday afternoon as a result of your message and your presence with us. Comments were repeatedly made on the high point that was reached as the result of your message."

Later, Father O'Hara was appointed to the Board of Directors which included Henry A. Wallace and Henry Morgenthau, Jr.

It was under the mantle of this national rural association that Father O'Hara made a move that was considered rather daring at this state of general Catholic apathy on rural matters. In the summer of 1923, he called a nationwide meeting of Catholic rural leaders and thereby brought to birth the National Catholic Rural Life Conference.

The importance and the eventual significance of the step Father O'Hara was about to take can perhaps be emphasized by a quotation from the 1954 autobiography of Father John LaFarge, S.J., who, as a rural pastor in Maryland and later as editor of *America*, was actively interested in the Conference from its first years. He writes:

> The question of land ownership—its distribution, its title, its use—which three modern Popes have treated but which seemed to be the affair of only a few country pastors like myself and friends meeting in St. Louis or Baltimore—has today become the great social problem of our time, in the words of Archbishop Antoniutti, Apostolic Delegate, of the

Holy See in Canada (Sept. 8, 1952, at St. Boniface, Manitoba). Land-hungry millions of migrants in Latin America, other millions legal and illegal to the United States, look to the clergy and lay leaders and the teachings of the National Catholic Rural Life Conference, for their aid, guidance and protection. The idealistic seed of our home-grown rural life plans fell on many an acre of stony soil here in the 80% industrialized United States. But it is beginning to bear a harvest of aid to families in the 70% agrarian remainder of the world.

In conjunction with the work of the American bishops and that of Pope Pius XII, as well as with the agencies of the United States government and the United Nations, the Conference became a vehicle for working out the intricate problems of resettlement, and Conference experts served as consultants to the World Health Organization and FAO.*

But back in 1923 there was only one man with the vision to see, and the practical ability to take steps toward, such an American contribution to the rural welfare of the world. And those first steps required the courage and perseverance to proceed in spite of indifference which sometimes amounted to opposition. An example of the sort of thing that had to be overcome can be seen in a letter forwarded to Father O'Hara by Professor J. H. Kolb of the University of Wisconsin College of Agriculture in May of 1923. Professor Kolb was one of those who had eagerly accepted cooperation with Father O'Hara. He had, in the course of cooperation, invited the rural pastors of the state to participate in activities and conferences sponsored by the college. One of the pastors replied as follows:

> For the past few years I have been receiving circulars like the one enclosed and from a desire to save you postage and paper in the future I wish to inform you that I am not a Protestant clergyman but a Catholic Priest to whom your

* LaFarge, John, S.J., *The Manner Is Ordinary*, N.Y., Harcourt, Brace, 1954, p. 240.

system or conference can necessarily be of no value and very little interest. My time is so completely taken up with the work of saving immortal souls for God and for Heaven that I cannot afford to neglect it long enough to attend your conference.

So there was a strong possibility that any attempt at a national Catholic convention of rural leaders would turn out to be a blatant failure. No one, not even Father O'Hara, had any idea of how many—or how few—would attend.

In July, 1923, the pastor of Eugene hit upon an idea that would make possible the meeting he so strongly wanted while insuring it against obvious failure. The American Country Life Association was to hold its convention that year in St. Louis from November 9 to November 11. If the Catholic conference were called for the same time and place, the worst that could happen would be good; the Catholics who did come would benefit from attendance at the long-established meeting in addition to holding discussions of their own.

Although providing against failure, Father O'Hara planned for the success that came. He did not speak of a meeting of Catholics attending the American Country Life Association. He spoke of a separate Catholic Rural Life Conference (thus giving the future organization its name) to be held at a different hotel with its own distinct, though interlocking program of meetings and speakers.

Within three months he had conceived this course, obtained authorization for it, publicized it and gathered enough cooperation to make the meeting a success and the Conference a reality.

His procedure was once more a model of ordinary things done extraordinarily well. Before reviewing it, a word must be said of an important instrument Father O'Hara had already forged for working the fallow field of Catholic rural living.

It was a monthly publication called *St. Isidore's Plow*, the first number of which appeared in October, 1922. This four-page tabloid had as its basic mailing list the rural pastors who received the questionnaire of 1920, was an answer to the requests for further guidance following publication of the program of 1922, and served the triple purpose of sharing information, bringing active Catholic ruralists together and spreading propaganda on the movement. As the organ of the Rural Life Bureau of the NCWC, it went to all American bishops and represented Catholic thought to other rural life groups.

From its pages we can both read the details of the early work of the Bureau and see how it provided a sufficiently far-reaching medium to give Father O'Hara reasonable hope of a decent attendance at his conference in St. Louis.

The very first number provides rather breathtaking evidence of the rapidity with which the editor's single-handed effort had been covering ground. Under the heading "Our Editorial Staff" (one man with his brother John helping with layout and seeing the paper through the press!) it reports:

"The Director of the Rural Life Bureau visited last May, the agricultural colleges at Corvallis, Oregon; College Station, Texas; Manhattan, Kansas; Ames, Iowa; Madison, Wisconsin; Cornell at Ithaca, New York, and Amherst, Massachusetts. . . . Interest of members of the faculties was also enlisted at Purdue University, Lafayette, Indiana; Minnesota State College, Minneapolis; Montana State College, Bozeman, Montana; Washington State College, Pullman, Washington; Berkeley, California; the New Mexico State College, as also at the Catholic University of America, Notre Dame University, Marquette University and Loyola University (Chicago). . . . The Director of the Rural Life Bureau . . . extends his thanks for the cordial reception accorded him during the past year by the Very Reverend and the Right Reverend Rectors at: St. Paul Seminary, St. Paul, Minn.; St. Patrick's Seminary, Menlo Park, Cal.; St. Francis Seminary, Milwaukee, Wis.;

Kenrick Seminary, St. Louis, Mo.; St. Mary's Seminary, Baltimore, Md.; St. John's Seminary, Brighton, Mass.; Overbrook Seminary, Philadelphia, Pa.; Dunwoodie Seminary, N. Y."

Another item reveals the expansion of the correspondence courses under the Right Reverend Monsignor Victor Day, of Helena, Mont., who had become in 1921 the "Supervisor of Religious Correspondence Courses for the Rural Life Bureau." A new course on the creed was announced along with the news that the Monsignor's First Communion course had gone into another edition and was being translated into Russian. Monsignor had gone to Winnipeg to explain the correspondence courses to an annual meeting of the Catholic Truth Society of Canada.

Six months later, the April, 1923, issue contains a report from Monsignor Day which tells how far this activity of the Bureau had spread in this short time:

". . . Not to mention the home diocese of the course, Helena, nor the home of *St. Isidore's Plow*, the Archdiocese of Oregon City, the First Communion correspondence course also is used in the Baker City diocese of Oregon and in other dioceses belonging to the following states in the Union: Nebraska, Illinois, Arkansas, West Virginia, Idaho, Iowa, Oklahoma, California, Wisconsin, Washington, North Dakota, Colorado, Wyoming, New York, Virginia, Pennsylvania, North Carolina, Alabama, Ohio, South Dakota, Louisiana, Rhode Island, Missouri, Maryland, Minnesota, Texas and in far-away Alaska.

"The correspondence course has also found its way into the provinces of British Columbia, Alberta, and Saskatchewan among our neighbors to the North.

"No doubt this wide diffusion in so short a time is due in a great measure to *St. Isidore's Plow*. . . ."

So here was one means of spreading the word of the proposed Conference over the entire field Father O'Hara had covered in his three years of constant quiet activity. But an announcement by itself, no matter how many people it may reach, is never enough for a good salesman. The axiom "no organization without activity" applies first of all to the organizer. So the organizer went into action.

In July he wrote the first letter to Bishop Muldoon, chairman of the social action department of the NCWC under which the Rural Life Bureau operated. On receiving a favorable reply, he turned his attention to ways and means of holding the conference.

He was especially fortunate in that St. Louis was the site of the American Country Life Association convention that year. Archbishop John J. Glennon was both cooperative and very interested in rural matters. Then the Centraal Verein had its Central Bureau in St. Louis and at the head of that Bureau was Mr. Frederick Kenkel, the most able and experienced figure in the Catholic rural field and a colleague of Father O'Hara's on the executive committee of the Social Action Department of the NCWC.

On July 21 Father O'Hara wrote to Mr. Kenkel asking him to represent the Rural Life Bureau in St. Louis and take charge of local arrangements. The request was bolstered with good reasons why it was made and why it should be accepted. It was accepted and Mr. Kenkel's knowledge of rural life organization and of handling national gatherings gave backbone not only to that St. Louis meeting but to the Conference as a whole for many years to come.

Mr. Kenkel brought the strength of the Centraal Verein behind the organization and publicizing of the meeting, but the main work still lay with Father O'Hara and the Rural Life Bureau. The October issue of *St. Isidore's Plow* contained announcements and descriptions of the Conference. Several of its articles reflect other avenues Father O'Hara was traveling to ensure success. Letters he had sent to all members of the American hierarchy brought some interested replies like the one from an important church figure who was a very close associate of Father O'Hara's in later years. The Most Reverend John T. McNicholas, O.P., recently appointed bishop of Duluth, wrote:

"I am greatly interested in the Catholic Rural Life Conference. Before coming to Duluth I thought I knew something about the rural life problem of the Church. I realize now that I knew nothing. I do not know what the problem is in other dioceses, but I know that our greatest problems are in our rural parishes."

In the midst of his attention to the matter of quantity at the meeting, Father O'Hara did not leave to chance the question of its quality. He invited speakers, suggested topics, and in conjunction with Mr. Israel arranged a program which would allow attendance at all meetings of both conferences. In addition he gave much thought to the desired outcome of this first national gathering of Catholic rural leaders. The principles and aims on which he wanted agreement had already been substantially set down in his program and in subsequent statements. About organization, he was quite clear that some permanent organization should be set up, that it should take the form of a free Conference of leaders engaged in any aspect of Catholic rural life, that it should be distinct from the Rural Life Bureau which would continue as the official rural office of the NCWC while the new organization became an association of those active in the field. To keep the proceedings of the St. Louis meeting in focus, he invited a dozen priests to be members of a resolutions committee and drew up a tentative list of resolutions which was printed in the November issue of *St. Isidore's Plow*.

By the beginning of November, everything that could be done had been done. Archbishop Glennon, though appreciative of the work of Mr. Kenkel and Father O'Hara, was of the opinion that they would be doing very well if twenty people came. Actually the number of delegates who registered on the first day of the first meeting of the National Catholic Rural Conference was not very impressive statistically. There were seventy-five of them, and a number more seem to have attended without registration. This number, however, was quite satisfactory to the realist who had organized the meeting. He knew the difficulties in advance, understood that a long campaign of education would have to come before national recognition of the Catholic rural problem, and was pleased at the thought of starting out with such a good group of interested Catholic leaders.

In the seventy-five were one archbishop and four bishops. Six religious communities of men were represented: Jesuits, Benedictines, Oblates of Mary Immaculate, Servites, Basilians and Brothers of Mary. There were thirty-four diocesan priests among them, nine laymen and six women.

The general sessions had audiences of several hundred from the St. Louis area. Speakers included Archbishop Glennon (who addressed a joint luncheon of the two conferences with Henry A. Wallace, United States Secretary of Agriculture, as the other featured speaker); Bishop Peter Muldoon, Bishop Vincent Wehrle of Bismarck, N. D.; Bishop John T. Mc-Nicholas, O.P., Monsignor C. F. Kelley, of *Extension;* Monsignor Victor Day; Father O'Hara; Father M. V. Kelly, C.S.B.; Father Zirbes; Father Edward Garesche, S.J.; Father William McDermott; Mr. Kenkel and representatives of the Catholic Union of Missouri, the Knights of Columbus and the National Council of Catholic Women.

In the matter of organization, the lines suggested by Father O'Hara were followed. They would form a separate body called the National Catholic Rural Life Conference. Its only connection with NCWC would be that the director of the Rural Life Bureau was ex-officio executive secretary of the Conference and the chairman of the social action department its honorary chairman. Membership was open to priests, to the laity, and to societies. One dollar a year would cover dues and subscription to *St. Isidore's Plow*. An annual meeting in the month of November would select a governing board of seven directors. A diocesan relations committee was to consist of one representative of each diocese and archdiocese in the United States.

Father Thomas R. Carey, of Lapeer, Mich., was elected first president of the National Catholic Rural Life Conference with Father Henry F. Schuermann, Cape Girardeau, Mo., Secretary. Other directors were Fathers William McDermott, Evansville, Wis., Howard Bishop, Clarksville, Md., Edward B. Conry, Salineville, Ohio, George Hildner, Villa Ridge, Mo., Bernard Hilgenberg, Carlyle, Ill., Francis P. Leipzig, Corvallis, Ore., and J. V. Scheffer, Potosi, Mich. Father O'Hara, as director of the Rural Life Bureau, was executive secretary.

The establishment of this organization on a permanent basis was the foundation of that Catholic influence on national and international rural affairs described in the quotation from Father LaFarge. It was also a remarkable accomplishment for the Oregon parish priest who three years previously had been hailed as an authority on industrial social welfare and who had carved out this new achievement in a totally different field while building up his own rural parish.

It meant that within the space of three years, Father O'Hara had seen the situation, analyzed it and brought it to public attention. He had thought out remedies, put them into practice and encouraged others to use them. He had persuaded the hierarchy of the United States to establish an official Bureau for rural affairs and had made that Bureau a practical working reality. He had given the movement a periodical for intercommunication and instruction. He had won recognition for Catholic thought on rural matters. And now he had brought the nation's active Catholic rural leaders together in an organization which enabled them to share their experience, pool their efforts and clarify their common principles and aims.

His work in the rural movement was by no means finished. There were years of nursing along and encouraging yet to be gone through. But the foundation had been well and truly laid. There was already sufficient reason for the honor Pope Pius XII was to bestow upon him for his rural work. When the first International Catholic Rural Life Conference gathered to Rome in 1951 national Catholic rural leaders from all over the world, the man called by the Holy Father to preside over their sessions was the Oregon parish priest who had sat down to prepare a paper on the problems of Catholic education in rural areas.

CHAPTER IX

The Oregon School Question

FATHER O'HARA had not been long in Eugene before he found himself the center of a statewide attack on Catholic schools sponsored by the Ku Klux Klan and the Freemasons of the Scottish Rite, southern jurisdiction. There was nothing clandestine about this sponsorship. The lawyer who defended the Oregon School Bill, Mr. Wallace McCament, was engaged to represent both the governor of the state and the Scottish Rite Masons. Klansmen made open propaganda for it in their speeches and publications.

Time has lent irony to the picture of this body of men waging acrimonious war on the principle of parental rights in education which they are now, in 1956, making frantic efforts to defend as a means of defeating the desegregation laws in their own southern states.

Father O'Hara's part in this historic action was just the reverse of that he played in the minimum wage question. Both bills, though initially state measures, were backed by national interests with a view to nationwide expansion after their acceptance in Oregon. The state of Oregon was to provide the test of their constitutionality. In the wage bill, Father O'Hara had supported such a measure and seen it win national recognition. In the education bill, he opposed the legislation and saw it declared unconstitutional before it could be put into practice, even in Oregon.

The Oregon School Bill was presented and referred to the people under the harmless title of a bill for compulsory school attendance. Actually it was a bill for compulsory public school attendance designed to close all Catholic elementary schools. As the court before which it was appealed observed, "The compulsory school act could not be more effective for utterly destroying the business and occupation of the complainant schools if it had been entitled 'An Act to Prevent Parochial and Private Schools from Teaching the Grammar Grades.'"

Presumably because someone realized that teachers and schools to accommodate all Catholic school children could not be whipped up overnight, the Act, though approved in 1922, was not to take effect until 1926.

The situation was most serious for Catholic education. It was the answer to all the secularists demanded—and still demand today. Their principal argument, that separate schools are disruptive of unity and against the principles of democracy, was the same then as it is today. If they had not been opposed and defeated on strictly constitutional grounds in that battle over a relative handful of schools and children, the flourishing Catholic school system of the United States might have been forced to fight for the right to start all over again.

As archdiocesan superintendent of education, Father O'Hara was obvious champion of the Catholic cause. He went at it in his customary thorough manner. He could not hope for much from the legislature itself. His old friend Governor West was no longer in office and the ruling political power was under the influence of the anti-Catholic forces. So he started by preparing a clear study of the situation and analyzing the bill as a violation of the Fourteenth Amendment. He drew up a strategy which would, if necessary, take the matter to the Supreme Court of the United States. He called on all his friends both in Oregon and, since he saw the national implications, in Washington and elsewhere. One of the first he got in touch with was Father Ryan at Catholic University. Through him, the American Civil Liberties Union promised its aid. In a letter to Father Ryan, Roger Baldwin, on behalf of the Union, suggests a former Associate Justice of the New York Supreme Court "to handle the legal end of the attack on the Oregon law and perhaps to do some research for us," and he adds, "We shall go ahead with someone else for developing the strategy along the lines Father O'Hara suggests."

In Oregon, Father O'Hara enlisted influential people from among his non-Catholic friends to join in committees which he supplied with ammunition for a propaganda campaign to bring the facts to light. When they were finally ready to take legal action the appeal was presented by the Sisters of the Holy Names for themselves and the Episcopalian Hill Military Academy. Their attorneys, Judge John P. Kavanaugh and Mr. Dan J. Malarkey, presented oral arguments, supplemented by a brief prepared in conjunction with Hall S. Lusk and Frank J. Lonergan, before the three federal judges of the Portland Federal District Court. The decision, handed down on March 31, declared the Oregon Compulsory School Attendance Law unconstitutional and invalid and restrained Governor Pierce, Attorney General Van Winkle, and District Attorney Myers from threatening or preparing to enforce it.

Governor Pierce carried the case to the Supreme Court of the United States. National interest was strong. There was a straight clashing of two forces. It had been established that the bill had taken its origin from a resolution adopted by the Supreme Council of the Scottish Rite Masons of the southern jurisdiction for the United States in May, 1920. The resolution, which was also adopted by the Grand Lodge of Oregon, A.F. and A.M., in June, 1920, said:

Resolved, That we recognize and proclaim our belief in the free and compulsory education of the children of our nation in public primary schools supported by public taxation, upon which all children shall attend and be instructed in the English language only, without regard to race or creed, as the only sure foundation for the perpetuation and preservation of our free institutions, guaranteed by the Constitution of the United States. . . .

It was this bringing together of "compulsory" and "public schools" that aimed at the annihilation of Catholic schools.

But the unconstitutionality of the bill had been so well established that the decision handed down by the United States Supreme Court on March 17, 1925, was unanimous in supporting the appeal and declaring the legislation invalid. In summarizing the Sisters' case against the State, the Court established some very important points that are the constitutional foundation of the freedom our schools enjoy today. It said:

The enactment conflicts with the right of parents to choose schools where their children will receive appropriate mental and religious training; the right of the child to influence of the parents' choice of a school, the right of schools and teachers therein to engage in a useful business or profession, and is accordingly repugnant to the Constitution and void; and further, that unless enforcement of the measure is enjoined the corporation's business and property will suffer irreparable injury.

Appellees (the Sisters) are engaged in a kind of undertaking not inherently harmful, but long regarded as useful and meritorious. Certainly there is nothing in the present records to indicate that they failed to discharge their obligations to patrons, students or the state. And there are no peculiar circumstances or present emergencies which demand extra-ordinary measures relative to primary education.

Under the doctrine of Meyer vs. Nebraska, 262 U.S. 390, we think it entirely plain that the act of 1922 unreasonably interferes with the liberty of parents and guardians to direct the upbringing and education of children under their control. As often heretofore pointed out, rights guaranteed by the Constitution may not be abridged by legislation which has no reasonable relation to some purpose within the competency of the state. The fundamental theory of liberty upon which all governments in this Union repose excludes any general power of the state to standardize its children by forcing them to accept instruction from public teachers only. The child is not a mere creature of the state; those who nurture him and direct his destiny have the right, coupled with the high duty, to recognize and prepare him for additional obligations.

Father O'Hara's recognized role in the battle brought him many requests for information on the Oregon School Bill and on the Catholic stand on public schools in general. One of the latter came through Archbishop Christie from Upton Sinclair who had a book dealing with the American public schools just going to press and was rather afraid, from something he had read in *Our Sunday Visitor*, that "I have been misinformed on the Catholic attitude." Father O'Hara's reply left him no doubt that such had indeed been the case.

One of the repercussions from the Oregon school question was an editorial in the New York liberal periodical *The Survey* on October 15, 1922. After treating of the general question, it refers to another manifestation of bigotry against Catholics in education:

> One extraordinary manifestation of the Ku Klux spirit in Oregon is the sudden fire of criticism against the effort of the Roman Catholic Church to promote the spiritual welfare of its own students at the state university. It will be recalled that a few years ago a very well and very favorably known priest, Rev. Edwin V. O'Hara, was transferred by his own desire from Portland to the rural county in which the state university is located. The rural social problem is admittedly pressing and serious and the decision of a competent

and successful clergyman to move from what may have been a more congenial city pastorate to an experimental undertaking of this kind was greeted on all sides with enthusiastic interest. Incidentally it has given the opportunity also to establish in Newman Hall a religious center for Catholic students in the state university. This institution is not on the campus but is conveniently near. There is no charge that there has been religious propaganda from it, or any attempt at interference which the most sensitive critic could discover. Father O'Hara has not sought such privileges as the YMCA or YWCA have long enjoyed without objection. The natural and logical sentiment of those who believe in higher education by the state would seem to be one of satisfaction. . . . Instead of this we hear that there must be some sinister motive, some desire to displace Protestant regents or instructors by Catholics, some deep conspiracy reaching back, perhaps, to a subtle Italian brain or a Sinn Fein firebrand. It is absurd, of course, and it will probably be short-lived.

The accusations of trying to catholicize the state university is something of a wry tribute to Father O'Hara's standing in anti-Catholic minds as a piece of dynamite that was likely to go off any moment and explode Catholicism all over the place. One can almost imagine hooded figures scanning a map of Lane County and putting their fingers on the vital spot that must have been the objective of his strange move from the city!

The Newman Club had been one of Father O'Hara's first interests on coming to Portland in 1920. His brother John had given the university its first Newman Club while teaching there from 1912 to 1916. The few Catholic students had held quarterly meetings, usually literary discussions, in his home. It had continued in existence, holding a number of social affairs. Father O'Hara reorganized the group on a wider basis. The summer of 1920 started a tradition of communion breakfasts. In 1921, Newman Hall was opened just off the campus, overlooking the playing field. The second and third floors were used as a residence for women students. Informal lectures were given on the New Testament and on early Christian literature. A publication, *The Apologia*, was started. Its first editor became the managing editor of the university daily, *The Emerald*, and another Newmanite was editor of the 1923–24 Yearbook.

By 1923, the president of the university was praising the Newman Club as an excellent student organization and saying, "In addition to making its contribution to the social life of the campus, it has served a still more serious purpose by proving a valuable factor in stimulating the intellectual and spiritual interests of the students who constitute its membership." The Dean of Men, in the same June, 1924, issue of *The Apologia* (dedicated to Father O'Hara), said of the club, "It furnishes a meeting place where these young men and women can come in contact with each other and where they can meet their adviser, Father O'Hara, who is a friend not only to his co-religionists, but to any student seeking his advice."

The bitterness of the Oregon School Bill campaign, going on at the very moment the above statements were made, obviously had a source outside Father O'Hara's immediate orbit. His civic activities in Eugene were carried on in the same friendly relations with non-Catholics as he had enjoyed in Portland. This is obvious from something that took place in connection with the very matter that was drawing the Ku Klux fire, Catholics and the public schools.

When Father O'Hara arrived in Eugene, the city had no Catholic high school. So he started one which opened in October of that year. Before doing so he went to the school board and explained very quietly what he was going to do and why he was going to do it. He had no desire to take his children out of the school just for the sake of taking them away from the public school. But that was the only means by which he could adequately provide for their religious education. Then he went a step further. He pointed out that since the Catholic children had a right to a complete high school education in the public school, they therefore had a right to any part of it. So he was going to have the children from his school go over to the public school for chemistry and physics, subjects for which he had neither teachers nor equipment. They admitted the logic of this and the arrangement went into effect. At the end of the year, one of the public high school teachers who was under the influence of the current anti-Catholic wave, protested against the Catholic school having the use of their equipment and staff. He was upheld by a majority of the board. Father O'Hara accepted the decision, told the board he knew the decision was only a temporary one which he felt certain they would reconsider and arranged to have the subjects in his own school for the time being. The next year he again requested that the Catholic high school children be allowed to take advantage of the public school to which they were entitled. His request was approved. The same teacher again entered violent protest. The board heard him out and then asked if he meant that he wouldn't teach in the school if the Catholics were allowed to attend the science classes. He replied that he certainly would not teach if that were again permitted. So they told him that he didn't have to teach there if he didn't want to, and that was that.

The same arrangement continued, the Catholic high school pupils taking their physics and chemistry classes in the public high school, until Father O'Hara left Eugene and for some years afterward.

CHAPTER X

The Catholic Church
and the Rural Community

HAD FATHER O'HARA known when he returned to Eugene
after the first Rural Life Conference in 1923 that he
had only six more years to work as a parish priest, it would
not have made any difference to him. It would merely have
meant foreknowledge that he would be performing in a
different sphere his ordained function of a priest walking
through his immediate world carrying Christ among men.

From his ordination, Father O'Hara had a very simple and
direct concept of his function as a priest in the world. It was
to be a good and useful priest of the Roman Catholic Church
and a good and useful citizen of the United States. The best
thing he had to give his country was his Church. The best
thing he had to give his Church was his country. By giving
himself loyally to both, he would be giving the one to the
other. He would also be fulfilling his individual end as a
being created for one purpose, the service of God. He would
be using Church and State for what they are: two means for
serving man in his service of God, as they are accurately revealed in one of the Pope's titles, "Servant of the Servants of
God" and in the fact that the President of the United States.
is a paid servant of the people.

He was never confused about this and had little patience with anyone, Catholic or American, who would seem to suggest that being thoroughly one could make you any less the other. The particular world into which he had to carry his priesthood was the United States of America of the twentieth century. The particular things he had to do were the things that came to his hand. Neither that place nor those things were outside the orbit of the universal faith he held. His function was precisely to see that his faith informed his fellow men in whatever circumstances he met them.

Thus his city, his state and his country had benefited when he brought the teaching of his Church into their laws on housing, unemployment and wages. Thus his Church benefited when he worked for better farmers making better farms in the State.

Never at any time did he lose sight of the person, the individual soul, as the direct beneficiary of the priest's work. If he was the opposite of the secularist in his insistence that the religious element *must* enter into education and civil affairs, he was also the opposite of the sectarian in his clear understanding that being in error about the truth was not synonymous with being an enemy of the good. He was sectarian neither in his attitude toward his fellow Americans nor in his dealings with his fellow Catholics.

In Eugene, Father O'Hara continued to practice, personally and through the organizations he fostered, his belief that Catholic services should be services to the community at large.

Two of the Catholic community services he encouraged during the Eugene years attained notable success. One was that rendered by the hospital and by the services of a social service nurse going out to homes. The other was a traveling dental clinic. This clinic had its inspiration in Father O'Hara's wartime experience of such a mobile unit at work among the soldiers. There was a total lack of dental care for the rural people of Lane County. Father O'Hara received the fullest cooperation from the community in putting this project into operation. But it was quite openly designated as an activity of the St. Vincent de Paul Society of St. Mary's parish. The two field workers who sought out the needy cases, acted as dentists' assistants and kept the records, were nuns. They were Sisters Frances Paul and Regina, two of the Corpus Christi Sisters Father O'Hara had brought to Eugene. Working out of a permanent headquarters in Eugene, the traveling dentist's office went through the area setting up shop in schools, community centers, homes or in the open air, to attend to patients designated by the county nurses or the Red Cross. From the beginning the Willamette Valley Dental Association cooperated and gave professional advice. Dr. W. B. Lee, of the Lane County Health Association, also acted as advisor and arranged clinics. At first a number of dentists of the area gave their time and services free. Then the mobile unit was able to employ a dentist of its own for varying periods. Funds and other support came from the non-Catholics of the city as well as from the St. Vincent de Paul Society.

The whole venture was eminently satisfactory both from the point of view of the community and from that of the Catholic rural apostolate. A good thing looks good from any vantage point.

The only instance of anti-Catholic opposition was the occasion for a good community laugh rather than for bad feeling. One village, during the election year of 1928, refused to receive the St. Vincent de Paul dental unit on the grounds that it was an attempt to win votes for Al Smith!

There was a fine tribute to the standing of the Catholics in the community when Father O'Hara attained another goal and dedicated his new church on October 12, 1927. The Eugene *Morning Guard* gave the occasion front page headlines and as much space as any diocesan paper could have given a similar ceremony. Reverent, respectful and full of lyric praise as the account was, it betrayed rather amusingly that neither the reporter nor his editor were Catholics. At the dedication banquet, the president of the University of Oregon was one of the two principal speakers and most of the leading citizens of Eugene were among the three hundred who attended.

The new church was something of which the city as well as the whole parish might well have been proud. In place of the little wooden structure which Father O'Hara helped drag across the tracks, a Gothic stone-and-brick building now rose in dignity and beauty. It was 135 feet long, the transept sixty feet wide, and the nave rose to a height of forty feet. It could seat six hundred.

The interior, thanks to the pastor's good sense in leaving art to artists, was worthy of a place of worship. The tabernacle door, by the University of Michigan sculptor Avard Fairbanks, has since been reproduced in volumes portraying the best in American sculpture.

The dedication ceremonies were the occasion for a reunion of many of the pastor's friends. Archbishop Howard, Father O'Hara's classmate at St. Paul's who had succeeded Archbishop Christie, presided. The sermon was given by Father George Thompson. One of the attendant priests was Father Leipzig, his co-worker in the rural life movement, his successor at Eugene, and the future bishop of Baker City.

For the parishioners, there must have been a "now we are beginning to get somewhere" atmosphere about the ten days of celebration that preceded the dedication. They had a spacious new parish hall with facilities for the various activities of the men's, women's and youth organizations that had been set in motion or given new life. Ground had been purchased around the church with still greater expansion in view.

If one looked only at his parochial activity, it must have

seemed as if Father O'Hara was just settling down to his place at the heart of the Eugene and Lane County community. But his rural activities were pyramiding, and within two years they were to take him away from Eugene and out of strictly parochial work.

Every summer from the founding of the Rural Life Bureau, Father O'Hara had set aside one month for travel in its interests. Journeying by night and speaking or interviewing as often as he could through the day, he drew zigzag lines across the map of the United States, each line uniting one point of rural life activity to another, or to a place where there soon would be such activity. He met many people, made many friends—and piled himself up a lot of work.

There are two secrets about getting people to do things that Edwin O'Hara seems to have possessed from his youth. The first is that once you have persuaded someone to promise that he will do something your best chance of prompt action is to stand quietly behind him and make the first move for him. The second is that if you are to get things done quickly, you must never hurry.

So where the director of the Rural Life Bureau did get a promise of cooperation, he had an immediate job of organization on his hands; where he did not, he had the less interesting and more arduous task of following up with one new attempt after another. If the ground is too hard for the seed, you don't just leave it alone. You get out the plow.

In proportion as the work spread, so did the need for the centralizing and distributing functions of the Rural Life Bureau. Father O'Hara tried to divide the work. He had the Catholic Rural Life Conference set up its own office in 1924 and separate its executive secretaryship from the Bureau. Father Schiltz took the job on a part-time basis in Des Moines, Iowa. At the same time, he undertook the editing of *St. Isidore's Plow* which became the organ of the Conference under the new title *Catholic Rural Life*, one column being reserved on the front page for Father O'Hara under the old title. The arrangement lasted a little over a year. Father O'Hara had to reassume the office of executive secretary while Father William McDermott undertook the editing of the magazine from Racine, Wis. In 1927, Dr. Frank O'Hara took over the editor's chair and published *Catholic Rural Life* from Washington, D.C.

The Conference was at the calf-legged stage in which most new organizations begin to wonder if it is all worth while. A substantial proportion of the American clergy looked upon it as a collection of crackpots riding a hobby of some kind. It needed more people with Father O'Hara's deep conviction about the reality of the problem and his courage to keep pushing toward a solution.

If there was no great rush of numbers in those early years, the people who did come were worth while. The dynamic personality of Father Luigi Ligutti and the strong intelligence of Father John LaFarge, S.J., brought added strength to the pioneer group at the second meeting of the Conference at Milwaukee in 1924. Father Ligutti, who has been for the later stages of the Catholic Rural Life Movement what Father O'Hara was for its first nineteen years, Father LaFarge and others like Bishop Kelley of *Extension* have become widely known through their own writings and from public recognition of their work.

But that early group of Catholic ruralists had more men of similar caliber. One of these was Father Howard Bishop, a founding director of the Conference and its president from 1928 to 1934. Father Bishop, a man of great zeal, initiative, and organizational ability, was at that time stationed in the rural parish of Clarksville, Md., close to the ridge country where his fellow Harvard graduate, Father LaFarge, spent his fifteen years in the rural apostolate. He had founded the Little Flower League to solicit assistance for rural parishes. In 1939, under the sponsorship of Archbishop McNicholas, he was to found the Glenmary Missioners who work for the conversion of souls in neglected non-Catholic areas of the United States.

It was as the representative and spokesman for such people that Father O'Hara obtained a three-month leave of absence from his diocese and crossed the Atlantic to make a survey of Catholic rural efforts in European nations. He visited Holland, Belgium, Germany, Italy and Spain as well as the British Isles and France. The two first-named countries and the Catholic provinces of Germany provided an excellent lesson in what the organized application of Catholic principles might do for rural life. His findings were summarized in a special chapter of a book *The Catholic Church and the Rural Community* which he wrote on his return and had published in 1927 by the Macmillan Company of New York.

This immediately became accepted as a standard American work of reference on Catholic rural thinking. In addition to a general statement of his Catholic rural life philosophy and the program of the Catholic Rural Life Movement, Father O'Hara's book had chapters on such practical matters as Farming as a Business, Catholic Principles of Land Ownership, Cooperatives, and Credit Unions. It also had a chapter on the nature and organization of the religious vacation school.

The book was widely and favorably reviewed by influential periodicals. A reviewer in the Irish Jesuit quarterly *Studies* took occasion to chide his fellow countrymen that an American book containing a survey of European Catholic rural activities had no word about Ireland for the very sad reason that there was nothing worth reporting.

Father O'Hara had indeed gone to Ireland and spoken with the leaders of the Irish Agricultural Organization Society. Count Plunkett he had already known in the United States, George Russell (AE) was at the office of his newspaper, *The*

Irish Statesman, full of romantic ideas without practical application, and a Jesuit veteran of the vain campaign answered his request for the names of priests active in rural work by telling him that in rural Ireland he couldn't name any.

By the autumn of 1928, the Catholic Rural Life Movement in the United States had reached another critical stage. The prodding of the pioneers was taking effect and a great number of rural pastors were asking for aid in launching their own programs. The religious vacation schools in particular were increasing and prospering in direct proportion to the effort put into their encouragement. It became apparent that the work could no longer be adequately instigated, supported and directed by the part-time effort of a parish priest.

It had to be one thing or the other. Father O'Hara decided in favor of the wider field.

He obtained Archbishop Howard's permission to resign his parish and moved the office of the Rural Life Bureau to the side of its parent NCWC in Washington, D.C.

His departure from Eugene was marked by general tribute similar to that he received on leaving Portland. Once again he was on the front page and the newspaper reported at length a farewell banquet at which civic, educational and ecclesiastical leaders joined in his praises. It tells us that Archbishop Howard spoke "in highest praise of Rev. Father O'Hara whom he had known since their days as classmates at St. Paul's Seminary." Dr. Arnold Bennet Hall, president of the University of Oregon, linked three phrases which have frequently been applied to Edwin O'Hara when he paid tribute to his "profound spirituality," his "high courage," and his "human compassion." Other speakers included the city's leading industrialist, R. A. Booth, who "has been his friend for many years," Father George Thompson, and the new pastor of Eugene, Father Frank Leipzig.

CHAPTER XI

A Year of Transition

FATHER O'HARA left Eugene at the end of December, 1928. In the beginning of January he started from Portland by car with his brother John, and in a cross-country drive south to the Gulf of Mexico and east to Washington, he called on every bishop on the way to tell the rural life story. When he arrived in Washington in time for the inauguration of President Hoover, he had completed arrangements for more than fifty religious vacation schools.

This result of Father O'Hara's first effort as full-time director of the Catholic Rural Life Bureau was a clear demonstration that in the rural field his primary interests lay in the same direction as in every other, in the teaching of Christian doctrine. He was scarcely settled in Washington when this became more evident than ever.

He was asked to teach in the summers of 1929 and 1930 at the University of Notre Dame and during the academic year 1929–30 at the Catholic University of America. He laid the foundations of a parent-educator movement. He was asked to fulfill a request from Rome for a survey of Catholic apologetics in the United States and his application to this assignment was to have effects analogous to those resulting from his study of labor conditions in Portland and his paper on rural education.

His teaching assignment at both universities required him to join his rural and urban experience in presenting a new field of Catholic study, parish sociology.

How new this field was in 1929 is indicated in a book published in 1951, *The Sociology of the Parish,* by C. J. Nuesse and Thomas J. Harte, C.SS.R. In a preface, His Eminence Samuel Cardinal Stritch, archbishop of Chicago, calls the book, "an exploratory study, a sort of pioneering in the field." In their introduction, the authors refer to this pioneering aspect of their study but add: "The sociology of the parish has something of an academic history, however, since as early as the second semester of the academic year 1920–30, the present Bishop of Kansas City, Mo., the Most Reverend Edwin V. O'Hara, offered a course in 'Parish Problems' in the Department of Sociology at the Catholic University of America. His Excellency offered a similar course at the University of Notre Dame the following summer."

The assignment from Rome, however, was one in which words like "urban," "rural" and "sociology" were merely accidental terms. He was asked, in effect, to make a study of the functioning of the Teaching Church in the United States.

The request came to Father O'Hara through the Catholic University of America from the Apostolic Delegate to the United States. A note from Monsignor Marella, auditor at the delegation, outlined the area he was supposed to cover. He was to make a survey:

1. about apologetical preaching in the various dioceses of the United States (sermons, conferences, lectures, debates)
2. on the teaching of apologetics
   a) in the seminaries
   b) in the Catholic University of America
   c) in our other higher institutions (colleges)
   d) in the higher institutions conducted for women by Sisters

The job was tackled with customary dispatch, deliberation and thoroughness. When completed under the title *Catholic Evidence Work in the United States,* it turned out to be at once a survey, an analysis and a program. Bishop John F. Noll, founder of *Our Sunday Visitor* and one of the nation's leaders in apologetics, saw a copy of the report—which he later published in pamphlet form—and wrote to its author: "I have received and read your 'Catholic Evidence Work in the United States' with a great deal of interest. I hardly understand why it is necessary for me to head a committee of bishops to deal with the subject 'Popular Apologetics' after the thorough presentation of the subject you have made. It would seem that all our committee could do would be to supplement your recommendations a little bit."

The report is necessarily dated in its facts. But its findings and recommendations are as much the primitive charter of the national Confraternity of Christian Doctrine as the paper on Catholic Rural Education was that of the Catholic Rural Life Conference.

The study began with a chapter on "Analysis of Means for Catholic Evidence Promotion in the United States." After defining Catholic Evidence as "the testimony of the Catholic Church to Jesus Christ as the Way, the Truth and the Life of mankind," it tabulated the classes of people, within and without the Church, to whom Catholic Evidence is directed. Then it spoke of the threefold apostolate of prayer, example and the word. It enumerated Catholic Evidence agencies under the headings Persons, Institutions, Literature and Organizations. It went on to a detailed survey of the field of contact with Catholics and non-Catholics and ended with a special paragraph listing radio stations carrying Catholic programs.

The second chapter was a "Survey of the State of Apologetics in the United States." It described the American heritage of a British anti-Catholic tradition and added: "There are two possible policies in this connection open to the Church. 1) to draw within itself, to edge off into a corner, to withdraw from participation in the national life, to paddle into a backwater and let the current of national life sweep by unheeded and unheeding, or 2) to confide in the Divine promises and set up the missionary standard; to embark boldly in the current of national life and call on the high-minded to follow Christian leadership."

It came out strongly against the timid course, saying "such a policy in the United States today can only prolong the Anglo-American tradition—long discarded in England—that the Catholics are a *gens lucifuga*." A paragraph on *Attitudes* bewails a tendency to be negative and nasty, ". . . what is needed is exposition of Catholic teaching and not an attack upon others, much less any questioning of their sincerity. Most converts have been made on their discovering some positive values in Catholic life; not by an attack on something they hold to be the truth. Besides being positive and constructive, the Catholic Evidence movement must above all be charitable."

On *Lay Leadership* the report says, "To assume that the laity are to act simply as rubber stamps for the clergy is to deny them leadership. . . . In general, it may suffice to say that the intelligent layman must be allowed a certain freedom of action. He must not be held in constant check, under penalty of losing his service altogether."

In speaking of *Teaching Children* the author was on a favorite theme: "At once the largest and most hopeful field for Catholic Evidence is provided by the children of Catholic parents. Over two million of them are being cared for in Catholic schools. It is unnecessary to say that the ideal is 'Every Catholic child in a Catholic school.' Another two million Catholic children, however, are in the public schools. There are in the United States about eighteen thousand Catholic parish and mission churches, and about eight thousand

Catholic schools. Thus ten thousand groups of Catholic children have no opportunity to attend parish schools. For these the Confraternity of Christian Doctrine organized by parishes and dioceses (Canon 711) with a well-rounded program of religious vacation schools and year-round religious instruction is an immediate necessity." Here we are at the heart of Father O'Hara's personal conclusion from his study.

The third chapter was on "Diocesan Plan of Organization." It spoke briefly of the Catholic Truth Society and the Catholic Evidence Guild, then said: "In a strong diocese with highly differentiated activities both of those types of organization would find important spheres of work, each under its own trained executive. In most dioceses for the present, and in many for considerable time in the future, such differentiation of function may not be deemed practical. Meanwhile both types of work can be carried on in connection with the work of the Diocesan Confraternity of Christian Doctrine." There followed a statement of what the confraternity was and an outline of its diocesan organization.

The statement lays down with admirable brevity the concept of the confraternity held by the man who was to spread it throughout the United States: "The official organization named by Canon Law for the promotion of Catholic teaching to those not well instructed in its tenants is the Confraternity of Christian Doctrine, which according to Canon 711, is to be established by episcopal authority in every diocese and parish. The Confraternity is enriched with many spiritual favors. Moreover, it is particularly suited to the task of transforming each parish into a missionary agency, addressing the Gospel message to every soul within its borders, instead of being a functionary institution serving only those who present themselves for its ministrations."

The outline for a diocesan organization required a diocesan director over centers in each parish run by a lay committee under the direction of the pastor.

The first of six listed functions of a parish center was "to organize the teaching of religion to a) Catholic children in public elementary and high schools; b) non-Catholic children; c) fallen-away and careless Catholics; d) non-Catholic adult groups." The second was "to train laymen and women as a) teachers of religion; b) public speakers on religious subjects; c) writers on religious topics; d) organizers of study clubs, etc.; e) pamphlet-rack tenders."

It is obvious that such an organization in every diocese, even if it fell considerably short of the ideal, would go a long way to solving the Church's perpetual apostolic problem of using available Catholic strength to spread Catholic truth. Father O'Hara saw this and, from that moment on, he set himself to bringing it about.

The detailed story of how he did so would require a lengthy volume of its own and would involve tracing the substantial contributions of many individuals and groups. But it would show Bishop O'Hara either in the lead or smiling gently behind the scenes at every step of the way. It is similar in many ways to the story of the National Catholic Rural Life Conference. A man comes into a field already being excellently worked in isolated patches, he finds ways and means of collating and extending the activity, he uses an already existing national organization as a stepping stone and brings the previously unformed movement to a national and international unity and effect of its own.

The confraternity also marks a further step in Bishop O'Hara's own story. It finds him reaching to the roots all over the United States and watering the growth of an ideal of Catholicism and citizenship similar to his own. It sees him serving his Church and his country on a larger scale than ever before.

The confraternity was not new in the United States. Father O'Hara's first contact with it went back to his earliest visits to New York after ordination. There he observed the work of groups like the Paulist Fathers who used confraternity methods in a few parishes and published in 1906 a confraternity manual. But his practical working with it began in 1926 when he was invited to Los Angeles to read a paper on rural problems to the National Conference of Catholic Charities. There he found an active group of Confraternity of Christian Doctrine workers who joined him in round-table discussion on methods of teaching religion.

The Los Angeles confraternity had been particularly concerned with the large number of Mexican children attending public schools and in danger of losing their faith through lack of instruction. The usual technique was to wait outside the schools and gather as many children as possible. Though their zeal was bringing good results, they were not satisfied with the method. Father O'Hara's description of the religious vacation schools particularly impressed them as a technique that would work in the city as well as in the country. Thus the vacation schools became the point of union between Father O'Hara's rural work and his fostering of the confraternity.

The then Bishop Cantwell, who became an important ally in the formation of the national confraternity, was so impressed that he invited Father O'Hara to return to Los Angeles and instruct the entire confraternity membership on the method of running a religious vacation school. Father O'Hara did so, conducting three separate sessions for priests, nuns and laity. The following summer, the diocese of Los Angeles had thousands of public school children in religious vacation schools.

The diocesan director of the Los Angeles confraternity was Father Leroy Callahan who had succeeded its founder, the future Archbishop Lucey. His principal lay aides were the Misses Blanche and Alice Vignos. From that time on, these people were working closely with Father O'Hara and the Rural Life Bureau. The services already being provided for the rural schools were useful to them and their active confraternity served as a laboratory for developing texts, teaching aids, techniques and programs for religious vacation schools.

By the summer of 1930, these schools were functioning so well in Los Angeles that Father O'Hara invited Father Callahan to that year's National Catholic Rural Life Conference at Springfield, Ill., to describe a diocesan religious vacation school organization.

That Springfield meeting was one of the cornerstones of the future national confraternity. Here for the first time, the sessions devoted to religious education were formally listed as Confraternity of Christian Doctrine meetings.

The same meeting put another link in the chain joining Father O'Hara's rural activities to the future national confraternity. It authorized publication of a pamphlet on parent education upon which Father O'Hara had been working that summer, and for which he wrote the introduction. This was published as Volume One of *The Parent Educator*. A second volume made up of articles plus discussion outlines by half a dozen experts was written in 1931 and published in 1932. A third came out in 1933.

Thus the first activities of the Rural Life Bureau, its vacation schools and the correspondence courses which had brought parents to working with their children at religious instruction in the home, drew a straight line between the Bureau and the confraternity. It would be quite proper to say that one grew out of the other in continuation of Father O'Hara's constant preoccupation with bringing the truths of religion to those who needed them most.

The months between departure from Eugene and episcopal consecration were, in fact if not in intention, direct preparation for national organization of the confraternity. In addition to conducting the survey, teaching teachers at two universities and launching *The Parent Educator*, he was getting together the first 1930 edition of the *Religious Vacation School Manual* and extending his circle of cooperation with other leaders in various aspects of religious education.

The manual, which was used as a means of spreading the confraternity idea, was a work of collaboration. In the first edition, Father O'Hara's co-workers were such prominent organizers as Father Felix N. Pitt of Louisville, Ky., Father Leon A. McNeill of Wichita, Kans., and Father Leroy Callahan of Los Angeles. In the 1931 edition, Father Aloysius Heeg, S.J., was added to this group. The 1932 revision was made under the editorship of Father McNeill by a committee which included Father Raymond J. Campion, Sister M. Ignatius Hayden, C.S.J., Ellamay Horan, Miriam Marks, John H. Good, Mary E. Spencer and Alice Vignos.

During this period, too, Father O'Hara established several other relationships that were to be important to the founding of a national confraternity. As a concrete result of his Catholic Evidence survey, the man who was to become the first national director of the confraternity was appointed to a special chair of apologetics at the Catholic University. Father Francis A. Walsh, O.S.B., Father John Forest, O.F.M., of the St. Anthony's Guild Press, began a long list of confraternity publications by producing and distributing with no security about financial return, *The Parent Educator*. Miss Miriam Marks, then on the guild staff, was to become the executive secretary and pivot of the national confraternity.

There appeared to be some danger, indeed, that the director of the Rural Life Bureau had freed himself from the responsibilities of a parish only to be caught up in other duties that could prove equally demanding.

But the question did not arise. He was taken away both from the classroom and from the Rural Life Bureau.

While giving his lectures at Notre Dame in the summer of 1930, he received a letter from His Excellency, P. Fumasoni-Biondi, Apostolic Delegate to the United States, which began:

> Reverend and Dear Father:
> I am pleased to inform you that it is the intention of Our Holy Father, Pope Pius XII, to appoint you Bishop of Great Falls, Montana.

So it was as a bishop-elect that Father O'Hara attended that important Springfield, Ill., National Catholic Rural Life Conference. There he was presented with a token of appreciation from the Conference he had founded, the episcopal crozier he carried until he died.

CHAPTER XII

Bishop of Great Falls, Montana

BISHOPS OF THE CATHOLIC CHURCH occasionally greet new-comers to their rank with the wry phrase, "I hear you have resigned from the human race." They are referring to the loneliness that falls upon the man who becomes a symbol of authority and actual arbiter of the destinies of those around him. As symbol, he must accept, and even demand, the formal respect due the authority he represents. As arbiter, he is inevitably feared for his power even when he is loved for his personality. Conversations grow brittle around the edges as sensitive people realize they must not slip over the thin edge of due deference. Good people shrink from anything that might seem like pleading their own cause. The other kind seek to ingratiate themselves by servility and flattery.

In such circumstances it is easy for one type of man to con-fuse his person with his position, accept the flattery and thus cut himself off forever from the truth about himself. Another may reach a similar, though more wholesome, isolation by sacrificing the personality to the post, removing consideration of the man from the matter, and making his rule an all but im-personal fulfillment of his office. In either case, the person in power is a lonely man.

This remains true of the Catholic bishop even in the more general instances where neither extreme of attitude is reached.

The power he holds is sacred and unshareable. He participates fully in the absolute power of the Church. He is Rome in his diocese. He is High Priest as well as administrator of a given geographical area. Within his breast are locked up— and his subjects can never forget this as they speak to him— the intimate details of every major spiritual and material, personal and institutional problem in the diocese. His role is as responsible as it is exalted: to govern, teach and sanctify in the name of the Universal Church, in the name of Christ.

Consecration to the episcopate of the Roman Catholic Church brings a priest a burden he must carry alone. He can carry it only as the man he is.

On November 5, 1930, the Ed O'Hara who shucked corn on a farm in Amherst township and studied so intensely at St. Paul's Seminary, the Father O'Hara who became so well-liked in his parishes at Portland and Eugene, the Dr. O'Hara of urban and rural sociological reputation, the lecturer O'Hara of Catholic University and Notre Dame, the war chaplain O'Hara and the writer O'Hara were all consecrated under the new title of the Most Reverend Edwin Vincent O'Hara, D.D., Bishop of Great Falls, Montana. They all wore a mitre, carried a crozier and extended an episcopal ring to be kissed on bended knee. But they were all the same unchanged person. And they all went to work at the job of being bishop of Great Falls.

Congratulatory messages from men in many fields reflected a widespread hope that his episcopal appointment had significance beyond the ordinary. One telegram summed up the common refrain: "Joyful congratulations your appointment is providential for church and country. John LaFarge."

Another was typical of the satisfaction of the various groups with whom the new bishop had worked: "Pastoral sociology rejoices our sincerest congratulations to our new bishop. Raymond Murray, C.S.C."

Father J. Elliot Ross, writing from Ohio, was more

pointed: "Do you remember that in answering your query about Catholic 'apologetic' agencies I suggested that one of the fundamental things to do was to get Rome to choose the right sort of bishops? At that time I was pessimistic about doing this. But I have just learned from *The Commonweal* that you have the secret. I congratulate the state of Montana and the Church in the United States for getting you as a bishop. Do you remember the Henry Adams dictum 'a friend in power is a friend lost'? I trust this will not hold in your case."

Gordon O'Neill, of the San Francisco *Monitor*, wrote: "Your elevation, however, is a sign that the Church does not regard a man as a Don Quixote because he takes the long range and radical view, the appointment puts an imprimatur on your pioneering, and gives your voice added authority."

If any of his many friends had fears that Bishop O'Hara would be different from Father O'Hara, those fears were not based on any thought that his dignity might "go to his head." They must rather have risen from doubt that he would be forceful enough to exercise the full authority of his position. For they knew Father O'Hara as the quiet, gentle, perpetually considerate and always unassuming person he always remained. Only those who had worked with him or under him or made a careful study of his achievements, realized the strength, the courage and the perseverance over principle that lay beneath the gentle manner toward persons.

Great Falls was a missionary diocese. Its thirty-two thousand Catholics (about five thousand of them Indians) were scattered over an arid area of 94,158 square miles. Of its forty-five parishes and eighty-eight missions only five parishes were very far removed from serious poverty and many of them were close to destitution. Any picture of the man who worked at being bishop of that area would have to show him in his shirt sleeves changing a tire on a rocky deserted road or flipping a coin with a pastor to see who would take the one bed the "presbytery" afforded. And Bishop O'Hara did work at it.

He studied at first hand the conditions in his Montana diocese much as he had those in his Lane County parish. The pastor, the educator and the sociologist guided the administrator in a program of churches, organizations, schools and social services.

In the record of Bishop O'Hara's activities in Great Falls, his organization of the confraternity must take first place. And that for two reasons. First, it was his primary instrument for organization of apostolic activity in the diocese. Secondly, it was the vehicle by which he was to accomplish, as a bishop being a good bishop, work that quickly assumed national dimensions as wide as those reached by his labors as a priest being a good priest.

In this he was simply putting into effect on a diocesan level the recommendations of his own *Catholic Evidence* survey-analysis-program. And he was to keep on implementing this program until he had sponsored national organizations of the Confraternity of the Christian doctrine, revision of the Baltimore Catechism, revisions and a completely new translation of the Bible, and the first use of English in the ritual. The first of these was a matter of organizing the spreading of truth to the uninstructed. The second and third were concerned with clarifying that truth at its twin sources of revelation and tradition. The last was a means of bringing the faithful closer to the Church in Her liturgy.

It is difficult to think of a Catholic priest or bishop perceiving his teaching function in larger terms.

Great Falls was the same sort of laboratory for the confraternity movement that Lane County was for Catholic rural life. On the afternoon of his installation, Bishop O'Hara gathered his priests together, informed them that he was about to erect the confraternity canonically in every parish of the diocese, outlined what each parish was to do, promised detailed instructions and aid on how to do it, and set a deadline for the first progress reports from each pastor.

On the first Sunday of Advent, the bishop who had taken *Sinite Parvulis Venire* as his episcopal motto issued his first pastoral letter. Its subject was the canonical erection of the Confraternity of Christian Doctrine in every parish. Its opening paragraphs clearly and succinctly set down the bishop's motivation for making this his first public episcopal pronouncement:

"The greatest need of humanity in any generation is to make the teaching of Jesus Christ live in the lives of men and women. To accomplish this is the supreme task of religion. Now the greatest hope of humanity in any generation lies in the rearing of children to noble manhood and womanhood through the knowledge and love of Jesus Christ. . . .

"It is as an agency for meeting this need and fulfilling this hope in our diocese of Great Falls that we charter on this first Sunday of Advent the Confraternity of Christian Doctrine in our cathedral church and direct all pastors of the diocese to proceed without delay to the canonical erection of the Confraternity in every parish and mission under their charge."

This 1930 pastoral went on to broach a subject on which the writer obviously felt strongly and about which he was to do much down the years through the cumulative effect of his quiet but persistent efforts:

"Let it not be supposed that the purpose of the Confraternity is merely to promote the arid memorizing of formulas which it is hoped the children will one day come to understand—a process which may as well repel the child from religion as lead him to practice it. For the teaching of religion to children is required a double competency, namely, a deep understanding of religion and a capacity to enter into the heart of the child."

Parish priests usually read pastoral letters from their pulpits on the day appointed. But they do not always carry them out in their parishes in the appointed manner. This pastoral, however, was characteristically tied to action by a paragraph that made excuse difficult and neglect obvious:

"Pastors will therefore establish the Confraternity in their respective parishes and missions according to the plan of organization accompanying this letter and will report progress to the bishop before February 1, 1931."

Since the letter was to be read in the churches on Sunday, December 7, 1930, this left ample time for action but little for delay.

The "plan" was quite specific. The confraternity was to be under the patronage of the Christ Child among the Doctors. Officials were to consist of the pastor as director and a lay executive committee appointed by him. It had items like:

"Training classes for teachers and other members who can attend will be held at least twice a month from the first of February until Pentecost Sunday when diplomas for faithful preparation issued by the Bishop will be distributed."

"While the detailed program of the Confraternity will contain many other features which will be developed in time, the immediate work for the Society will be the conduct of the Vacation Schools next summer."

"The Confraternity is not to be identified with any other society in the Parish. Nor is a large membership to be sought. In the very small missions two or three may suffice. In parishes ten or fifteen zealous members are preferable to a much larger merely nominal membership."

The final item was apparently designed to see that the pastor would not lack help—and perhaps, here and there, a little prodding:

"The cooperation of the women's societies of the various Parishes and Missions will be sought by the Confraternity in carrying on the work. Suggestions as to how they can cooperate most effectively with the Confraternity will be made to these Societies by the Bishop in a separate communication to them."

The old lesson learned from the Portland Cathedral Men's Club had evidently sank deep, "No organization without activity." Just how deep, and just how serious their new bishop was in intending that his diocesan organizations be kept healthy by action, must have been apparent to the parish priests of the Great Falls diocese when a second letter appeared, not too long after the date set for their first progress reports.

It was on the same subject and any lingering doubts or hesitations must have been cleared away by the first points under the heading "General Suggestions":

I take this occasion to emphasize the following points:

1. The Confraternity is an official agency of the Diocese and each pastor is charged with the responsibility of creating an effective Confraternity in his parish and in each mission of more than twenty families. The establishment of the Confraternity in missions of less than twenty families is left for the present to the prudent judgement of the pastor.

2. The Confraternity is no perfunctory organization, but is the authorized agency for home mission work within the Diocese, and the effectiveness of the Confraternity will be regarded by the Bishop as one of the major tests of the quality and effectiveness of the pastoral work being done in a parish or mission.

The remaining eleven points under this heading dealt principally with immediate preparation for the sixty vacation schools the diocese would need that summer. Then came an equally long and more detailed list of "Specific Suggestions."

Such directives piling up on a single subject during the first few months of a new bishop's episcopacy might well have sounded like the cracking of a whip or the overambitious sweeping of a new broom. But they were not. And they did not sound as if they were. The bishop was putting more work into the confraternity than he asked from any of his priests. And it was quite obvious to all that this work, far from being a sudden ambitious notion, was a simple and natural continuation of the sort of thing he had been doing for years.

In addition, the directives had been focused on a single, most desirable and reasonably attainable immediate objective and the man who issued the directives was always on call to lend sympathetic and understanding aid.

Edwin O'Hara was making his transition from priest to bishop in a way that showed he neither feared to exercise his authority nor isolated himself from the men under his command.

Within the year, Great Falls had given the United States one diocese in which the Confraternity of Christian Doctrine was erected according to the requirements of canon law in every parish. Not only were the parish confraternities canonically erected but they were working as living and growing centers of apostolic activity. The sixty religious vacation schools planned for the first year had by 1937 grown to 140 schools with nearly six thousand children. The spring of 1930 started sixty-five study clubs. There were 150 clubs that fall and two hundred in the spring of 1931. By the spring of 1932, some parishes had twenty and some as many as thirty of these study discussion groups. Every parish had a chairman of study clubs, appointed by the pastor, and a total of about four thousand adults were studying the life of Christ in four hundred such groups.

The unified functioning of so many groups in the widely separated churches of an area twice as large as New York State was something of a triumph of good organization. It was reflected in the greater unification of all Catholic activities in what was still very much a missionary diocese.

Bishop O'Hara began building the parish-district-diocesan pyramid structure of Catholic Action we will later see working in Kansas City. Diocesan councils of men, women and youth, formed on the model of the national councils sponsored in Washington by the bishops of the United States, began holding biennial conventions. Isolated groups of active lay people felt that a great step toward a feeling of Catholic solidarity had been taken when they could attend district meetings of similar souls from some twenty parishes or missions scattered over perhaps two hundred miles.

One of the fruits of an organization that could readily call upon the help of every group in the diocese was the great success of the first Great Falls Diocesan Eucharistic Congress in May, 1938. The careful planning of this event so impressed Archbishop Joseph Rummel, of New Orleans, that he wrote Bishop O'Hara a note of congratulations beginning: "With your usual genius for thoroughness and high spiritual ideals, Your Excellency sets before us a plan for Diocesan Eucharistic Congress which is truly inspiring."

The 1930's were notoriously bad years for starting anything. The depression had upset Americans almost as much psychologically as economically. Montana was doubly depressed in both ways by a prolonged drought which brought slaughter to the cattle it depended upon and a feeling of irritated hopelessness to the people. These conditions made what might be called the normal building up of a young diocese especially difficult for its second bishop. Yet Bishop O'Hara succeeded in finding means for accomplishments that were of lasting value to Great Falls.

When he arrived in his diocese only two of his fifty-one diocesan priests were products of the diocese. Most of the others had come from Ireland or other European countries. He applied himself seriously to this prime concern of any bishop with such success that he could say in a pastoral letter of September 15, 1937, "In the diocese of Great Falls, we have ordained seventeen young men during the past five years, and twenty students for the diocese are now pursuing their studies in various colleges and seminaries."

He also made one of those "good farmer" decisions in which present profit is sacrificed for future yield by sending a number of his best young priests away for postgraduate studies. This was done in immediate cooperation with another long-sighted project in one of his favorite fields.

There was at that time no institution of higher learning, either Catholic or non-sectarian, in the Great Falls area. The Sisters of Providence conducted a large hospital and an orphanage in which they taught children up to the high school grades. These Sisters had their Mother House in Montreal and no institution in the United States for the academic training of their own young nuns. They had the space in a roomy hospital which they had just left for a new one. They were willing and able to supply the basic personnel. Best of all, they had as their superior a brilliant and capable woman, Sister Lucia.

The bishop saw the need, the possibilities, and the opportunity for Catholics to take the lead in higher education in Great Falls. He encouraged them to begin the college, one year at a time. He assigned priests he had sent for special studies to chaplaincies in the city so that they could collaborate in the teaching and administration.

The emphasis was first upon teacher training and the orphanage classes were available for practice teaching. Thanks to the high academic standard set and maintained from the beginning, the College of Great Falls had no difficulty obtaining full accreditation as soon as the successive years brought it the full four-year program with the requisite courses. Proximity to the hospital enabled it to build a reputation not only in the training of teachers but also in preparing medical technicians and laboratory assistants. With a full arts course, it kept its high standing while growing to today's five hundred enrollment. It is coeducational and, as Great

Falls' only college, has many non-Catholics among its students.

His early contact with Catholic journalism had made the bishop conscious of the value of a diocesan newspaper. If small numbers and large distances made such a paper a practical problem for Great Falls, they also made its unifying influence that much more desirable. So the bishop made arrangements with his friend Father Matthew Smith for a local edition of the Denver *Catholic Register*, and had the paper going into nine thousand homes in his diocese.

He arranged for this Eastern Montana edition of the *Register* in cooperation with his neighboring prelate, Bishop George J. Finnigan, S.S.C., of Helena. For the first two years of his episcopacy, until the bishop of Helena died in 1932, Bishop O'Hara enjoyed a close personal friendship and a profitable official collaboration with Bishop Finnigan. The two were kindred spirits who had several things in common— the University of Notre Dame, service in World War I and the fact that they had only recently been consecrated bishops. Together they extended the invitation and made the preparations for Archbishop Howard of Portland to hold, against the splendid background of the Montana Rockies, the first and only provincial synod convened in the United States since the last Council of Baltimore.

Almost immediately upon his consecration to the episcopacy, Bishop O'Hara had been named a trustee of the Catholic University of America, and chosen by Bishop Lillis, of Kansas City, Mo., to be his assistant episcopal chairman on the Social Action Committee of the NCWC.

It was in the latter capacity that he went to Rome in 1931 and represented the United States at a world congress of Catholic leaders in social action. The gathering was in celebration of the *Quadragesimo anno* of Pope Leo XIII's encyclical *Rerum Novarum* and Bishop O'Hara read America's tribute.

But his journey to the Eternal City in 1934 was made officially as bishop of Great Falls. It was the first of his episcopal quinquennial visits *ad limina apostolorum* to make personal report to the Holy Father on the affairs of his diocese. Traveling with his classmate of seminary days, Archbishop Howard of Portland, he planned that they would extend their trip to the Holy Land. Then, instead of retracing their steps, they would come home by way of the Indian Ocean and the Pacific.

This meant that he saw Europe and the Orient at a moment when all the seeds of World War II were stirring to life. Mussolini and Hitler were on the march. India, China and Japan were seething in protest against the white man's presumption of superiority.

Several things stood out above the rest of a journey that was interesting all the way. Rome and a thirty-minute private audience with the Pope was the highest moment. In the Holy Land, Bishop O'Hara said Mass both at the holy sepulcher and at the manger in Bethlehem.

In Singapore, Manila, Hong Kong, Shanghai and Tokyo, he visited places and made friends who enabled him to feel in personal terms the upheavals that were to erupt in those lands. On leaving the University of Tokyo to head back for the western world, he made this note of his impressions of the Orient: "Very hostile to foreigners. They want the Orient for Orientals. They are edging the foreigners out. The future of the Church in the Orient will depend upon Oriental clergy."

One pleasant feature of the journey was a meeting in Rome with an old friend, the distinguished President of St. Mary's College at the University of Notre Dame, Sister Madaleva, C.S.C. The famous poet and educator and her companion made the pilgrimage to the Holy Land with the two prelates. A decade later, the American translators of the Old and New Testaments were to hold two of their most important meetings at St. Mary's. When Sister Madaleva took a pioneer step and established the nation's first full school of theology for women at St. Mary's, she paid tribute to Bishop O'Hara as one of the principal supporters who made this possible.

It would not have been Bishop O'Hara had he not taken his work along on the trip. He even conceived and completed along the way an entirely new project that had **not** as much as entered his mind before he started.

In Lyons, France, he was browsing with the inveterate reader's insatiable hunger for books through a bookshop near the little shrine of Notre Dame de Fourviere. Dipping into a French book of meditations for priests, he became intrigued by the contents and thought what good material it would make for the priests' retreat he was due to give at the seminary in Denver. He bought it and slipped it into his pocket for reading and meditation on his journey.

By the time he had left the Holy Land, he was convinced that this retreat for priests was very much worth translating and adapting for American reading. Since "I can do" did not wait long upon "I shall" with Bishop O'Hara, he completed the translation during a slow voyage down the Red Sea and across the Indian Ocean on a German freighter loaded with machinery for China. The manuscript was typed in Manila by a young Igorot studying law while living in the archbishop's palace.

The book, which had its fourth printing in 1955, was published in 1939 as "*With the Divine Retreat Master* by Joseph Schrijvers, C.S.S.R., translated and adapted from the French by Edwin V. O'Hara, Bishop of Great Falls (St. Anthony's Guild Press)." A glance through its pages reveals some of the reasons why it appealed to the bishop of Great Falls:

"Your gentle and disarming approach will gain more souls for Me than your most eloquent sermons."

"Do not proudly wait until sinners come to seek you; show

your goodness and willingness to serve them before they ask you."

"Do not complain of the fruitlessness of your efforts. Have you sufficiently cleared the field, have you pulled up the weeds, have you plowed the earth deeply enough?"

"Do you give special attention to the young plants, to the children who form the choice plots of my garden?"

"Do you explain the truths of catechism to them clearly, patiently and with perseverance?"

Among the benefits of this trip had been leisure for thought on the progress then being made toward a national Confraternity of Christian Doctrine.

CHAPTER XIII

Toward a National Confraternity
of Christian Doctrine

THE WORK of the Confraternity of Christian Doctrine had never been far from Archbishop O'Hara's mind since he first saw it as the Church's own answer to the situation revealed by his study, *Catholic Evidence Work in the United States*. By the time that report was published in pamphlet form in 1932, he had already tested its recommendations and proved them practical. His diocesan confraternity program was printed along with the report and soon became a familiar term of reference as "the Great Falls Plan."

Two years before this, Miss Miriam Marks had come to Great Falls on loan from St. Anthony's Guild to serve as a field worker to help set up the various confraternity units. The bishop of Helena, working as always in close harmony with his colleague in the Montana episcopate, adopted the straight Great Falls program. Miss Marks carried her organizational lectures and her explanations of the workings of the plan into Helena, then throughout the Northwest and over the border into Canada. The confraternity was on the march.

In 1931 the Wichita convention of the national Catholic Rural Life Conference devoted its first day to rural education and appointed confraternity men to three key posts. In 1933 a regional meeting of the Rocky Mountain and Pacific Coast Confraternity of Christian Doctrine planned parish units throughout the ecclesiastical provinces of San Francisco and Portland and discussed the need of a central CCD headquarters. At the Milwaukee NCRLC convention later the same year, Bishop O'Hara announced that the CCD would soon have its own national headquarters at the Catholic University of America.

The three different paths along which the bishop had been working toward a national confraternity began to converge. In his own diocese he had been finding a workable basis for parish units on a diocesan scale. Through the vacation schools and correspondence school aspects of the Rural Life Bureau he had been correlating his work with that of other confraternity leaders. And as a bishop among bishops he had been preparing the way for acceptance on the highest level of the need for an officially approved national central office.

This last was made easier by the fact that Bishop O'Hara was already widely and favorably known among his fellow bishops. Their trust in him was shown particularly by two appointments that came in the year following his consecration. Bishop Lillis of Kansas City, Mo., was then episcopal chairman of the NCWC social action committee. He immediately chose Bishop O'Hara as his episcopal assistant. This meant that the new bishop immediately had a seat at the sessions of the administrative board, the executive voice of this conference of the bishops of the United States. He was also made a trustee of the Catholic University of America.

The university had set up an Institute of Apologetics after recommendations made in the bishop's survey of Catholic Evidence work in the United States. The bishop had taught at this and worked closely with Father Francis Augustine Walsh, O.S.B., at nursing it along. It was in effect a center of higher education for the training of confraternity leaders.

When the question of a central office came up at the north-western regional conference in 1933, the bishop at once turned his mind to the institute and to Father Walsh. The procedure he followed in this first official step toward a national confraternity was a model of his courteous and prudent respect for the proper authority, not only of the hierarchy, but also of those working with him.

There was at that moment no national organization of the CCD. So the bishop decided to request that the national shrine of the Immaculate Conception at Catholic University be named as the headquarters church of the Confraternity of Christian Doctrine in the United States. This headquarters would be in charge of Father Walsh and his office would take over the clearing-house and distributing functions which had been thus far done, at least nominally, through the Rural Life Bureau.

The great zeal of Father Walsh led him to add to his existing duties this work which he was to carry for the next six years. The bishop then spoke privately with the ordinary of the shrine, Archbishop Michael J. Curley of Baltimore, but the official consent was given to the man who was to be in charge of the work. A letter from Archbishop Curley to Father Walsh, dated November 23, 1933, said:

"Bishop O'Hara spoke to me about establishing a Headquarters Church for the Confraternity of Christian Doctrine. . . . This authorization brings with it my approval of the work you are about to undertake."

Under date of December 13, 1933, Bishop O'Hara received from Father Walsh a letter sent to all bishops of the United States, saying:

"A National Center has been established for the Confraternity of Christian Doctrine. Diocesan and local units may call upon this Center for such assistance as their particular localities may require. As this Center has just been inaugurated we would be pleased to learn from you the needs of the

Confraternity as it exists in your diocese. It will be found desirable to affiliate all centers with the National Center.

"A Confraternity has been set up under the authority of His Excellency, Archbishop Michael J. Curley of Baltimore, in the National Shrine of the Immaculate Conception of the Catholic University of America. This Confraternity will hold regular meetings, attend to the details of the National Office and be controlled by the National Direction. . . ."

Father Walsh signed the letter as "Director of the Confraternity of Christian Doctrine." This placed him, except for the lack of direct affiliation to the NCWC, in the position Father O'Hara had been in with his one-man part-time Rural Life Bureau during the first years at Eugene.

Bishop O'Hara's reply to the above letter was addressed to "Reverend F. A. Walsh, Confraternity of Christian Doctrine, National Center, Catholic University of America, Washington, D. C." Its contents revealed that the center had existed in the bishop's mind before it became an actuality and promised the further action which was already in preparation:

"At the meeting of the Rural Life Conference in Milwaukee I asked the Conference to make a contribution toward the work of the National Center, Confraternity of Christian Doctrine. We voted to allocate two hundred dollars to this purpose for the year 1934 . . . which I am herewith enclosing. . . .

"I have received your letter of December 13 announcing the establishment of the Confraternity in the national shrine. I think the work should go forward very satisfactorily, although, of course, it is to be expected that there will be some difficulties."

The prudence which minimized the anticipated difficulties is well revealed in a letter Bishop O'Hara wrote to Father Walsh on July 19, 1934. This letter is an important document. It outlined the complete plan, with strategy and tactics, which brought about the national organization of the Confraternity of Christian Doctrine under an episcopal committee representing the bishops of the United States. It said:

"Your letter of July 10th reached me here in St. Paul where I am discussing with Archbishop Murray and Father Bandas the Confraternity program in November. Archbishop Murray is organizing the Confraternity in the archdiocese and has Dr. Rudolph Bandas in charge as Director and Miss Marks is to come to St. Paul January 1 to spend some months assisting Father Bandas with organization work. This I regard as a tremendous promotion of Confraternity development and will have many consequences. . . .

"There now arises a practical question about which I wish to consult you. The Apostolic Delegate, on more than one occasion, has said that he would be happy to get a special word from Rome approving of the Confraternity development in the United States. Archbishop Murray and others agree with me that the St. Paul meeting will be a most appropriate occasion for the commendation of the Holy See to be presented. The Archbishop is inviting all of the Bishops of the United States and Canada who are interested in the Confraternity or who have established it to be represented on this occasion either personally or by delegate. Now, while allowing all reasonable margin for negligence or indifference, the St. Paul meeting can fairly be called the Conference of the National Union of Diocesan Confraternities, and from the St. Paul meeting should emerge the Committee of Bishops, with an Archbishop as Chairman, who will lend their names to the work of the National office.

"The practical question now arises as to the proper procedure in requesting the Apostolic Delegate to secure from Rome a definite approval of the Confraternity development projected in this country. I have discussed the matter at length with Archbishop Murray and the following points are noted as important:

"1st. That your office at the Catholic University has been set up in direct response to the suggestion of the Apostolic Delegate himself and that, consequently, the appeal for papal approval could obviously be made to the Apostolic Delegate by yourself.

"2nd. The question arises whether there should be an Episcopal Committee authorized by the hierarchy at whose head should be some Archbishop. Obviously, your ecclesiastical superior at the University is the Most Rev. Chancellor who has shown a fraternal interest in the Confraternity. Whether he would desire to be Chairman of the Bishops' group would have to be learned from himself. He might have reasons for not wishing to accept that responsibility. In view, however, of the approval he has given your office and at the same time because of his absence in Europe this summer, it would seem that you could with propriety present the request to the Apostolic Delegate without further intermediary.

"3rd. Archbishop Murray is deeply interested in the development of the Confraternity and is willing to make any requests for the blessing or approval that are within his propriety. He can, of course, quite properly ask the Holy See for a blessing on the meeting in St. Paul, but that is a different matter from asking, through His Excellency, the Apostolic Delegate, for the formal approval of systematic development of the Confraternity in the United States. In regard to this latter, he would not wish to make any requests unless he received intimation that it was entirely within the field of propriety. . . . Will you, yourself, give this thought and bring the matter to the attention of His Excellency, the Apostolic Delegate?

"You may use this letter in whatever way you see fit in presenting the matter to His Excellency as I am confident that he will understand fully that we have no motive except to proceed in such a way as will bring the blessing of the

Holy See and of God on the development of the Confraternity in the United States."

Under Archbishop Murray, Confraternity Day at the St. Paul Rural Life Conference turned out to be a very great attendance success. This led to a decision to hold a separate CCD convention the following year.

A letter from the Apostolic Delegate, His Excellency, the Most Reverend Giovanni Cicognani, was read to "the Confraternity of Christian Doctrine in session at St. Paul, Minnesota, November 7, 1934." It included these words: "The Holy Father has desired to place among the principal ends of Catholic Action participation with the clergy in the teaching of Christian Doctrine, under the direction of the Bishops. . . . It is my earnest prayer that the Confraternity of Christian Doctrine may meet with every success in the extension of its important work and I wish the Confraternity, its members and its disciples, every abundant blessing."

CHAPTER XIV

An Episcopal Committee
and a Central Office

AT THE ST. PAUL MEETING a petition was drafted to the NCWC administrative committee requesting the appointment of an episcopal committee on the Confraternity of Christian Doctrine.

The annual meeting of the bishops of the United States took place that same month. There was little time. But Bishop O'Hara's four years of careful preparation for this moment rendered everything in readiness for a full statement of the confraternity case for its own episcopal committee.

It was perfectly understandable that there should have been some objections when Archbishop Murray presented the petition to the administrative committee. The NCWC would become a rather unwieldy organization if it kept on multiplying episcopal committees for every aspect of Catholic activity. It would be simpler to let the confraternity function under an existing committee. One distinguished prelate summed up his objection by saying that he did not think the confraternity was "important enough" to justify an additional episcopal committee. This was answered by a simple question from Bishop O'Hara. Referring to the number of

Catholic children not in Catholic schools, he asked, "Aren't two million children important?"

Meeting one day, the administrative board approved the request to have the matter referred to the body of bishops by Archbishop Murray. On the morning of the next day, the bishops took favorable action and the presiding officer, Cardinal Mundelein, named the first NCWC episcopal committee on the Confraternity of Christian Doctrine: the Most Reverend John T. McNicholas, O.P., S.T.M., Archbishop of Cincinnati; the Most Reverend John G. Murray, S.T.D., Archbishop of St. Paul, and the Most Reverend Edwin Vincent O'Hara, Bishop of Great Falls.

Immediately after the meeting of the bishops, the committee of two archbishops and one bishop met at NCWC headquarters and the two archbishops chose the bishop as chairman. The same afternoon saw an episcopally approved national Confraternity of Christian Doctrine established, given a physical headquarters, staffed, and started working.

As committee chairman, Bishop O'Hara conferred there and then with Monsignor John Burke, C.S.P., General Secretary of the NCWC. He was allocated space at NCWC headquarters for a national confraternity office. Father Francis A. Walsh, O.S.B., as national director, and Miss Miram Marks, as executive secretary and field representative, entered upon their duties immediately, though actual occupation of the office space was delayed pending formal approval.

Since no funds were available for rent of the office, stenographic service, postage and printing, Archbishop Murray immediately that afternoon gave Bishop O'Hara a check on his personal account which was deposited to the credit of the National Bureau of the Confraternity of Christian Doctrine.

With these arrangements made and only awaiting necessary confirmation, Bishop O'Hara put all his previous experience of organization to work at keeping things moving with a sweep that would gather sufficient momentum to guarantee steady progress.

By December 10, he was writing to tell Father Walsh of this progress in drawing up a comprehensive program for presentation to the bishops. In January, 1935, he was acting as chairman of a CCD publications committee making a list of all available confraternity literature, drafting a constitution for approval by the bishops, formulating instructions for directors and officers of parish units, and in general preparing for preliminary discussions or publications to explain the confraternity and aid those who wished to put its principles into practice. He was also planning for the first full national convention of the Confraternity of Christian Doctrine to take place the following October.

He wanted to have everything in readiness for the Easter meeting of the bishops. Before that meeting took place, Rome had issued a decree on the teaching of Christian doctrine that made the timing of Bishop O'Hara's effort seem inspired.

On January 12, 1935, the Sacred Congregation of the Council issued its decree *On the Better Care and Promotion of Catechetical Education*. It was spreading through the United States exactly at the same time Bishop O'Hara was sending out his proposed constitution and program of activities for the criticism or approval of the individual American bishops. Thus the bishops had before them a plan for the erection of the Confraternity of Christian Doctrine in every parish of every diocese of the United States while they were reading the following "command" from the Vatican: "But in order to give effect more readily to all of this, throughout the whole world, this Sacred Congregation, with the approval of His Holiness Pope Pius XI, commands that in all dioceses the following be observed:

"1. In every parish, besides the Confraternity of the Most Blessed Sacrament, there must be established before all others the Confraternity of Christian Doctrine, according to canon

711 #2. It should embrace all who are capable of teaching and enkindling love for catechism, especially teachers in schools, and all who are equipped with the knowledge of teaching methods. . . .

"Finally, with the approbation of His Holiness, Pope Pius XI, this Sacred Congregation commends all Bishops that . . . every five years they shall make an accurate report to the Sacred Congregation about catechetical education in their dioceses, according to the questions which follow. . . ."

The questions to be answered each five years by every bishop in the Universal Church included these:

"6. Is the Confraternity of Christian Doctrine established in every parish, and in what manner does it assist the pastor in teaching Christian doctrine to the children?

"10. Whether and with what fruit are assemblies of catechists or other meetings for schools of religion held?

"19. In what public schools, and for what reason is Christian doctrine not taught, and how is provision made for the religious instruction of these students?

"20. What means are used or can any be used in order that Christian doctrine be taught in public schools?"

The decree, however, much as its promulgation at the providential moment helped, did not do all Bishop O'Hara's work of propaganda and persuasion. In spite of the absolute sound of the paragraphs quoted, it also took cognizance of a bishop's authority to interpret and apply within his own territory. It cited the prescription of Canon 1336: "The Ordinary of the place has the right to regulate in his diocese all that pertains to the instruction of the people in Christian doctrine." Then it added, "Let each Ordinary consider in the Lord what is to be provided; what still remains to be prescribed for this most holy and necessary work; by what means he can most readily secure and achieve his desire in this regard." It remained for Bishop O'Hara to demonstrate that the confraternity plan he was drawing up provided for "what still remains" and offered a practical means by which each bishop could "most readily secure and achieve his desire in this regard."

He had, of course, many strong allies. To begin with, there were the two outstanding archbishops on his episcopal committee. Then there were such thriving diocesan confraternity centers as Los Angeles, under Father Leroy Callahan; Denver, with Father Gregory Smith; Monterey-Fresno, with Monsignor John J. Crowley; St. Paul, with Dr. Rudolph Bandas; Wichita, with Father Leon McNeill, as well as Great Falls and the rest of the recently organized Rocky Mountain-Pacific region.

In addition, there were other confraternity groups which preferred to work out from a strong center rather than by erection of a confraternity in every parish. One of the earliest and strongest of these was the Missionary Confraternity started as far back as 1908 in the diocese of Pittsburgh.

In the diocese of Brooklyn, N. Y., Monsignor Timothy A. Hickey had in 1921 evolved a different confraternity technique in meeting his problem of seventy thousand Catholic children in the public schools. He enlisted in the confraternity Catholics teaching in the public schools, particularly within the boundaries of city parishes. Within ten years he had more than two thousand of them in 120 active confraternity centers. They carried out the usual confraternity activities of teaching, visiting and investigating to such effect that in one instance confraternity investigators located in one school three hundred children of Catholic families who had never been to Mass and did not know where the Church was.

The confraternity in the archdiocese of Santa Fe was reaping the benefits of the community founded at Huntington, Ind., by Bishop John F. Noll—the Society of Missionary Catechists of Our Blessed Lady of Victory. These Sisters, in addition to their own catechetical work, trained lay catechists who would go back to their out-of-the-way villages and carry on the confraternity work in places the Sisters could not regularly reach. Their director, Father J. J. Sigstein, was already widely known for his success with the congregation, the institutes they conducted, and his magazine, *The Missionary Catechist*.

Then there was the Catholic Instruction League, founded by Father Lyons, S.J., in Chicago in 1912. This had the specific confraternity purpose of organizing the teaching of religion to Catholic children in public schools. It used the Summer Schools of Catholic Action, conducted by the Jesuits in various sections of the country, as a principal means of spreading its work. In 1925 it had received the approval of a special papal brief granting "a lasting permission rightly to aggregate to themselves any other Unions of the same title and institute, canonically erected in any part of the world." Its Director General in 1935 was Father Aloysius J. Heeg, S.J., who had collaborated with Bishop O'Hara in the 1931 *Religious Vacation School Manual*.

The attitude of cooperation which prevailed is shown in a letter from Father Heeg to Bishop O'Hara three weeks before the Rochester convention. The Director General of the Catholic Instruction League wrote: "The question is sometimes asked me: 'Aren't you afraid that the Confraternity will put you out of business?' And my answer is: 'No.' It is the cause that I have always been interested in and not the name of the Catholic Instruction League. I was interested in catechetical work long before superiors put me in charge of the League, and I would maintain that interest were I removed from that position."

It is a measure of Bishop O'Hara's capacity for organization and leadership that he was able to keep a steady course toward his goal through the rough seas of opposition or indifference from bishops, parish priests or fellow leaders in the Christian doctrine field. His understanding of one good man's right to differ from another worked like oil on troubled waters. He steered prudently away from both the laissez-faire and the all-or-nothing attitudes which might have wrecked the project. Some advice he received in a congratulatory letter from Monsignor M. J. Lavelle, the revered pastor of St. Patrick's Cathedral in New York, is a rather good description of his habitual philosophy on the launching of a good work:

". . . There is a French proverb which says, in effect, 'The best is the enemy of the good.' It means that when in our efforts we fail to reach the ideal, we disdain to take, even for the time being, the lesser blessing which is at our hands. This has a marked application to our problem. . . . There may be a temptation to pass over the foundation and to begin at the upper stories of the building. The real teaching of the catechism is our first essential work. Be wary of overtheorizing and regimentation."

All through 1935 Bishop O'Hara moved steadily along his single-minded but conciliatory path toward a functioning national CCD.

His newly formed CCD publications committee was effective during these organizing months as a publicity and propaganda instrument. It clarified the nature and objectives of a national CCD by drawing up and disseminating the draft of a suggested constitution, instructions for directors and officers of parish units, plans for the development of activities. It saw that the new Roman decree was distributed throughout the United States.

From the suggested constitution everyone could plainly see that the central office was to be a clearing house and a service for diocesan directors and parish units, not an executive giving orders for regimented action and that the whole was safely under the direction of all the bishops through the episcopal committee. From the other literature it was evident that a workable plan of operation had been arrived at through planning and experimentation and that practical help would be available to anyone engaging in this important work.

By February 9, Bishop O'Hara was writing to Father Walsh: "I have been getting certain basic suggestions together which I am submitting to all of the Bishops prior to the Easter meeting. I enclose a copy for a suggested constitution of the confraternity for local units and suggested plan of organization. I am working on a series of leaflets supplementing those in reference to Study Clubs, Vacation Schools, etc., so I can submit to my committee of Bishops a rounded program for them to approve."

In March, definite arrangements were made and authorization obtained for the formal opening of the central office.

On April 10, another letter to Father Walsh showed Bishop O'Hara continuing his work of shaping a constitution in cooperation with the bishops after he had collated their comment and suggestions on his first draft: "I am sending you a tentative draft of considerable Confraternity material, which I have just sent to about fifty Bishops as well as to Archbishops Murray and McNicholas."

The same month saw the Apostolic Delegate showing his continuing interest in the confraternity in a letter approving the use of seminarians in the vacation schools, as recommended in the manual.

On May 10, an NCWC press release made public announcement of the opening of the central office:

> In accordance with the authorization given at the annual meeting of the Bishops last fall, a National Center of the Confraternity of the Christian Doctrine was established at the headquarters here of the National Catholic Welfare Conference. Dom Francis Augustine Walsh, O.S.B., of St. Anselm's Priory at the Catholic University of America, has been named Director and Miss Miriam Marks, field representative, is Secretary.

Also in May, the episcopal committee drew up its policies regarding the publication and distribution of CCD literature.

It accepted the offer of St. Anthony's Guild Press to print and distribute at cost any literature approved by the committee. Any profit that might be made in time was to go to the central office.

That summer, the *Journal of Religious Instruction* invited the central office to fill a regular CCD section of the publication every month. The issue of September, 1935, carried an editorial signed by Bishop E. V. O'Hara of Great Falls.

All this preparation insured the success of the first national congress of the Confraternity of Christian Doctrine, held at Rochester, N. Y., on October 31, 1935, at the invitation of Cardinal Mooney, then Archbishop-Bishop of Rochester. The New York City congress of 1936 brought the national confraternity wide publicity as a thoroughly established organization, and it held its third congress at St. Louis in 1937 in an atmosphere which took for granted the existence of a national CCD.

But Bishop O'Hara took nothing for granted. After the Rochester congress and the acceptance of a constitution, he worked steadily at consolidating the CCD position, particularly among his fellow bishops. It became more and more recognized that this was something more than just another way of doing what every bishop and every pastor had always been doing. Many of the letters Bishop O'Hara received after the St. Louis congress reflected the increasing appreciation of what had been accomplished.

The letter from Monsignor Lavelle quoted above had begun by saying: "For many years this work of giving adequate and universal care to the spiritual interests of our children who attend secular schools has been my dream. Many intelligent and devoted efforts have been made in this direction. At last the keen interest of all has been aroused. Thanks be to God for this blessing. . . ."

The Most Reverend Gerald P. O'Hara, then Bishop of Savannah-Atlanta, wrote: "I trust that I may be permitted to give expression to the profound admiration that we all have for you, for the truly amazing work that you are doing for souls through the Archconfraternity of Christian Doctrine and the Rural Life Bureau. When I consider the great work that you and others are doing throughout the country, how microscopic I feel!"

Speaking for the laity, the Catholic publisher Mr. Frank Bruce wrote from Milwaukee: "The St. Louis Convention is another milestone in a tremendously important development in the service of the Catholic Church here in America. A mighty oak has grown from a very small acorn, and you deserve the appreciation of the clergy and the laity for your magnificent contribution."

These tributes are particularly impressive when we realize that just as the foundations for the Catholic Rural Life Movement were laid on the work of a priest providing for his own parish, so the shape of the national confraternity grew from the pattern set by a bishop providing for his own diocese. The tremendous job of planning and organization had been done while the bishop was setting an enviable record of accomplishment within his diocese of Great Falls, Mont. His episcopal duties had always come first. He had kept up his educational, social and literary activities. He had continued his active interest in bringing an understanding of Catholicism to people not of his faith and in seeing that the influence of Catholic thought and teaching was brought to bear on contemporary America.

Although the actual organization of the national confraternity was strictly an ecclesiastical matter, it was in its effects perhaps the most important of the many things Bishop O'Hara had done for his country in his capacity as a useful citizen. And he was again acting in concert with good men of other faiths to fill a disturbing national need.

For the serious thinkers of the nation were gravely concerned about increasing godlessness and an apparent desertion of moral principles. The chaos of the Roaring Twenties was being assessed along with the despair of the Great Depression. Leaders of all faiths were searching themselves to find ways of bringing faith and principles to millions who had slipped away from them. Totalitarianism was on the rise in other, morally bankrupt, nations and thoughtful Americans saw that their own cherished democratic freedom could be saved only by preservation of the moral goodness on which it was founded. For only the good are free.

This meant a serious examination of conscience for some of the nation's leaders who had themselves fallen into easy and even materialistic interpretations of the absolute moral values they professed to honor. But the Catholic Church had kept those principles intact. To serve the nation in its crisis of faith and freedom all the Church needed to do was bring those principles to more Americans. In founding a national confraternity of the Christian doctrine and getting it working smoothly, Bishop Edwin Vincent O'Hara of Great Falls, Mont., had supplied the machinery for doing that job.

The distribution of truth is one thing, and though the two are inextricably tied together, the truth itself is another. The truth of the Catholic Faith is securely contained in the twin vessels of revelation and tradition. Revelation means, first of all, the scriptures. Tradition is a vast body of the continuing teaching of Christ in His Church. Its essentials are summarized in the catechism.

The truth itself does not change. But the manner of its presentation must, in the nature of things, be a matter for the representatives of Christ in every different country and in every different age.

No sooner was the national confraternity established than Bishop O'Hara found himself shepherding a re-examination of the versions of the Bible and the catechism then in current use in the United States—the Challoner-Rheims version of the "Douai Bible" and the Baltimore Catechism.

CHAPTER XV

Revision of the Baltimore Catechism

THE AVERAGE CATHOLIC acquires his formal knowledge of what the Church teaches from the catechism. If he belongs to the majority, this is the only course in theology he ever has. The questions and answers of the catechism, insofar as he remembers them, remain fixed in his mind as standards to which he constantly refers. Even when he does not remember them, those answers have had such an early formative influence that they continue to affect his whole life.

The catechism is both dogmatic and moral theology. It teaches not only what to believe but also what to do. It gives direction to a man's attitudes and conduct as well as to his belief.

In the United States, the Baltimore Catechism, issued after the Third Plenary Council of Baltimore of 1855, has been the predominant and authoritative text ever since. In the 1930's approximately two million copies of it were coming off the press each year. For three generations of Catholic Americans its answers had set the standard for their relationship with God, themselves and their fellow men. Any text which has such a fundamental influence on the lives of almost one-fifth of a nation's population is of significance to that nation. So when Bishop O'Hara set in motion a revision of the Baltimore Catechism he was working at one of the main wellsprings of contemporary Americanism. What the revised catechism said, millions of Americans would believe and do.

Widespread dissatisfaction with the 1855 text had brought about a state of confusion in which cutting, patching and rewriting had led to about a hundred different catechisms bearing various local seals of approval. But nothing had been done about complete and authoritative revision of the text approved for the whole nation through the Baltimore Council.

This was the work that Bishop O'Hara initiated, fostered and saw to a successful conclusion. When it was finished, millions of American children were being taught the old truths of their fathers' faith with a new emphasis on things like the action of the Holy Spirit in the soul of the individual, the responsibilities of a citizen and the spiritual brotherhood that binds one man to all men whoever and wherever they are. They were also being protected from learning merely by rote truths they were intended to know in their hearts.

It goes without saying that Bishop O'Hara's preoccupation with the teaching of Christian doctrine had long made him aware of the problems surrounding teaching from the old Baltimore. But the actual moment that touched off the revision has an almost amusing casualness about it.

He was in a Pullman car traveling west from Washington after the 1934 meeting of the bishops. The Apostolic Delegate came through his car and stopped for a chat. There was some casual talk about the possibility that there might be a fourth council of Baltimore in the not too distant future. Then the Delegate suggested that "this might be a good time to study the catechism with a view to its revision should the council be held."

That was enough. The bishop had good reason to know Archbishop Cicognani's close interest in the work of the confraternity. He understood that Rome's representative in the United States was speaking to him as the newly appointed chairman of its episcopal committee and he saw at once that this was a major work in which the confraternity could take the lead.

So, as the bishop worked toward organization of the first CCD national congress of October, 1935, he was thinking of that meeting as an opportunity for firing the first shot in one of his typical broad-based and well-planned campaigns.

He clarified his ideas on what should be done and on how to do it. He discussed the matter with his colleagues on the episcopal committee, Archbishops Murray and McNicholas. The Dominican was an outstanding theologian who commanded the respect of his fellow bishops, the obvious member of the committee to take primary responsibility for determining the final content of any revision.

The three bishops knew that much of the criticism of the old Baltimore had been made at cross-purposes. Theologians were approaching it from one point of view, pedagogues from another. Many of the previous attempts at alternative catechisms had suffered from being compiled either by theologians untrained in pedagogy or by pedagogues untrained in theology. But worse than this was the too prevalent misuse of the catechism by teachers who made it serve as a text—which it was never intended to be. The catechism is an exact statement of doctrines. It is not a method of teaching them.

By the time the Rochester meeting opened, Bishop O'Hara knew exactly what he had to work for: approval of the bishops to engage in the work, the collaboration of competent theologians on its content, recommendations from teachers on the wording chosen by the theologians, and some insurance that the catechism questions and answers would be surrounded by sufficient additional pedagogic material to make their meaning come alive in young minds.

At Rochester, Archbishop McNicholas explained the project of revision and suggested the desirability of a resolution that would set things in motion.

On December 27, 1935, a letter from Bishop O'Hara to

Archbishop McNicholas reveals that the desired resolution had been passed and the work set on foot: "At the Rochester meetings of the Confraternity, one of the sectional committees, with Bishop Gerow as chairman, drew up a resolution asking the Episcopal Committee of the Confraternity to take some preliminary steps looking toward a revision of the Baltimore Catechism. With a view to presenting something definite for discussion by the Episcopal Committee, I have drawn up a page of 'Suggestions for Preliminary Steps' which I enclose herewith."

The wording of this letter is to be noted. The committee had not been asked to make a revision. It had been asked to "take some preliminary steps looking toward a revision." Bishop O'Hara with his page of "Suggestions" was not acting on the resolution but merely preparing for the committee to act on it. Nobody was stepping out of line. But the job was getting itself done.

On January 24, 1936, the printed page headed "Suggestions for Preliminary Steps toward a Study of the Baltimore Catechism," with large-size worksheets on which every question of the old Baltimore Catechism was printed alongside two wide blank columns for comment and suggested wording, went out to all the bishops of the United States accompanied by a letter signed by Bishop O'Hara.

April 14, 1935, was set as a deadline for return of the worksheets. On May 13, Bishop O'Hara was able to write to Archbishop McNicholas: "I enclose a report to date on the study of the Baltimore Catechism and the copy of a proposed letter to the Apostolic Delegate to accompany the report, with a view to securing a word of approval from the Catechetical Office. Will you kindly send me at once any criticisms that may occur to you on form or content of the letter and of the report. His Excellency, the Apostolic Delegate, is desirous of having it at an early date. I have asked three committees (i.e., one on Creed, Commandments, Sacraments and Prayer) to collate the reports which come in, giving in parallel columns the various corrections. With few exceptions, the suggestions can be reduced to three or four readings."

The reply came at once in a telegram from Archbishop McNicholas, "Letter and report entirely satisfactory can offer no suggestions." So the report was sent with a letter to the Apostolic Delegate for forwarding to Rome.

The report of the first returns was indeed surprisingly good. It was summarized in these facts:

1. Fifty-five archbishops and bishops either replied personally or appointed theologians to make the study, in every case expressing gratification that the study was being made.

2. Every ecclesiastical province in the United States was represented by at least one report.

3. Responses, for the most part very carefully detailed, came from groups of theologians in ten major seminaries.

4. Other theologians cooperating represented twelve major religious orders of men, and in some cases several provinces of the same order. The orders reporting included Jesuits (four provinces), Dominicans, Franciscans (three provinces), Benedictines, Capuchins, Passionists, Viatorians, Precious Blood Fathers, and Vincentians.

5. Not less than 150 theologians were engaged on the reports received.

6. A number of bishops, in addition to those submitting written reports, made recommendations orally.

The report also noted a striking unanimity in regard to the principal points raised and said that no unfavorable response had been received from any bishop.

Bishop O'Hara kept things moving with extraordinary speed for a work of this nature. In June 1936, he called a meeting of a committee to discuss the whole catechism on the basis of the reports received. This was a working committee. It consisted of himself and Father Walsh of the CCD along with the three theologians charged with collating replies on the three main divisions of the catechism—Father Keenan, S.J. (Sacraments and Prayer), Father Cagney, C.P. (Commandments) and Father Ratigan, O.F.M. (Creed). Besides unifying the results of the reports, the committee decided on papers to be read at a session of the coming New York Catechetical Congress on "The Doctrinal Background of the Teacher of the Catechism." Archbishop McNicholas would give the general address and Fathers Keenan, Cagney and Ratigan would speak on the divisions they were collating.

The unified report, with alternative suggestions entered on worksheets opposite the old text, was passed on to another committee of theologians and then to the veteran professor of theology, Father Francis J. Connell, C.SS.R., of the Catholic University of America.

That same summer, Father Connell was at work on the comprehensive job of drawing up a preliminary revision, with detailed explanation of changes, to be submitted for discussion at the New York meetings. Father Connell had been assigned to the work by his provincial in response to Bishop O'Hara's first letter. He was one of the first to offer, in a letter dated February 12, 1936, substantial suggestions. He played a key role, under the episcopal theologian, Archbishop McNicholas, throughout the work and stayed with it till the end.

The Apostolic Delegate acknowledged Bishop O'Hara's report on June 9, 1936. Rome's real interest in the work may be gauged from the speed of its reply. July 10, 1936, was the date on the letter addressed to Bishop O'Hara from the catechetical office of the Sacred Congregation of the Council over the signature of the prefect of the Congregation. The letter told of the response given by Pope Pius XI in audience on July 7. It was a strongly favorable statement saying that the work of revision of the catechism *"vehementer gratulari dignatus est"* and expressing the hope that the work so happily begun would go forward successfully. It conveyed the apostolic benediction to the bishops of the committee and to all engaged in the work.

The Sacred Congregation need not have worried about the work going forward. A man was in charge who did not believe in waiting for the ultimately perfect before doing the immediate good. By the end of August, Father Connell had finished his work and Bishop O'Hara had sent it to the printer. (St. Anthony's Guild Press again did the job without charge.) This first draft appeared as a "manuscript—printed not published" in an edition of 540 copies for examination by bishops and theologians. At the bottom of each page was a blank space for "Notes and Criticisms." The title page called it *First Draft of a Study of the Baltimore Catechism prepared by Committees of theologians as a basis of discussion for the sectional meeting on the study of the text of the Baltimore Catechism at the National Congress of the Confraternity of Christian Doctrine to be held in New York October 3-6, 1936, under the patronage of His Eminence Patrick Cardinal Hayes.*

On September 8, this "printed not published" first draft was sent to the bishops and theologians with a letter signed by Bishop O'Hara. The letter was a summary progress report and an advance notice of the New York discussions. It said in part:

"Notwithstanding a wide range of personal opinion, there was substantial agreement in the reports, centering in several important suggestions;—e.g., (1) a slight re-arrangement of chapters; (2) elucidation of several points of doctrine; (3) elimination of certain complicated phrases; (4) conforming certain answers to the Code of Canon Law; (5) a few additional questions. . . . The points to be discussed will be (a) the accuracy, (b) the clearness, and (c) the comprehensiveness of the theological presentation."

Attention was drawn to the fact that the work was being

done on the basic Number Two Baltimore designed for the upper elementary grades. The Number One and Number Three were to be studied later.

At the New York congress, attendance at the discussions was restricted to bishops and theologians appointed to the work. Forty of them spent an entire day of the congress going over every single question in the first draft of the proposed revision.

At its annual meeting in November, 1936, the body of bishops of the United States discussed the project and decided that the confraternity episcopal committee should proceed to complete the revision.

At this point Bishop O'Hara asked Archbishop McNicholas to take charge of the work. The archbishop engaged the interest of the Right Reverend Rector of the Catholic University, Monsignor Corrigan, in forming a group of theologians who devoted every Sunday afternoon for the entire year of 1937 to preparing a second draft. All previous suggestions and criticisms were placed at the disposal of this group. When their work was completed, it received the personal attention of the Archbishop of Cincinnati.

This manuscript, considerably changed from the first draft, was again prepared in a "printed not published" edition. That there were hopes that this might be the final form of the revision can be seen from the title on its cover: *A Catechism of Christian Doctrine prepared and enjoined by Order of the Third Plenary Council of Baltimore (Revised Edition)*.

But the project was not to be closed without every possible precaution against error in form or content.

On January 25, 1938, almost two years to the day from his page of "Suggestions" and the worksheets, Bishop O'Hara sent this second draft to the bishops and theologians with a letter which once again explained the scope of the work and asked for further comment and criticism.

The letter described the nature and purpose of the revision

as follows: "First, to revise the Baltimore Catechism text (No. 2) only to the extent demanded for a correct and clear statement of Catholic doctrines; and Second, with such simplicity of language as would make it generally intelligible to children in upper elementary grades, leaving to a revision of Baltimore Catechism No. 1 the presentation of religious teaching in language intelligible to younger children."

It closed by asking for prompt action. "May we hope to receive Your Excellency's criticisms, if any are deemed necessary, within a month, in order that the work may be carried to completion." Replies were to be sent to Archbishop McNicholas.

Though the matter of content was in the hands of the archbishop of Cincinnati, Bishop O'Hara was still the administrator of the project and was doing the pushing and prodding to keep things on the move.

Evidently intending the one-month interval as the final period for further revision, and anticipating only minor changes, he wrote to the Apostolic Delegate on February 15, 1938, reporting progress, informing him that "a typewritten copy of the changes will be submitted to Your Excellency" and asking his cooperation in securing "such approval as may be extended to a work of this character by the appropriate Roman Congregation."

He also optimistically attempted to set Rome a deadline: "Owing to the importance of releasing the text to the publishers at an early date if it is to be ready for use in the schools next September, our committee indulged the hope that the subsequent changes would be forwarded in typewritten form at an early date; such changes being probably few."

The Apostolic Delegate was rather appalled at the time schedule. In his reply he wrote: "However, to be quite frank with Your Excellency I must say I foresee that it will be almost impossible to obtain the final approval of the text by the

Sacred Congregation before the end of May. Indeed, I doubt whether approval can be obtained in time to have the Catechism in use during the coming scholastic year. The revision of the Baltimore Catechism is a great and important undertaking. The work thus far has progressed very well and I think it would be fatal to attempt to rush it at this point. The text, when finally approved by the Holy See, will probably be used in this country for many years and stand as a monument to the enterprise and work of the Episcopal Committee."

As a matter of fact, Rome did not have an opportunity to cause delay for some time yet. By this time every bishop, priest and teacher of religion in America was awake to the major importance of what was being done. And almost all of them wanted to have a hand in it. No fewer than ninety-eight bishops sent their comment on the second draft to Archbishop McNicholas. The year 1938 passed in further collation of suggestions from theologians and teachers.

By February, 1939, Archbishop McNicholas had on his desk proofs of the third draft. But he was holding them from final printing until he felt the body of bishops would be satisfied that there should be no further changes.

This resulted in the unusual situation of Rome writing America to hurry on its own catechism. A letter from the Apostolic Delegate to Bishop O'Hara on April 29, 1939, said: "In a letter from the Sacred Congregation of the Council, received this morning, His Eminence, Cardinal Marmaggi, asks of the progress being made in the revision of the Catechism of the III Plenary Council of Baltimore. If it would not cause Your Excellency too much inconvenience at this busy time, I would be pleased if you would send me a brief report in duplicate on this matter, so that I can forward the good copy to the Holy See. I heard from Monsignor Binz of your information that almost all of the Bishops have given replies regarding the Catechism; but I would be pleased to have something more than this to say to His Eminence, Cardinal Marmaggi, to satisfy the interest he has manifested in this project."

The summer brought some last-minute delays in submitting the revised proofs to the printer. One example was the appeal made in May by the head of the Propagation of the Faith, the Right Reverend Thomas J. McDonnell, that some questions dealing with the missions be inserted, and its solution by bringing the matter in as part of the Christian's obligation in spreading the faith.

In July, Archbishop McNicholas asked Bishop O'Hara to urge the three American Cardinals to join in requesting Rome's approval of the revised text. He did so and favorable replies were received from Cardinals Dougherty and O'Connell.

On November 7, 1939, the third draft finally appeared in another "printed not published" edition of 551 copies. It was sent to the bishops, the theologians—and to the Sacred Congregation of the Council, over the signatures of 130 bishops of the United States.

When the text went off to Rome, there must have been many who felt as did Father Connell who opined in a letter of December 5, 1939, to Archbishop McNicholas: "Outside of the decisions of an oecumenical council, I doubt if any statement of Catholic faith was ever so carefully prepared or had so extensive a composite authorship."

Europe was at war. It was no time to expect a quick reply from Rome. But the delay stretched out till it became critical. A full year passed with no word. On February 8, 1941, Bishop O'Hara wrote the Apostolic Delegate a letter that was obviously intended rather for Rome's reading than for Archbishop Cicognani who was already well informed on the situation and just as anxious as the American bishops. It pointed out the difficulties caused to publishers by the day-to-day expectation of an official text which would make the one they were using obsolete.

The Apostolic Delegate forwarded the letter to Rome and by the beginning of April the Sacred Congregation of the Council had replied. It gave its approval for the publication of the revised catechism and made thirty-one suggestions for changes in the text.

Almost all the Roman suggestions were verbal. Some were for precision, like replacing "thinks" with "sincerely believes," "help" with "dispose" or "to remain ever on our altars as our constant friend" with "to remain ever on our altars as a proof of His love for us, and to be worshiped by us."

One change that came from Rome pleased many. It was the suggestion to substitute "The Lord's Day" in the Third Commandment for "the Sabbath Day." In addition to agreeing more closely with the Latin, this avoided unnecessary confusion with the Jewish Sabbath.

All the suggestions were followed to the letter.

So when the revised Baltimore Catechism Number Two was published by the St. Anthony's Guild Press on June 21, 1941, under copyright of the Confraternity of Christian Doctrine, it was a statement of Catholic belief drawn up by the collaborative effort of 150 American bishops and theologians and approved in detail both by them and by the Universal Church through its Sacred Congregation of the Council. Both the collaboration and the authorization were unique. Never before had a catechism been composed by the cooperation of so many authoritative people. Never before had Rome granted such approval of a catechism in the vernacular.

Bishop O'Hara's guidance of the work he initiated had brought it to a conclusion successful even beyond his own hopes. From now on, America's Catholic millions would be formed in the truths and obligations of their faith by questions asked and the answers given in this revised catechism.

For many years to come the thoughts and acts of one-fifth of the nation's population, as individuals and as citizens, will be influenced by what they learn from this little book.

For the secular press in the United States, the most newsworthy feature of the revision was its inclusion of questions on citizenship. *The New York Times* for October 6, 1938, carried a three-column report of the second draft under the headline, NEW CATECHISM TELLS CATHOLIC DUTY AS CITIZEN. The subhead said, TENTATIVE VERSION STRESSES RELIGIOUS OBLIGATIONS AS VOTER, TAXPAYER, HOLDER OF OFFICE, AND SOLDIER.

But these were only some of the more obvious results of a deep change in emphasis which was perhaps the principal achievement of the revision. There was a general policy of positive more than negative presentation of the virtues; the goodness of God was emphasized; more attention was given to showing the operation of the Holy Ghost in individual souls as well as in the Church; a whole chapter, "Why I Am a Catholic," was added to aid children in explaining their faith reasonably to others.

Virtually all the changes from the old Baltimore, except those that were verbal, had profound theological implications. The exercise of jealous care that these were all in complete conformity with the definitive teaching of the Church was at the heart of the prolonged discussions that went into the making of the revision. Throughout these discussions, Bishop O'Hara was the mediator, the man in the middle. The final decisions about content he left to others. But the work of placating, of smoothing differences into agreement and acceptance, he kept for himself.

It was no easy job. In any given diocese or religious order, the theologians assigned to work on the revision were men of standing, used to having their decisions respected. They labored over a question they thought should be changed, gave of their best to make it theologically accurate and verbally clear; their bishop put his authority behind their suggested change—and then it might be, and sometimes was, rejected. You just don't do things like that to men like these. It says much for their humility as well as for that of the episcopal committee that the work was ever finished and given the unanimous episcopal approval it received before being sent to Rome.

Bishop O'Hara's share in the determination of the content of the revised catechism is literally inestimable. It cannot be estimated because so much of it came through personal contact with most of the key collaborators. He was continually in touch with Archbishop McNicholas and Father Connell. The original three committees who collated the first suggestions were of his choosing. Many of the bishops and theologians who made those suggestions were men with whom he had previously discussed the direction revision should take. It is not merely coincidence that many of the changes reflected views Bishop O'Hara held all his life.

Placing of the copyright for the revision in the hands of the bishops (through the episcopal committee of the confraternity) was the means toward another end the bishop had desired.

His first pastoral letter had come out strongly against relying only on brute memory in the teaching of catechism. In another article, "Suggestions for Lay Teachers of the Confraternity of Christian Doctrine," he had elaborated the fact that the catechism was the matter, not the method.

He was not, of course, alone in this attitude. Most thinking Catholics realized that much of the criticism heaped on the catechism really belonged to incapable teachers who had tried to make it do their work. But with control of permission to publish the official text of the approved Baltimore, it was possible to do something about it.

This was accomplished through a contract which licensed publishers to use the revised Baltimore text only if an equal amount of additional pedagogic material was printed with it.

Today a typical Baltimore Catechism will be divided into lessons corresponding to the chapters in the bare text. An illustration will depict the theme and an introductory paragraph explain what the lesson is about. A word list with pronunciation and definitions will precede the questions. They will be followed by a number of study helps or exercises which demand an exercise of student activity, an understanding of what the questions mean, and a knowledge of how they apply to daily living.

Even before the appearance of the finally approved catechism Number Two, work had begun on Number One, the First Communion catechism, and on Number Three for more advanced students and for the laity in general.

For the Number One and the First Communion version Bishop O'Hara turned to the leaders in teaching religion to primary grades with whom he had already been working in connection with *The Parent Educator*, vacation schools, and other aspects of confraternity work. For these more elementary texts, answers were in general shortened or simplified and their number substantially reduced. The revised Number One appeared in the fall of 1941 and the First Communion text in October, 1942.

Catechism Number Three was designed as a serious and substantial work which would be a brief but complete theology for the layman. The questions were the same as in Number Two but the answers were expanded to include scriptural proofs and additional explanatory text.

Father Connell worked intensively on this under Archbishop McNicholas as principal theologian. It was 1947 before the archbishop was assembling all the criticisms and suggestions for this fuller version of the revised Baltimore. The work was published in 1949 just in time to play an important role in the "No Salvation Outside the Church" controversy which had been nationally publicized through the activities, and the subsequent excommunication, of a prominent New England priest.

The priest had been maintaining a very narrow interpretation of the doctrine that there is no salvation outside the true Church. Many non-Catholics saw in his teaching a verification of the old charge that Catholics believed all non-Catholics were damned.

The appearance at this moment of the revised Number Three Baltimore Catechism brought the true teaching to equal prominence in the public press and made it impossible for any man of good will to misinterpret the Church's stand. Publication of the relevant questions and answers, their wording approved by Rome and their explanatory notes authorized by the bishops of the United States, was decisive.

The Number Three revised Baltimore gave even more attention than the revised Number Two to the twentieth-century revival of the importance of a lay apostolate. The extent of this attention is indicated in a memorandum from Archbishop McNicholas to Bishop O'Hara: "We have studied seriously the question of using the term 'lay apostles' instead of 'soldiers' in Confirmation, but we could not justify it. Pope Pius XI said that Baptism and Confirmation impose the duty of being 'lay apostles.' This statement we have incorporated in question 314 b [the final question in the chapter on Confirmation]."

Today, there are, on a conservative estimate, five million copies of the revised Baltimore Catechism, or texts based on it, in circulation within the United States. About three million of these are being pored over every day by young people absorbing their first clear notions of religious truth and moral responsibility. The others are on the shelves and in the cupboards of American homes where they are not infrequently hauled out to settle some disputed point or to clarify a half-forgotten teaching.

That is no little thing in the life of the nation.

As early as 1942, the revised Baltimore was being translated into French and Spanish and it has since gone into Canada and Latin America to spread its influence over all the Americas.

One man's initiative and the patient collaboration of many brought a great result from a Pullman car conversation with Archbishop Cicognani.

CHAPTER XVI

Revision of the New Testament

O N JANUARY 1, 1932, Bishop O'Hara issued a pastoral
letter to the priests and people of the diocese of Great
Falls, Mont., in which he said: "I am addressing you, my
dear Fathers and beloved faithful to invite your zealous cooperation in a work to deepen our knowledge of Jesus Christ,
to strengthen our Faith in His heavenly doctrine, and increase
Christian Charity among us. It is no other project than the
systematic study of the Life of Jesus Christ from the inspired
pages of the Holy Gospel."

Similar exhortations, it is quite safe to say, have been given
to the faithful by every bishop from the time of St. Peter.
There was little about this one to indicate that it would lead
to an important event in the history of the Catholic Church
in the United States: a new version by American scripture
scholars of the then current three-hundred-year-old English
translation of the Old and New Testaments.

It did so because of certain characteristics of the man who
wrote it.

In the first place, the exhortation was tied to action as part
of the Great Falls plan of the Confraternity of Christian Doctrine. It was issued as a directive and program for the parish
study clubs which formed the core of the adult education
part of that plan.

In the second place, the man who wrote it was not in the habit of throwing out directives without having previously provided means for implementing them.

In the third place, Bishop O'Hara was not a man to leave a desired good unattained through lack of any effort he could make. He had the courage to initiate action toward it, the simplicity to take whatever means were open to him and the perseverance to see the action through to its end.

In regard to this pastoral, those things meant not only that Bishop O'Hara had a well-trained organization of study clubs already prepared and the texts and methods ready for them to use, but also that he followed their progress to see what was lacking for their better understanding of the scripture and what could be done about it.

He found, as others had before him, that the untrained laity experienced much apparently unnecessary difficulty from the antiquated wording and verse by verse arrangement of the Douai-Rheims text.

So the first remote step toward the present erudite work now being done by American scholars toward a completely new English translation of the scriptures from the original texts was the effective desire of one bishop to get a more readable text for the members of his diocesan confraternity study clubs.

Before he was finished, Bishop O'Hara was involved in a lot more than asking a simple question. But his first actions are another insight into one form of greatness—the ability to combine large vision with simple acts placed in persevering single-mindedness.

He did not consider himself a scripture scholar. The only priests of standing in that field with whom he was in personal touch at that time were the professors of scripture at the seminaries to which he had sent candidates for the priesthood: Father Edward P. Arbez, S.S., of Catholic University, who had been at Menlo Park, Calif., during the bishop's Portland days, and Father Joseph L. Lilly, C.M., of Denver, Colo., where the bishop was sending his seminarians from Great Falls. He asked them about the possibility of getting out a more easily understandable text. His first suggestions were extremely modest: printing in sense-paragraphs rather than by verses, modernizing spelling and perhaps changing a few definitely antiquated words.

He learned that scripture scholars were in complete agreement about the need for revision of the old translation and that individuals had already done much work toward it. But there had as yet been no episcopal authorization of an official revision. In fact, there had been no real attempt at cohesion in various individual studies. There was no organized body of scripture scholars in the United States, no common medium through which they could meet in discussion.

After he had become chairman of the episcopal committee of the CCD and had seen the national confraternity safely launched at the Rochester congress of 1935, Bishop O'Hara conferred with his fellow committee members, Archbishops McNicholas and Murray and decided to take action on revision of the Bible.

He drafted a letter asking comment on how to go about a revision which "should not go beyond necessary correction and modernization" of the Challoner text.

Then he pulled over the *Catholic Directory* and addressed the letter to sixteen professors of scripture teaching in the major seminaries of the United States. Each letter included an invitation to attend a meeting for preliminary discussion at the Sulpician Seminary, Catholic University of America, on January 18, 1936.

This letter went out and the meeting was held even before the mailing of the page of "Suggestions" which launched the revision of the Baltimore Catechism.

The infant confraternity, in other words, during the first year of its existence, within three months of its first national congress, was fostering a contemporary revision of the twin source books of Catholic teaching, the Bible and the catechism. And the prime mover in all three instances, the confraternity, the catechism and the Bible, was the same man.

Fifteen scripture scholars attended the Washington meeting. With few exceptions, they had not met before. Bishop O'Hara, who knew most of them only by correspondence, introduced them to each other.

Their discussion was based on the suggested procedure toward a revision which had been contained in the bishop's letter. They came to quick agreement on both the advisability and the opportuneness of such a revision; on the willingness and the ability of American scripture scholars to start work on it immediately; and on a rather complete set of principles dealing with the basic text to be used, the manner of treating it, the extent of the revision and other matters of procedure.

The same meeting went on to nominate, by authority of the episcopal committee of the Confraternity of Christian Doctrine, some twenty American scholars to begin revision of different sections of the Challoner revision of the Douai-Rheims translation of the New Testament. Following the meeting, these men were notified of their nomination and provided with copies of the adopted principles.

A second meeting was held in Washington in April and the work of revision actually set in motion. The principles governing the revision were given final formulation and a copy of them sent to the Pontifical Biblical Commission in Rome and to some fifty biblical scholars in the United States.

This April meeting also decided on the preparation of a one-volume commentary on the entire New Testament to be issued as a companion volume to the revised text, appointed an editorial board to divide responsibility for definite phases of the work and heard, from Father Butin, S.M., the first suggestion for a permanent organization of American Catholic biblical scholars.

The workmanlike speed with which these initial steps were taken provided abundant proof that the men concerned had already given much thought to the desired revision. The document they sent to the American biblical scholars was headed "Principles Governing the Revision of the New Testament." It began by defining the project. Then a paragraph on the organization of the work contained a sentence, "The whole project is ultimately under the direction of this committee [the Episcopal Committee of the Confraternity of Christian Doctrine], and will be issued with its authority."

Ten further paragraphs dealt in detail with the actual principles governing the division under the headings "Basic Text," "Extent of the Revision," "Language," "Prefaces," "Footnotes," "External Form," "Illustrations," "Commentary," "Preparation of Manuscript" and "Time."

The basic text was to be the Clementine Vulgate. The work in its relation to the Rheims-Challoner text was to be determined by four principles of which two were: "All real paraphrasing must be restricted to the footnotes" and "While free to make whatever changes he deems justified, the reviser should retain, as far as possible, the diction, style and rhythm of the present text. All defects in language of the present text should naturally be corrected."

The reviser was asked to eliminate obsolete words and forms: "E.g., omit 'ye,' but retain 'thine' and 'thou.' "

The paragraph on time must have sounded to some a little like "There's no hurry about this. Tomorrow morning will do." It read: "No time is fixed for the execution of this work. It will depend upon the individual reviser and the demands of thoroughness. It has, however, been suggested that the Revision Committee be summoned for a meeting early in September, 1936, at which time most of the preliminary work could have been accomplished."

In point of fact, the work took five years. The confraternity New Testament was published on May 18, 1941. The one-volume commentary followed one year later.

To the non-scholar, announcement of a projected revision of the English bible was merely a news item about a more or less mechanical academic undertaking. To the dedicated men who give their lives to the investigation, preservation and explanation of the revealed Word of God, it was a call to battle. They were jealous guardians of the Sacred Book. They knew what harm had come to the world through tampering with it lightly, and they girded themselves for its defense.

They knew, as few laymen did, that the translation of the Bible authorized for use by Catholics of English-speaking countries had come to occupy an unauthorized position of untouchability. No translation into any vernacular language is recognized by the Universal Church as the "official bible." That title was reserved by the Council of Trent (in a sense soon to be clarified in the encyclical *Divino Afflante Spiritus*) for the Latin Vulgate. An authorized translation is one that has been guaranteed by theologians as theologically sound and approved by bishops who exercise the authority of the Church in regions where the translation is used.

In some nations this distinction was clearly kept through the ages. A French preacher, for example, would be aware that he was quoting Grampon's translation in preference to another and he would traditionally accompany his French quotation with the corresponding Latin text.

In English, however, a single translation had held the field so long that no other was ever cited. Generation after generation grew to look upon its familiar phrases as the one and only wording for revelation.

This translation was originally made by a group of English scholars in exile from Elizabethan persecution at the English College in Douai, France. The New Testament was published at Rheims in 1582, the Old Testament at Douai in 1609.

Some hundred and fifty years later much of its language had become obsolete. Bishop Challoner, Vicar Apostolic of the London District, with the assistance of others, made a revision, not a new translation, of the Douai-Rheims text.

This mixture of sixteenth century and eighteenth century English prose was given some early nineteenth century touches by Canon Haydock and that was substantially the form in which twentieth century America was reading "the Douai Bible."

There was obvious need of a revision (or of another translation) and no good case against it. Those who are habitually suspicious of change—and there are certain to be a good many of them in a tradition-preserving institution like the Catholic Church—denied this. There were also some who recognized the advantages of modernization, yet still opposed it. Some of these maintained that the obsolete biblical phraseology had remained clear because of familiarity with its meaning and indeed possessed, through association, a near sacramental value of its own. Others felt that increased clarity for lay readers would not compensate for their disturbance at finding consecrated phrases suddenly changed.

Bishop O'Hara's part in the new English bible, which had begun with his instigation of the whole project, entered another phase with his unsentimental resistance to this kind of opposition. As chairman of the episcopal committee, he was able to place the protective authority of the hierarchy between the revisers and those who cried out, "Leave our Bible alone! It was good enough for our fathers and it's good enough for us!"

But his longest, most difficult and most typically Bishop O'Hara contribution was shepherding a sometimes unwieldy flock of people, problems and attitudes toward the fold of a single acceptable and accepted "confraternity bible." He took no part in the actual revision of the text beyond his first letter with its suggested procedure. Yet he was probably more important to its steady and successful progress than any other individual. He was ambassador from the revisers to the hierarchy and spokesman for the hierarchy to the revisers. He stood in much the same relation to the total effort as a producer does to a film. Directors, writers, actors and technicians have freedom in their own fields but turn to him in their relations with each other and with the outside.

This can be seen from the beginning in the correspondence of the first few months which saw the revision started and a permanent organization of America's Catholic biblical scholars formulated.

Father William Newton brought enthusiasm and great energy to his work as secretary of the editorial board. When he wrote on March 13, 1936, to each man who had accepted assignment to some part of the revision he began his letter, "In the name of the Most Rev. E. V. O'Hara let me thank you for . . ."

When he sent out invitations for the editorial board meeting of April 18, he said that the meeting was called, "by His Excellency Bishop O'Hara."

On July 14, he was reporting to the bishop that two revisers had already sent in their work.

A constant correspondence during the intervening months recorded Father Newton's close collaboration with Bishop O'Hara in every step he took. He writes, for example, to say that he had received, along with a list of all Americans who had passed through Rome's Pontifical Biblical Institute, personal approval of the revision project from the Reverend J. B. Frey, Secretary of the Pontifical Biblical Commission.

The progress toward the Catholic Biblical Association of America can also be followed in these letters. On August 28, 1936, Father Newton wrote to all the revisers and other scripture scholars a letter which began: "Some months ago the Most Rev. E. V. O'Hara, chairman of the Episcopal Board of the Confraternity of Christian Doctrine, initiated a revision of our Rheims New Testament. Two meetings were held on the project and to them were invited such Scripture scholars as were readily available. At the second of these conferences the need and advantages of a wider organization of our Catholic Scripture scholars was brought under discussion. The Bishop contributed the tempting offer of forming such an association to function as a section of the Confraternity, and under the authority of its Episcopal Board."

A first draft for a constitution of the proposed Catholic Biblical Association of America came with a note to Bishop O'Hara saying that the draft was "formulated by Fathers Butin and Donze at your appointment."

This draft was the constitution actually adopted for the CBA by its founding members. In Article Two, under "Purpose," it states:

"1: *Primary:* To place at the disposal of the Episcopal Board of the Confraternity of Christian Doctrine a body of men qualified to study and work out Biblical problems.

"2. *Secondary:* Better acquaintance among our Scripture men; mutual encouragement and support in the Biblical field; to afford the laity an opportunity to cooperate in the advancement and diffusion of Biblical knowledge."

Some fifty scripture scholars held sessions during the second national congress of the CCD at New York in October, 1936. They discussed the revision in detail, heard a report on its progress, and decided to form the American CBA which would have its first formal meeting at the following year's CCD congress.

This made the New York congress something of a sweeping triumph for the one-year-old confraternity. It meant that the new organization had gathered Catholic leaders from all the nation to discuss religious education all the way from kindergarten techniques, through the function of Newman Clubs in secular universities, to the most erudite biblical research. It meant that the confraternity was presenting at its second national meeting, by way of high-level concrete accomplishment, the "printed not published" first draft of a revision of the Baltimore Catechism, the first sections of a revision of the New Testament, and the first permanent organization of America's biblical scholars.

That was a lot of quality production for one year. It is illuminating to consider together the importance of that year for the confraternity, the catechism and the Bible and think of how much it meant in terms of work for one man who was very actively involved in all three.

At this point, a busy bishop might have been fully justified in saying to himself, "Now the goal has been set, the work is started, the men are organized to do it. I can ease out of it and let someone else carry the load." But that was not Bishop O'Hara's philosophy. He was too wise in the ways of organization. He knew too well the necessity for a leadership as sustained as the effort it was inspiring. He understood what another notable organizer, Father Daniel Lord, S.J., once described in a blackboard lecture: "Every new organization zooms upward like *this*. Then it takes a sharp turn down. The secret of success is to be there with a basket and catch it before it falls beneath the level you want it to maintain."

A major danger in the collaborative effort of New Testament revision was that of collapse through intensely held differences of opinion among the revisers, editors and consultants. This showed itself in matters theological, historical, semantic, grammatical, literary and in virtually every branch of knowledge that subserves the Queen of Sciences. Every man was an expert in his own field and clashes were inevitable.

There was an early echo of this in the next meeting of the

editorial board, held in Washington on April 10, 1937. After a progress report which told that only six of the twenty assignments had not been completed and that three books had already been examined by all the editors, there was a lively discussion over the method of handling the submitted manuscripts. The result was a motion to the effect that after having been seen by all the editors, a manuscript would go back to its reviser who would incorporate the corrections and resubmit it, with or without justification for any disagreement with the editor. The resubmitted manuscript was to be at the discretion of the editorial board. They would reexamine it in this order: a) Fathers Arbez, Butin and McClellan for comparison with the original; b) Father Callan for improvement of English expression; c) Father Plassman as final consultant; d) the other editors, Fathers McHugh, Donze and Steinmuller for the details for which each had been appointed.

Fathers Thomas Plassman, O.F.M., and William H. McClellan, S.J., were new appointments to the board made at this meeting. Bishop O'Hara presided over that meeting as he did over a meeting of the CBA held the same day. There is no telling what protests about "the other fellow's" cavalier treatment of "my" manuscript were poured into his ear. Such things do not appear on the record. But they are the very stuff from which diplomacy reconciles divergent opinion to unified action.

There is a phrase in a letter from Cardinal Tisserant to Bishop O'Hara on March 6, 1941, which betrays Rome's understanding both of the situation and of the part the bishop played in it. The Cardinal closed his first paragraph by saying: "I wish to congratulate you most heartily on the prompt completion of the revised version of the New Testament, prepared by the Committee appointed by the Hierarchy of the United States, a Commission over which Your Excellency, laboring *fortiter et suaviter* so efficiently presides."

One may read a lot into that "laboring *fortiter et suaviter*." A combination of strength and calm on the part of a single man in an executive position was the only thing that could have kept the work moving. Bishop O'Hara supplied this time after time when it looked like things had reached an impasse on some particular point. For keeping the work moving, he had an able lieutenant in the secretary of the editorial board, Father (later Monsignor) William Newton, of whom he later said, "Without Father Newton, there would have been no revised New Testament."

Father Newton, in addition to doing his own share of the revising, kept incessantly after revisers, editors and consultants alike. In 1938 he journeyed to Rome and to England in the interests of the revision. At Rome he was successful even beyond his hopes. The individual members of the Biblical Commission not only confirmed Father Frey's previous approval of the work on the New Testament and encouraged reference to the Greek from the Vulgate, but also gave their blessing to the project for a similar revision of the Old Testament.

In England, he was not quite so successful. The English were themselves engaged on two new translations. At Oxford, Father C. Lattey, S.J., was heading a group of scholars working on the Westminster version. On assignment from the bishops of England and Wales to do a new English translation of the New Testament, Monsignor Ronald Knox was working at his gigantic solitary task.

Father Newton did not succeed in meeting Monsignor Knox, but he had mutually profitable discussions with Father Lattey. The Jesuit was most cooperative and these meetings were the beginning of a prolonged correspondence between Father Lattey and Bishop O'Hara. The Englishman politely indicated his fear that his country would not take kindly to a revision worded in America. Although he and a colleague, Father Barton, offered to cooperate with the editorial board, there was little attempt to disguise his wish that the cooperation might be the other way around. Could not the confraternity put its influence behind American distribution of the Westminster version to which some American scholars might be asked to contribute their advice?

At this stage of the game, however, Bishop O'Hara would not have accepted a ready-made non-American revision if an angel had told him it was excellent. This attitude was not a mere matter of using the American idiom. He saw that work on the revision, and the new translations to come, would be the foundation of something the United States needed and had not previously been able to claim, a continuing body of highly competent, experienced and respected Catholic biblical scholarship.

On his return, Father Newton prepared a scholarly "Brief for the Revision of the New Testament" for presentation to the committee of biblical scholars.

By this time, the work had reached a stage at which some judgment could be passed upon its quality. A complete text of a first revision had been given to the editors by the spring of 1938. The editorial board decided to print, as a trial balloon for circulation among scripture students and competent critics only, the revised text of St. John's gospel. When this was brought out, it drew generally favorable comment from both religious and secular sources. But its very appearance in print was a signal for everyone, from scholar to crank, who had any strong ideas on what form the revision should take, to rush in with his contribution.

Much of the comment was both authoritative and important. Some of it was neither. And not all of it was offered with the dispassionate calm one likes to see among scholars.

As the man in the middle, and in accordance with a long-standing principle of loyalty to his co-workers, Bishop O'Hara was a bulwark of strength and confidence for the revisers at this time.

Another major and constant problem, that of keeping the project staffed with the best available men, fell squarely on his shoulders. When the CBA, at a meeting during the confraternity congress at Hartford, Conn., in 1938, came to the conclusion that work could be started on the Old Testament revision, this problem was more than doubled. It meant appealing to diocesan seminaries and religious orders for the use of their very best men. Nor was it long after the undertaking of the Old Testament before it became evident that the work would be unbearably prolonged if done only in the spare time of professors already burdened with teaching and priestly duties. Bishops and religious superiors sometimes had to be begged to release the one man they could least spare for full-time work on the confraternity bible.

When the Catholic Biblical Association of America held its first annual general meeting apart from a confraternity congress at Toronto in August, 1940, Bishop O'Hara presided over a meeting of the board of revisers of both Testaments. He received Father Newton's report that the revised New Testament would be in the hands of the booksellers by spring, 1941.

The Toronto sessions also saw the CBA voting to sponsor a book of gospels and epistles for Sundays and Holydays whose publication during the following spring had been authorized by Bishop O'Hara. The association reported a membership of six hundred, with seventy members of the hierarchy on its rolls in some capacity. It took pride in the fact that its publication, the *Catholic Biblical Quarterly*, started in 1938 on the instigation of Bishop O'Hara, was the first periodical devoted to scripture in the English-speaking world.

Preparation for completion of the confraternity New Testament saw Bishop O'Hara directing the work of sales and distribution. The book was published by St. Anthony's Guild Press "for the Episcopal Committee of the Confraternity of

Christian Doctrine." For distribution, the bishop organized a national New Testament Committee sponsored by the Holy Name Society whose members would undertake the actual distribution through their parish units all over the nation. The national spiritual director of the Holy Name Society, Father Harry C. Graham, O.P., was executive secretary of the committee.

The long-term preparation included winning official approval and confirmation by more than three-quarters of the bishops in the United States that Sunday, May 18 (the official date of publication), would be celebrated as Bible Sunday. Some archbishops and bishops issued pastorals on the day. St. Bonaventure's College, New York, marked the occasion by celebrating, from May 11 to May 18, the "First Bible Week in America" and had a special postal cachet for St. Bonaventure Post Office which was requested by President Roosevelt and many other philatelists.

At the same time, Francis X. Sadlier published the confraternity text edition of *The Epistles and Gospels for Sundays and Holydays* and the new text was read in churches for the first time that first Bible Sunday. (Later Septuagesima Sunday went into America's church calendar as the annual Bible Sunday.)

It was a job of promotion, distribution and sales to arouse the admiration of the best professionals in the business world. It was the first time in history that a single Catholic-sponsored edition of the New Testament had sold half a million copies.

All this paid off in the kind of coin Bishop O'Hara valued most. The nationwide publicity in the secular press swept out of many of the dark corners of the United States in which it still lingers that monstrous calumny that the Catholic Church does not believe in the Bible. And the systematic distribution, the concentrated appeal from so many pulpits, the minimal price at which the handsomely produced book was

offered, left little excuse for any Catholic home to be without a New Testament phrased in words the family could understand.

The expected criticism of the wording of the revision was
not long in coming. It was sometimes irresponsible and often
self-contradictory. The people who rushed to make it might
have been less impetuous had they been able to read just one
of Bishop O'Hara's communications with Archbishop Cicognani.

They would have learned that they were basing their criticism on the false premise that those who authorized its publication believed the revision to be perfect and the last word.
Nothing could be further from the truth. Disagreement over
the final wording had been so prolonged without final group
decision that the editorial board had finally given the whole
manuscript over to one man, Father William McClellan, S.J.,
and agreed to accept his phraseology. It is quite likely that not
one other person connected with the revision would have
agreed with every word Father McClellan accepted. There
was no doubt of the authenticity of the work as a translation
of the Vulgate. The only question was one of English prose
style. Perfection in that is a most difficult, if not impossible,
matter for any group to decide upon. The editorial board did
not decide that this was perfect. It decided that it was good
and proved that it did not think it was quite good enough by
immediately forming a committee for revision of the revision
after all criticism of the first edition had been received and
evaluated.

The general public was not aware of this. It must have required great reticence on Bishop O'Hara's part to listen si-
lently to casual criticism offered in ignorance of the fact that
he himself was working on those very things. As always he
was working with his revisers, editors and consultants. Since
the planned improvements in phrasing will now likely be incorporated in the current project of an entirely new transla-

tion from the original languages, it may be permissible to refer to some evidence of what was being done along these lines immediately following first publication of the revision.

The best example is perhaps the communication from Bishop O'Hara to another prelate which enclosed two confidential reports on the revised New Testament, one from an outstanding American theologian, the other from an Englishman famed both for his learning and for his mastery of the English language.

The two were in agreement on virtually all the points they brought up. One or two quotations will give an idea of the direction their suggestions took. It is not without interest that they turn toward the more traditionalist view which agrees with Bishop O'Hara's own preference for smooth-flowing prose.

In a detailed report requested confidentially by Bishop O'Hara, Father Thomas Plassman, O.F.M., one of Catholic America's best all-round scholars and a principal in the work of revision, began his "General Observations" with praise for the new work:

"The New Revision represents a noble, practical and apostolic effort to render the New Testament into the language of the day, i.e. into correct, readable, clear, up-to-date and, as far as may be, literary English. The general consensus is that this purpose has been largely accomplished. This sacred Book may now be taken in hand and read intelligently from cover to cover, and even the common man will understand and relish what he reads."

In his particular examples, however, he rather qualifies his statement about it being always literary (or even correct) English. He regrets for instance a certain loss of rhythm and quotes as one of "numerous examples" Matt. XXIV, 37:

> And as it was in the days of Noe
> Even so will the coming of the Son of Man be.

He shows the loss of the Hebrew balance which the Greek and Latin had maintained and objects to the awkwardness of the final, suspended "be." He would prefer the last line to read "Even so shall be the coming of the Son of Man."

He states, "Frequently the new Version, in its effort to be *scrupulously exact* offends against good literary taste." As an example, he says:

"Hence, the expression 'Get up' (which has a tinge of Americanism) might just as well be exchanged for 'Arise' or 'Rise.' In fact, the verb 'to get' seems to have been given far too much prominence. Instead of 'getting into' or 'getting out of' (a ship), the verb 'to go' might have been used with more propriety. Both the Greek and Latin imply this.

"At times this tendency leads dangerously close to what may be taken as irreverent, if not ridiculous. Instead of saying that Our Lord had 'slipped away,' one would prefer to use the more dignified form, 'He had withdrawn' (*deviavit*). . . ."

He thinks the auxiliary verb "do" is used with unusual frequency and sometimes fails to carry the emphasis which was evidently intended. "Do not fear" appears weak and wobbly alongside the forceful "Fear not." Examples are numerous.

About the use of "shall" and "will," he first defers to the decision of the revisers and then goes on to speak rather strongly about the need for using "shall" to express "the unutterable finality" of all Christ's statements.

His particular comment goes verse by verse through the four gospels, noting each place in which he would like to see the phrasing changed.

The English poet Alfred Noyes backed him up in almost everything he said. Frequently he added additional emphases of his own. Both much preferred, for example, "Before Abraham was I am" to the revision's "Before Abraham came to be I am." Mr. Noyes added, "It compresses into a brief, incisive form, a clear statement of Our Lord's transcendence of time. Moreover, the way in which the word is balanced against the words *I am* enhances the whole effect by its subtle suggestion of the transitory nature of mortal life. . . . 'Before Abraham was I am' seems to convey its own evidence of the supernatural power whereby it was uttered. 'Came to be' is more like a labored and merely human utterance. I would regard alteration here as of the utmost importance. If the 'ordinary man' does not understand it, it is because the idea is beyond him, not because the language has failed. . . ."

Mr. Noyes was invited to make his comments on a purely unofficial and personal basis. He was one of many who made their contributions to the continuing work of revision by placing the results of their thinking at the disposal of Bishop O'Hara for the revisers and the editorial board.

CHAPTER XVII

A New English Bible
from the Original Languages

THE APPEARANCE IN 1943 of Pope Pius XII's encyclical *Divino Afflante Spiritu* was momentous for the whole world of Catholic biblical scholarship. The encyclical was an invitation, even a directive, for Catholic scholars to work on translations directly from the original languages rather than through reference to the Vulgate.

His Holiness stated that when the Council of Trent decreed that "all should use as authentic" the Vulgate Latin version, it was speaking in reference to other, erroneous Latin versions then current. The Pope pointed out that this approval did not "in any way diminish the authority and value of the original texts."

The encyclical recalled that the Council of Trent had projected authorized editing of "first a Latin, then a Greek and Hebrew edition which eventually would be published for the benefit of the Holy Church of God" and added, "If this desire could not then be fully realized owing to the difficulties of the times and other obstacles, at present it can, we earnestly hope, be more perfectly and entirely fulfilled by the united efforts of Catholic scholars."

American scholars, thanks to the project on which they

were engaged, were ready for this. In fact they were over-joyed. They did not in the least mind putting aside their five years of work on the revision of the Old Testament if the way was open to a completely new translation from the orig-inal languages. Their work was by no means lost. All the re-visers had been using the original texts while working from the Vulgate and keeping an eye on the English they were to revise.

Divino Afflante Spiritu was issued on September 30, 1943. By December Bishop O'Hara was able to inform the trans-laters of a favorable reply from the Pontifical Biblical Com-mission to the specific question whether scholars could now proceed with a new translation from the original texts.

He conferred among his fellow bishops and verified by correspondence what he already knew to be the wishes of the scholars. On February 21, 1944, for example, Bishop O'Hara wrote to Father Arbez: "The Episcopal Committee of the Confraternity has been giving consideration to the re-sponse of the Pontifical Biblical Commission. . . . We are considering whether it is not almost a directive to base the translation on the Hebrew text. . . . Should we decide to base the translation on the Hebrew text, do you foresee any serious disadvantage to the translaters, or would you rather welcome such a decision? I should appreciate an expression of your views in the matter."

The reply was enthusiastically in favor of working from the Hebrew. How little time was wasted in acting may be seen in a letter to Father Lilly dated just eight days later, March 1, 1944:

". . . I have just written Father Arbez that the Episcopal Committee concerned with revision of the Scriptures has, after full consideration, unanimously decided to base the re-vision of the Old Testament upon the Hebrew text. . . . I am sure that all of the Scripture scholars will rejoice at the change."

A meeting of the CBA at St. Mary's College, South Bend, in the summer of 1944 formally announced the undertaking of translating both Testaments from the original languages. A letter from the Apostolic Delegate gave his approbation of what is possibly the most important work of scholarship in the history of American Catholicism.

The work was planned without any attempt at a timetable. It was to take as long as the scholars required.

Actually, the Book of Genesis appeared in 1948. The Book of Psalms and the Canticles of the Roman Breviary came out in 1950.

The complete authorized text of the new American translation of the Old Testament will be in four volumes. The first, Genesis through Ruth, appeared in 1952; the third, Job through Sirach, in 1955. Volume Four, the Prophetic Books, is expected in 1957 and Volume Two, the remaining historical books, in 1958 or later.

The completely new translation of the New Testament from the original languages will be added to the Old Testament to make an entirely new English translation of the Bible by American Catholic scholars.

This is indeed a continuing work. Archbishop O'Hara was engaged in it right up to his death. All the problems of the revision—material, personal, scholarly or literary—came up again and were even intensified in the new translation. The archbishop was still striving to shape from the best advice he could obtain a definitive set of canons for the translaters. In a letter he wrote as preface to Volume One of the new translation of the Old Testament, he fashioned a sentence with a classic ring to it, one that was eagerly seized upon by several of the translaters: "The supreme goal to be sought in rendering the word of God into the vernacular is rigorous fidelity to the meaning of the original, expressed in simple and intelligible language."

That this goal was being approached was indicated in a

review of Volume One which appeared in the weekly Book Review section of *The New York Times*. Comparing modern English versions of the Bible, the reviewer said: "At its best, the Revised Standard is a faithful trustee of the Tyndale-King James heritage, whereas the Confraternity edition often achieves strikingly fresh and powerful effects by forgetting about literary considerations and aiming at nothing more than digging the meaning out of the Hebrew and putting it into plain words."

Twenty years after he called that first meeting in Washington, Archbishop O'Hara was still poring over proofs, meeting with translaters, editors and publishers, and winnowing suggestions. He had read proof on every single one of the successive publications of the revised catechism and of the revised and newly translated Bible.

As he waited for the last pages of a new English Bible translated by a band of American Catholic scholars he had been instrumental in bringing into existence, he might well have recalled the combination of personal and official respect conveyed in a letter of December 26, 1943, by Father Lilly, speaking on behalf of the Catholic Biblical Association of America:

"I shall ever remember the evening in Denver when Your Excellency first suggested to me the project of revision. It was what I had been hoping for, but such an undertaking could only have succeeded under the patronage of the Hierarchy, and it was Your Excellency's efforts which secured that for us. While Your Excellency expresses gratitude for our work, we cannot but acknowledge the debt of gratitude that the scripture men owe to Your Excellency for having initiated such an undertaking and making it possible for us to organize ourselves into the Biblical Association."

In 1954, the CBA made formal recognition of its debt to one man in the wording of an illuminated scroll it presented at its annual meeting:

. . . Archbishop O'Hara brought the Association into existence. For the past 17 years he has watched over its growth and has been its constant champion and advocate among the hierarchy of our country.

It was through his efforts as Chairman of the Episcopal Committee of the Confraternity of Christian Doctrine . . . that the revision of the Rheims-Challoner New Testament was begun and completed and that the present work of translating the entire Bible from the original languages or their oldest extant form into Modern Eiglish, was undertaken and is now nearing completion.

Be it resolved we

. . . Name him officially what he has always been in fact, the Father and the Founder of the Catholic Biblical Association.

Of the many living monuments he left behind him, this must surely be one of those he held closest to his heart.

CHAPTER XVIII

English in the Ritual

A LONGSIDE THE REVISED CATECHISM and the new translation of the Bible stands a third slender work which will find a place in the history of the Catholic Church in America. It is the "Ritual with English" or, as it was entitled in its first edition of 1954, *Collectio Rituum Anglicae Linguae*. And Bishop O'Hara had a central role also in the preparation, approval and publication of this milestone in encouraging participation of the laity in the liturgy.

There was a special liturgical section at the fifth national congress of the CCD held at Cincinnati in November, 1939. Its sessions included discussions on topics like "Using the Liturgy in the Teaching of the Eucharist" and "The Liturgy and the Confraternity." But, more important, they brought together Catholics from all over the nation who were keenly interested in the study of the liturgy. These men already had an American center of the churchwide liturgical revival in the Benedictines at St. John's, Collegeville, Minn. Now they determined to perpetuate the group effort of this meeting at the confraternity congress by establishing an annual Liturgical Conference. These conferences were held in subsequent years apart from the confraternity congresses because they were interested in every aspect of the liturgy, not only its teaching function which was naturally the primary concern of the confraternity.

At the Liturgical Conference held in Portland, Ore., in 1947, a motion was passed calling for study of the possibility of having some of the Sacramental Rites in English along the lines of permissions recently granted other nations. At the Chicago confraternity congress of 1951, Monsignor Joseph Morrison, of Chicago, approached Bishop O'Hara with the suggestion that he lay this proposal before the meeting of the American bishops to be held in Washington the following week.

Bishop O'Hara was strongly favorable to the idea. Just that summer, he had received from Archbishop Jaegers, during a visit to the latter's home in Paderborn, Germany, a copy of the new ritual in which the use of German in certain rites had been authorized by the Holy See. He had already been giving some consideration to the most prudent and most likely successful procedure for bringing a similar use of the vernacular to the United States.

He knew that current movements for the use of English in the Mass—from which he had not altogether held himself apart—had reached a stage at which rather firm lines of opposing opinion had been drawn. There would be little chance for unanimous approval of anything submitted under the large heading of "Use of the Vernacular in the Liturgy." But there was an area in which the Confraternity of Christian Doctrine had a legitimate interest, in which the question of English in the Mass had no part, and in which the Holy See had already spoken.

This was the use of the vernacular English on such public or semi-public occasions as baptisms, weddings, sickbed prayers and burials. There was not only the consideration of fuller participation by the Catholic laity in such rites, but also the possibility of taking full advantage of the instructional value

of such occasions for non-Catholics. It was certainly a matter falling within the scope of the CCD.

So, rather than present the motion as an individual, Bishop
O'Hara first placed it before the episcopal committee of the
confraternity. The committee agreed that they could sponsor
it and it was as a confraternity measure for the better promotion of Christian teaching, not as a move for more vernacular
in the liturgy, that Bishop O'Hara placed his proposal before
the bishops' meeting.

After serious discussion by the prelates present, the motion
was passed and the chairman of the meeting appointed the
episcopal committee of the CCD to "the task of studying the
desirability of presenting a request to Rome, for the optional
use of English in connection with Baptism, Marriage, the Last
Sacraments and Burial, and of reporting the same at the 1952
meeting of Bishops."

As was his habit, Bishop O'Hara lost no time in availing
himself of the commission. He immediately got in touch with
Father Gerald Ellard, S.J., of St. Mary's, Kans. They discussed working procedure and decided that the study would
consist of two things: first, the formulation of a brief on the
project, to be amplified and revised for presentation to the
entire hierarchy; secondly, the drawing up of a *Collectio
Rituum Anglicae Linguae* on the model of the *Collection
Rituum I* approved for Germany in 1950.

For Father Ellard this was a real labor of love. He threw
himself into the work with an intensity that matched even
Bishop O'Hara's desire for dispatch. On January 29, 1952,
the bishop was able to send a first draft of the proposed brief
to a list of consultative scholars and authorities with a covering letter whose ending indicated that anyone who wanted
to take part in the work would have to be prepared to travel
fast:

"Will you please give us the advantage of your suggestions either on the margin of the enclosed rough draft or in

a separate statement. I should be grateful if I might have your reply by February 15, 1952."

There was a good response. The number of consultants in the work grew during the year to sixty-two and included liturgical authorities in Europe as well as in the United States.

The first draft of the brief also went to the bishops even before the reports were in from the consultants. Bishop O'Hara explained his reasons for this in a letter to Father Ellard: "I think this procedure is better since it sends the original statement in a frankly tentative and preliminary form and will indicate that the Committee is earnestly engaged in its task. Secondly, it will give an opportunity to follow up with the compilation of the scholars' opinions."

The brief in its final form traced the history of papal guidance on the use of the vernacular in certain rites. It cited the Vatican approval of the 1935 *Collectio Rituum Archdiocesis Viennensis* which Propaganda recommended in 1941 as a model for compiling rituals with vernacular for certain mission territories. It quotes Pius XII's *Mediator Dei* of 1947: "The use of the Latin tongue prevailing in a great part of the Church affords at once an imposing sign of unity and an effective safeguard against the corruption of true doctrine. In spite of this, the adoption of the vernacular in quite a number of functions may prove of great benefit to the people. But to make such concessions is for the Apostolic See alone."

It went on to refer to the German *Collectio Rituum* as an interpretation of this statement. Then it defined the scope of the indult that might be asked for the United States: "It is contemplated, then, that the Holy Father will be asked to express his mind on granting a similar indult in favor of the United States for the optional use of English with reference to Baptismal, Marriage, Sick Call and Funeral Rites.

"The scope of the indult envisaged is thus limited strictly

to the Sacraments and situations named. The proposal does not in any way concern itself with any wider question of the partial use of the vernacular at any parochial function. It bears no reference to the topic of the introduction of English into the Mass, or the Office (Vespers, Compline), or elsewhere. It *does* contemplate enriching Catholic life, for the evident good of souls, in the personal-and-group associations involved in the situations mentioned."

The brief also discussed the general direction of the specific changes contemplated in each rite, giving reasons for each. Under baptism it pointed out that more than a million baptisms at each of which an average of five or six people were present took place in the United States each year. "Thus several million instances for a deep and moving *religious instruction* were present—and were almost wholly missed."

In its conclusion, it again had recourse to Pius XII in *Mediator Dei:* "It is true that the Church is a living organism and therefore grows and develops also in her liturgical worship; it is also true that, always saving the integrity of her doctrine, she accommodates herself to the needs and conditions of the times."

The rapid progress of Father Ellard's work on the proposed ritual can be read in a letter Bishop O'Hara sent to the Cardinals, archbishops and members of the episcopal committee on June 30, 1952:

"While seeking for a Ritual text to accompany the study which the Episcopal Committee of the Confraternity of Christian Doctrine has been asked to submit to the Bishops this Fall, we have been offered very generously the results of several years of cooperative work by a group of liturgical and literary men on both sides of the Atlantic. The Bruce Company of Milwaukee has accepted responsibility for setting this up in good type.

"I have requested the Bruce Company to send Your Eminence galley proof of this text for your information and comment.

"Comments on this galley proof received during July will be in time to be considered before the book is printed.

"Our Liturgical Committee is at work on the final draft of the study which will be sent to the Bishops together with the text of the Ritual (printed not published) in September. . . ."

The replies were prompt, constructive and generally very favorable. On July 30, 1952, Bishop O'Hara sent all the bishops mimeographed copies of the revised "Statement Explaining *Collectio Rituum Anglicae Linguae*" in which the principal suggestions made by the bishops and consultants had been incorporated. The careful attention given by most of the metropolitans to the galley proofs of the ritual itself, induced Bishop O'Hara to have proofs sent to all the ordinaries of the country.

Suggestions were collated and in a number of instances adopted in page proofs which were again sent out for scrutiny. By mid-September, final texts for both the statement and the ritual were in the hands of the Bruce Publishing Company which brought out both volumes in "printed not published" editions the first week of October.

On October 3, 1952, Bishop O'Hara wrote to all bishops, ordinaries and auxiliaries of the United States a letter in which he said:

"I have requested the Bruce Publishing Company of Milwaukee to send to Your Excellency the final draft of the study made by the Episcopal Committee of the Confraternity of Christian Doctrine at the request of the Bishops at their meeting last November. The report is in two sections; first, the Statement in reference to the desirability of petitioning the Holy See for permission to use English more extensively in the administration of certain Sacraments and Blessings, and secondly, a Sacristy Ritual embodying the suggestions made in the Statement. Though printed for the convenience of the Bishops the report is not published:

". . . The Co-Chairmen of the Liturgical Committee were Father G. Diekmann, O.S.B., Editor of *Worship*, Father G. Ellard, S.J., author of many books on the liturgy, and Father J. C. Selner, S.S., of St. Mary's Seminary, Baltimore. The literary editor was Mr. H. P. R. Finberg of London, favorably known both in England and America for his translation of liturgical texts. . . ."

When the bishops met in Washington for their meeting of November, 1952, they were quite fully informed on the progress of the work on the proposed ritual. They were also armed with their own suggestions and those of the experts they had called on for advice. The statement met with general approval but it was decided not to vote on the submission of the actual text to Rome until further revision had been made.

These revisions concerned three suggestions that came out of the bishops' meeting: first, to restore the "Thou" address-form in reference to the Divine Persons; second, to break down two long prayers into shorter ones; third, to consider the translation in the light of studies on the medieval Latin texts of the ritual prayers.

Father Ellard's health had begun to feel the effects of having carried the main burden of the year's intensive work without secretarial assistance of any kind. He asked to be relieved of the heavy responsibility and given some less demanding role in the further revision. The text finally approved was substantially that of the Jesuit liturgist.

Bishop O'Hara turned for aid to Father Theodore Hesburgh, C.S.C., president of the University of Notre Dame where a liturgical institute and a medieval institute could provide the two branches of scholarship needed for the work. With the approval of Father Hesburgh, Father M. A. Mathis, C.S.C., head of the Liturgical Institute, was appointed to the chairmanship of a committee formed from members of the faculties at both institutes.

This committee worked throughout 1953 in collaboration with consultant scholars. When their completed work was submitted to the bishops at their 1953 meeting, the prelates voted to submit it to the Holy See with their united request that it be considered for approved optional use in the United States. The ritual then passed into the hands of the administrative board of the NCWC whose chairman, Archbishop Karl J. Alter, of Cincinnati, brought it to the Apostolic Delegate for forwarding to the Holy See.

On June 3, 1954, the Sacred Congregation of Rites completed its study of the proposed ritual and returned a rescript on it to Archbishop Cicognani. The Apostolic Delegate forwarded this to Archbishop Alter as administrative representative of the bishops of the United States who had made the request. Archbishop Alter delegated Bishop O'Hara and his episcopal committee of the confraternity to see to the corrections suggested by the Sacred Congregation and to supervise the publication of the amended and approved ritual.

From the arrival of the favorable rescript, Bishop O'Hara began to receive congratulations from those who knew how much he had to do with the work.

Bishop Mark K. Carroll, of Wichita, added to his congratulations "for a job well done" the statement: "To my way of thinking, this is the greatest stride made by the Catholic Church in America since its missionary beginnings."

From the Apostolic Delegation in London, England, Archbishop Gerald P. O'Hara wrote: "This generous grant is something for which we are indebted, in large measure, to your own good self. Congratulations on having succeeded in obtaining it."

There was a note of fraternal understanding in Archbishop Lucey's letter from San Antonio: "I think that this indult from the Sacred Congregation will bring general satisfaction throughout the country to clergy and laity in spite of the fact that when you first brought up this matter at the meeting of the Bishops a few years ago many of them were not frantically enthusiastic about the project. All of which only goes to show that time marches on."

Other English-speaking countries soon sought to follow the path broken for them by the United States. When Canada, Australia, India, Ceylon and Burma in turn petitioned for use of English in the ritual it was the careful work done by the United States liturgists that won it for them. In the rescript replying to the request of the Australian bishops, the Sacred Congregation of Rites specifically stated that permission was granted for the approved text as published by The Bruce Company for use in the United States.

In December, 1954, Catholic newspapers across the nation carried a photograph of Archbishop O'Hara handing a copy of the newly published ritual to the Apostolic Delegate. Everyone who knew the story of the Ritual understood that this picture symbolized the part Archbishop O'Hara had played in giving the Church its first approved Ritual-with-English.

CHAPTER XIX

Bishop of Kansas City

W HEN BISHOP O'HARA was appointed to the See of Kansas City, Mo., on April 15, 1939, he was in the full maturity of his manhood and his priesthood. At fifty-seven, in his thirty-fourth year as a priest and his tenth as a bishop, he had proved his natural abilities and established himself in his chosen vocation through a constant succession of significant activities. There had been no wavering from the line he had started to follow from the farm in Minnesota. Day after day, year after year, he had gone steadily about the work he had chosen, the work for which God had chosen him—being a priest among men. The years, far from diminishing energy or zeal, had brought an increased capacity for work and a greater desire to do more of it.

It was to be expected that the habits of thought and action these constant years had formed should reveal themselves in some distinctive fashion during his spiritual leadership of an area that has been called the heartland of the United States. His new diocese was a place in which all his previous experience could stand him in good stead.

Kansas City is situated on the northern half of Missouri's western border. The diocese stretched south and east down through the Ozarks to Arkansas and included the west-central and southwestern part of the state. It cut through the "bible belt" and embraced towns in which "Catholic" was a fighting word. Its people were with the South in the War Between the States, old slave cabins are still to be seen on some of its farms, one of its cities is Joplin where the KKK spirit had one of its more recent revivals. In 1939 it had whole counties without a single known Catholic in their population. Its cities had America's usual industrial problems accentuated by racial feeling.

Bishop O'Hara was once again, as in Portland and in Great Falls, at the commercial center of a predominantly rural area in which Catholics were very much in the minority. He was in a situation typical of the Catholic in the United States. His spiritual jurisdiction enclosed an almost ideal test ground for the sowing and cultivation of his ideas on rural and urban sociology, education, lay participation in the work of the hierarchy, the application of Catholic principles to contemporary social attitudes and Catholic contribution to civic life. He was in exactly the sort of place that would benefit most from a successfully functioning Confraternity of Christian Doctrine.

Proof that he lost no time working this ground may be seen in two of the tributes paid him on the tenth anniversary of his arrival in Kansas City.

One came from his Catholics in the form of a handsome brochure entitled "A Decade of Building in the Diocese of Kansas City." It contained pictures of no fewer than 150 buildings "constructed or acquired for religious, educational and charitable uses" in the ten years. The new buildings included forty-two churches, fourteen convents, sixteen grade schools, six high schools and two colleges.

The other revealing tribute was an official Civic Testimonial Reception at which leading citizens of all faiths joined in "honoring his decade of service as a Kansas Citian." The principal speeches were given by two Protestants, one Jew

and a Catholic businessman under the headings, "The Kansas
Citian," "The Humanitarian," "The Shepherd" and "The
Man."

A complete account of the activities that earned these
tributes will not be attempted in this book. Nor is one necessary. Every bishop in every diocese is a builder, an educator,
an apostle and an important member of the community. And
we are already familiar, from Portland, from Eugene and
from Great Falls, with Bishop O'Hara's pattern for "getting
things done" within the Church and making himself and his
Faith respected outside it. It will be sufficient for us to select
items that demonstrate in one more area of influence the universally wholesome effect of a good shepherd's devoted attention to all the needs of his flock.

As always, Bishop O'Hara's approach to his work in
Kansas City was that of a priest providing channels between
God and man. As always, he started immediately, simply
and directly. His very first words to the priests and people
of Kansas City were spoken in his installation sermon at the
Immaculate Conception Cathedral on June 8, 1939. He used
the text from which he had taken his espiscopal motto: "Per-
mit the little children to come unto Me and forbid them not,
for of such is the Kingdom of Heaven."

The principal message of the sermon was contained in one
simple sentence: "I charge you today, as your Bishop, with
the responsibility for the religious and moral training of all
the youth of this great diocese."

The sermon included an invitation to the non-Catholics of
the diocese to cooperate with him in working for the common good. There were quotations from Pope Pius X whom
the bishop called, fifteen years before his canonization, "this
Saintly Pope."

The Kansas City installation sermon was cut from the same
cloth as all the beginnings Edwin O'Hara had made in all his
years as a priest—the first sermons and talks around Lanesboro

in the weeks following his ordination; the catechism classes in the first months of his first appointment as priest in Portland; starting the rural life movement at Eugene with vacation schools and correspondence courses; his first episcopal exhortation to his priests and his first pastoral letter as bishop of Great Falls.

The continuity and the consistency was imbedded in his singleminded adherence to Christ's words, "Go ye and teach." Here in Kansas City he was putting into practice his own teaching (in Great Falls pastorals and elsewhere) about the primary importance of teaching Christ and (in *Catholic Evidence Work in the United States*) about the desirability of a positive attitude for Catholics living in a non-Catholic milieu. And he was doing it as the bishop of Kansas City, the First Pastor, anointed to the cardinal function of teaching the teachers and providing them with the means to go about their teaching.

Perhaps the most fascinating story in all of Bishop O'Hara's Kansas City apostolate is that of the "ten little churches." It is the story of one man's way of putting priests and churches into one of the areas Father Howard Bishop named "No-priest Land." A story that begins with a perfectly sane prelate writing to a New York architect that he had $50,000 at his disposal and with it wanted to build—during the labor and material shortage and the high prices of World War II— *ten* churches.

Its background is Bishop O'Hara's years of work and study in Catholic rural life and the Confraternity of Christian Doctrine. During his first months in Kansas City he made a thorough inspection of the diocese and noted the counties in which there was neither church nor priest. Before the year was over he had taken the immediate action of a series of forays into the priestless lands. These took the form of week-long street-preaching campaigns in each of the county seats and in other towns.

The project was entrusted to the Confraternity of Christian Doctrine under the "Good Will toward Non-Catholics" aspect of confraternity work. Every young priest in the diocese would be freed from parochial duties for two weeks of the year to go on such a mission at the call of the diocesan director of the confraternity. Direct preparation was given at a street-preaching institute conducted at confraternity headquarters.

The results were gratifying. The sharp edge of that prejudice which comes from ignorance and fear was blunted. Forgotten Catholics, who had been separated from the sacraments first by distance and then by time, came out of the woods and down from the hills. They all needed a church, a focus, a spiritual hearth. That meant not one church but as many churches as there were counties without one.

Bishop O'Hara took immediate steps to consolidate the gains of the street-preaching apostolate. Then he turned for aid to Archbishop William D. O'Brien, president of that great builder of churches in rural America, the Catholic Church Extension Society.

Archbishop O'Brien's reply gave promise of support which when added to the proceeds of a diocesan campaign gave a total of $50,000. The minimum number of chapels immediately needed was estimated at ten.

That was when a New York architect engaged on a multi-million-dollar building project received Bishop O'Hara's startling request to have ten chapels designed and built for $5,000 each.

The request reached Mr. Julian Whittlesley through the Monterey Guild which was headed by its foundress the well-known liturgical artist Charlton Fortune. Miss Fortune had already found in the bishop of Kansas City one of the few patrons sympathetic to her efforts for the improvement of Catholic church art and architecture. One of her collaborators was a Benedictine graduate in architecture from M.I.T.,

Dom Hilary Martin. Dom Martin was in the habit of "keeping his hand in" by occasionally working for a week or two with the Mayer and Whittlesley firm. That was how Mr. Whittlesley, himself not a Catholic and a man one would not normally approach with such a small job, came into the picture.

The architect was intrigued by the idea of building a church for $5,000. It challenged his talent and also appealed to him as something worth doing. By December, 1943, it was settled that the Monterey Guild would undertake the project with Mayer and Whittlesley as architects acting in consultation with Dom Hilary.

Mr. Whittlesley and Dom Hilary came out to Missouri to select the sites for each of the churches and find out about available material. In 1944, they produced a simple, attractive and functional set of plans which could be followed, within the specified cost, in frame, concrete blocks, stone or brick according to the material available.

The "ten little churches," their low price and their ingenious design aroused widespread comment (including an article in *Time*). But to Bishop O'Hara they were interesting only as a partial solution to his pastoral problem. His concern lay only in how well they would fulfill their function of keeping open that channel of truth and grace which joins man to God; how well they would do their job as churches.

He did not have to wait long to find out. Bishop O'Brien accompanied him to the dedication of the first two chapels in mid-summer, 1945. On December 19 of the same year, the president of Extension received a long letter which began like this:

"I have just returned from a two weeks Confirming trip in the southern part of my diocese in the course of which I visited the new chapels and confirmed in the two chapels which you assisted us in dedicating. All of the ten chapels are now complete. . . . Seven of them have been in use for more than two months and all of them will have Christmas services. When you were at Cassville blessing the church it was known that there were two Catholics, a brother and sister living about 8 miles from the church. I confirmed three adults there the other day and a baby was baptised just before the Confirmation ceremony. Father Lyons has about twenty at Mass each Sunday.

"When I blessed the chapel at Buffalo in September there was one Catholic woman known to live in the parish. Now Father Corbit has 11 families who come to Mass each Sunday. . . . The chapels have won their way with admiration by the communities also for their simple artistic value. . . ."

But the length of the letter was not from talking about what had already been done. It was from describing circumstances in the places Bishop O'Hara intended to build "seven chapels in the coming year."

The Catholic map of the Ozarks was changing rapidly. The little churches that were springing up all over it were so many centers where lay Catholics gathered around their priests for that active participation in the life of the Church which is their heritage and their duty.

The principal means for encouraging lay participation in the work of the hierarchy was the confraternity—already active in the diocese before Bishop O'Hara's arrival. There is no need to labor the point that a prelate who had been so intimately connected with the spread of the confraternity throughout the United States would give special attention to it in his own diocese. He followed the pattern he had set in Great Falls and gathered all lay organizations into diocesan councils of men, women and youth. He went further and took another pioneering step by seeing that each council had its own central office with a full-time secretary supported by the organizations themselves.

Thus both the confraternity and the diocesan councils in the diocese of Kansas City follow the national model. There is the harmony of unified action among all the groups within the diocese and a direct line of communication between them and the national headquarters in Washington.

The value of these central offices through which the men, women and youth of the diocese conduct their own activities goes much beyond paper unification. It is a most effective stimulus to sustained interest on the part of the leaders and therefore to the vitality of each group and each unit. Everyone knows how easy it is for an organization, or a unit of an organization, to curl up comfortably within itself and die. It is not unheard of for organizations to have life only in occasional conversations between the president and the priest. Many a zealous soul has been lost to Catholic Action because he could not find any action. But these things are less likely to happen where there is an active nerve center sending out its impulses to every member of a well-integrated body.

And integration, not regimentation, is the right word for Bishop O'Hara's concept of organization. This can be seen by taking a glance at the structure of Catholic Action organization in Kansas City and then watching how it works.

Under the central diocesan office, the ninety-one parishes of the diocese are divided into fourteen district groupings. Each district has its own council of men, women and youth. Then there are parish councils in which the separate organizations of the parish correlate their activities. The confraternity follows this same pyramid structure. From the broad base of every individual layman engaged in any active Catholic work, the pyramid ascends to leadership in the particular unit, then to leadership on the parochial, district and diocesan levels. On top of the pyramid stands the Executive Committee of Catholic Action. The composition of this executive committee is defined in such a way as to make clear that the diocesan effort is part of the national plan. It consists of the president and executive secretary of four boards:

1. The diocesan board of the Confraternity of Christian Doctrine.
2. The diocesan board of the National Council of Men.
3. The diocesan board of the National Council of Women.
4. The diocesan board of the National Council of Youth.

In February, 1940, Bishop O'Hara officially conveyed the mandate of Catholic Action to these four boards and "all groups affiliated with them." This mandate was a characteristic Bishop O'Hara action. It cut through a tangled knot of futile and frustrating discussion which was then going on over what was and what was not Catholic Action. The discussion has happily died down under the gradual realization of something Bishop O'Hara saw at once—that the rigid European classifications of "specialized Catholic Action" required translation into terms of American life and custom. But it was intense enough at the time to require courage to stay out of it and act independently of it.

The classic definition of Catholic Action, "the participation of the laity in the apostolate of the hierarchy," required two things: lay activity and an endorsement from the bishop that this activity was participating in the work of the hierarchy. The names or the number of the activities were not of the essence of Catholic Action. The bishops of the United States had already set up four national centers of Catholic Action in the National Councils of Catholic Men, Women and Youth and the Confraternity of Christian Doctrine. That was directive enough for Bishop O'Hara. All he need do in Kansas City was determine what groups fitted under these headings.

In deciding this, he had the definitive authority of papal statements from Pius X to Pius XII. These were constant and clear. In following them, he found it impossible to take any narrow view. He liked to quote Pope Pius XI's words:

"The field of Catholic Action is as vast as that of the hierarchical apostolate. Just as the hierarchical apostolate was confided to the Church, to the Bishops and to Priests for the expansion of the Reign of Christ, for the salvation of souls, for the glory of God, for the honor of Holy Church, so also in all these domains, a field of action is open to all the laity who, fully conscious of their duties to God and the Church, wish to consecrate their activity to the service of the Lord and their brethren, at the side of the Bishops and priests, under the direction and discipline of the hierarchy, that is to say, those who in our day continue the work of the apostles."

This statement (in an address to the bishops and pilgrims of Yugoslavia, May 5, 1949) was equally definite about the virtually limitless scope of lay activity and about the necessity of pastoral direction. Statement after statement by all the modern popes brought out the same thing in different ways. This was undoubtedly the mind of the Church; and one of the principal functions of a bishop is to interpret that mind in terms of the faithful who are under his charge.

So when Bishop O'Hara issued his mandate of Catholic Action for the diocese of Kansas City, he excluded no group that worked for the expansion of the reign of Christ, for the salvation of souls, for the glory of God or for the honor of Holy Church and placed its services at his disposal.

This meant objection from several contrary directions. Some said, "Do you mean to say that this amorphous group of people who hand in their names to some organization and then forget all about it, are in the lay apostolate?" Others complained, "You can't call that little bunch of screwballs who think everybody else is wrong Catholic Action!"

Such objections were met with a patient smile. One of the ways Bishop O'Hara most faithfully reflected his Church is that he was never disturbed by the fact that it is catholic. It is for everyone. And so is the lay apostolate. Deficiencies of apathy or uncontrolled enthusiasm can be all the better repaired when the ailing cell is joined to a healthy body. The bishop is the head of the diocesan body. He is the shepherd who not only guards and guides his flock but also feeds it and gives it strength.

Bishop O'Hara had never forgotten his early lesson that "organization without activity is useless." A series of directives were soon outlining work enough to keep every organization busy, to provide outlet for any man's zeal. These were not so many commands to be answered by a salute and a quick step into action. They were food for the spirit of the lay apostolate. They were matter for a season's study by the six hundred "Discussion Action Clubs" scattered through the diocese. And while they were being absorbed by study and meditation on their spiritual significance, they were tied to action by what the bishop called "in-service training" in Catholic Action. At council meetings on various levels and in the annual Catholic Action workshops, which gathered representatives of all the groups for several days of prayer, study and discussion, their application to specific situations was thrashed out against a background of deeper penetration into their meaning for the full Catholic life. Catholic Action diplomas were granted and Catholic Action awards bestowed. There was action in Kansas City's Catholic Action.

But most important of all in Bishop O'Hara's program of Catholic Action was his relentless insistence that it be rooted in the liturgy. His 1951 pastoral letter on Catholic Action showed his constant teaching in its title, "The Participation of the Faithful in the Apostolate and in the Liturgy."

This unusual pastoral (which was made a study club text) opened with a letter to the clergy of the diocese of Kansas City. Its three sections were "On the Teaching of Christian Doctrine," "Reconstructing the Social Order" and "Eucharistic Worship." Three popes wrote the text for the body of the three sections: Pius X in *Acerbo Nimis*, Pius XI in *Quadragesimo Anno* and Pius XII in *Mediator Dei*. To each section were added selected readings on the same theme and a numbered list of "pastoral directives" applying the papal statements to the diocese of Kansas City.

Each one of the directives made a point toward better participation by the laity in the liturgy that would make many Catholics jump with joy. Here are some of them:

"11. It is an abuse to have the school children sing a Requiem Mass morning after morning; this practice renders the Mass wearisome to the children. It would have an educational value for the children if they were to join more frequently in the singing of the Mass of the day or the feast.

"12. For the faithful, also, at the regular daily Parish Mass each morning to have nothing but Requiem Masses is to deprive them of the variety, the beauty and inspiration of the Liturgy. The people should be instructed that a Mass in the color of the day may be appropriately offered for the deceased.

"13. In parishes of such numbers that Masses are scheduled to begin at intervals of one hour there should be a parish bulletin distributed so it will not be necessary to take undue time with oral announcements. In this way fifteen minutes can be devoted to a well prepared Sermon which will encourage the faithful in their participation in the Sacrifice of the Mass."

To round out the story of how Bishop O'Hara fostered the lay apostolate, we must add to his encouragement of traditional organizations, his fatherly understanding of those individual efforts in which the young must so often try their mettle against the institutionalism of their fathers. He himself had had the word "radical" thrown at him too often to do anything but smile and wait when he heard it hurled at others. He knew that this ferment from the leaven of newly arrived enthusiasm was a necessary ingredient for the bread of life in any human organization. He welcomed rather than feared it.

When these individuals came to him, he knew from the

very fact of their coming that their desire to collaborate with the hierarchy was real. If the project was for the glory of God, his usual attitude was noncommittal assent. The noncommittal part did not exclude a little, often essential, material help. But his official attitude was hands off, until the people and the project had proved themselves. You might say they had a novitiate during which the attempt might collapse of itself either through impracticability or by the defection of its sponsors. If it proved good and the will to do it was evidently constant, he was only too pleased to help it sustain itself as a part of his Kansas City lay apostolate.

Thus when a few young people conceived the noble and quixotic idea of publishing, without capital or income, a Catholic daily newspaper, they found a home in Kansas City after they had tried in vain for approval elsewhere. Bishop O'Hara had been too long an administrator, too long conversant with the problems of publishing, to think that the paper had any reasonable prospect of success. But, like a few thousand other people across the United States, he admired the purpose and the spirit of sacrifice that lay behind it and he hoped against reasonable hope that it might by some miracle succeed.

The paper appeared as the Kansas City *Sun Herald*. It never occurred to Bishop O'Hara to say, "The first thing I did when I came to Kansas City was start a diocesan edition of *The Register*. It has access to worldwide and local news. What do I want another Catholic paper for?" All through its short-lived existence he was its friend and protector. When it moved to New York in a doomed attempt to carry on in a larger and more Catholic city, his approbation followed it and the editors were able to present themselves under the cloak of his sponsorship as an episcopally approved essay in the lay apostolate.

A young Catholic student in sociology at the University of Kansas began worrying about the "incorrigible" young boys who had been found too difficult to handle by the usual social agencies. So Al Allen took one homeless boy in to share his small apartment. Soon he had another, and another. The neighbors began to complain—and anyhow the place was much too small. By this time Allen had decided there was a job to be done. There was a need of a house of hospitality, a family atmosphere, for these boys of high school age.

Did Bishop O'Hara say, "We have Catholic charities for that kind of work?" Not at all. He recognized both the need for the work and the spirit of the man who was willing to dedicate himself to it. In point of fact, Al Allen was on the Catholic Charities staff. His work with the high school age boys was a personal apostolate in an area not covered by organized charity.

When he brought his plan to the bishop, it was encouraged in the personal-apostolate form in which he presented it. The bishop's immediate aid was to suggest that Allen form an auxiliary and to indicate that the auxiliary could call on him for help.

A farmhouse was found within commuting distance of Kansas City. Al moved in and soon had the dozen boys the place could accommodate. In a short time Ozanam Home, its personal, family atmosphere untouched, was an integral part of the diocesan organization. It had become Al Allen's full-time Catholic Charities job and he continued to run it out of his salary and whatever aid his auxiliary could bring. A recent extension has brought the capacity to comfortable quarters for twenty boys. Graduates are already coming back with their children. Some of them have gone on to further education in places ranging from a School for Baseball Umpires to St. John's Seminary.

There are other instances in Kansas City of young people finding in the CCD or similar organizations an outlet for the zeal which first drew them to more individualistic activities.

Several of these saw with Archbishop O'Hara an analogy between forms of the dedicated life in the priesthood and in the laity. Some lay groups function after the manner of a religious order. They embrace a "rule," a common way of living, and follow the specific ideals of their founder. Others are more like secular priests who operate as individuals at the disposition of their bishop.

A clear understanding of the "diocesan priest" form of lay dedication can do a lot to bring spiritual vitality into the lay activities of the diocese.

On his arrival in Kansas City, Bishop O'Hara also plunged immediately into another familiar body of difficult waters, that of formal education. He was installed in his new diocese in June, 1939. By March, 1940, he had planned, prepared and launched a diocesan campaign to raise funds for four new high schools.

There were cries of horror. It was an impossible burden. It would injure existing schools.

And that was not all. Bishop O'Hara was proposing to have boys and girls in the same school. Coeducation, no less!

The money was raised. The schools were built . . . and enrollment increased all around, fees went down from $10 to $3 per month. By 1945, the people of Kansas City were very happy about their high schools. Facilities and enrollment had doubled. Nothing but good had come out of having boys and girls in the same school.

In 1952 the National Catholic Educational Association held its annual meeting in Kansas City. At its general session, Bishop O'Hara, recalling that his first paper to these annual meetings had been read in 1909 and that his second had been that Catholic rural life study of 1920, read a paper in which he touched upon the matter of coeducation in the Kansas City high schools:

"We did not choose coeducation; we chose to have Catholic schools. But I should be willing to go further. As I have read the Papal Encyclicals, I find the objection to coeducation to be that it gives the same education to boys as to girls—not to the fact that they are educated in day schools under the same roof. After all, boys and girls are reared under the same roof in Christian homes—and our day schools are only an extension of our Catholic homes."

Formal education can sometimes be an island unto itself cut off from the mainland of total community life. This is not so in Kansas City. The diocesan organization of Catholic Action reaches into the schools and the schools reach out to the community. Rockhurst College has its Institute of Social Order. There are broad extension courses at St. Theresa's College. Many high school activities come under the CYC. The grade school children, as in the community Mass, can enrich the whole parish with the fruit of their classwork. The Parent-Teacher Associations enjoy a status of influence not always granted them in Catholic school systems.

In fact, the title Bishop O'Hara chose for the address quoted above was "The School and the Community." A major point he made in it was: "Let not our schools be afraid to associate intimately with themselves the fathers and mothers (for fathers are parents also) of such families in the mutual work of educating their children. Invaluable assistance in effecting this cooperation will be found in the Parent-Teacher Association."

An important link in this integration of school and community is the Catholic community library. Besides bringing children to the library, it circulates small lots of books through schools lacking adequate library facilities. It conducts book reviews, debating and other literary programs in the high schools in conjunction with the CYC.

Very few cities have sufficient Catholic library service from their public libraries. In Kansas City the situation was more difficult because the public library was under the same board as the public schools. Experience had taught Bishop

O'Hara the advantages of a Catholic library—as well as the difficulties of maintaining one. He set about getting one for Kansas City by turning over the centrally located former episcopal residence for this purpose, raising sufficient funds to stock and equip it, finding a staff, and giving the first impetus to an organization which would help support it.

He was very fortunate in being able to persuade the Sisters of Social Service to staff the library. As chief librarian, Sister Christine, S.O.S.S., became a most popular central figure in the intellectual life of Catholic Kansas City and has made her library a focus of Catholic literary activity.

CHAPTER XX

Apostle of Goodwill

CATHOLIC SERVICE to the community-at-large was a life-long theme in Archbishop O'Hara's ministry. In Kansas City, the clearest example of this is perhaps the Catholic Community Service.

Housed in a building with ample recreational facilities, this organization is just what its title states: a service provided by Catholics for the community. While acting as a center for many Catholic Action activities—Family Life Institute, Liturgical Institute, adult education committee and various clubs and groups—its rooms and services are available to any group in the city. The Council of Jewish Women, for example, uses one of its crafts rooms to conduct a weaving shop for the blind.

Its billiard tables and social evenings provide a much-appreciated center for soldiers on leave from the several camps around Kansas City. It became so much the soldiers' center that when the Korean War came, after other USO units had been abandoned, the Catholic Community Service became what it remains today, the official USO in Kansas City. Such patriotic groups as the Veterans of Foreign Wars Auxiliary, War Dads and Mothers, United States Army Mothers, American Legion Auxiliary, Irenic Navy Mothers, Silver Wing Mothers of Army Pilots and American War Mothers send representatives every week to wait on servicemen at this Catholic club.

A public recreational service is carried out against a liturgical and apostolic background. The soldier who goes to the notice board to find out about free tickets for the ball game will, likely as not, find himself scanning the announcement of a communion breakfast or a week-end retreat.

That is how Bishop O'Hara wanted it to be. But it wasn't altogether easy to keep it that way. Some of his Catholics found it difficult to understand that this really was a service for the community. There was a fuss when some group announced a dance to be held at the community center during Lent. But the bishop remained undisturbed. The CCS was for the community. And some members of the community do have dances during Lent. Besides, when they took a look around the walls of the building, they would at least know that it was Lent and perhaps learn what Lent means.

The apostolate of goodwill toward non-Catholics has many facets. And it invariably works both ways. In the CCS it not only brought reciprocal goodwill but also earned a substantial contribution to the budget from the Community Chest.

The same sort of process went on in Kansas City's Catholic youth activities. With the Catholic Youth Council functioning as the organization *of* Catholic youth, Bishop O'Hara formed the Catholic Youth Organization *for* Catholic youth. This was composed of Catholic, Protestant and Jewish businessmen who contributed their time, talent and money to running sports and recreational programs. The bishop held an appeal in all the parishes and raised $100,000 to build a CYC stadium for the use of the youth of the community without respect to race or creed. The CYO men took over the administration and maintenance of this along with guidance of the CYC athletic program. It is now, and has been from the first year of its existence, a civic center of amateur sport activities. In the baseball season it is used, not only by the Catholic high school and parochial leagues, but also by the Jewish Center, War Veterans League, American Legion teams and the Ban Johnson League. The CYC has been excellently administered by the interdenominational executive of the CYO and in the ten years of its existence it has not cost the diocese one cent.

Several of the non-Catholics who have sponsored this Catholic activity have become immersed in the work far more deeply than any surface interest could demand. In such an atmosphere it did not seem at all strange that a Jewish gentleman should be one of the finest presidents the Catholic Youth Organization in Kansas City ever had. And Mr. George Goldman is proud to wear the Benemerenti Medal Bishop O'Hara obtained for him from Pope Pius XII.

As it had been years ago in Portland, the cooperation Bishop O'Hara received from non-Catholics grew out of his willingness to associate himself with them in any worthwhile community effort. Far from fearing to put Catholicism alongside any other faith, he welcomed the opportunity to do so. (His priests have joined, and been presidents of, their local ministerial associations in various parts of the diocese.) This won himself and his Church a position of respect and influence in the dominantly non-Catholic region.

When the bishop began bestowing, in the name of the Catholic Community Service, annual "Citations of Distinction," these at once became highly considered honors proudly accepted as genuine marks of distinction by the prominent citizens who received them. These citations were not given for service to the Catholic cause. They were given for service to the community. In the year of the disastrous Kansas City flood, for example, they went to men who had been most notable in relieving the city's distress at that time.

The award, which consists of a simple certificate that most of the recipients immediately hang in a place of honor, is bestowed with full public ceremony. The occasion is televised and broadcast. It always gets prominent newspaper publicity as one of Kansas City's events of the year.

This sort of thing can easily turn into a specious good. It can become a matter of log-rolling. You scratch my back and I'll scratch yours.

But here again the Portland pattern repeated itself in Kansas City. There was never any doubt where Bishop O'Hara stood. He was a Catholic priest. He was *the* Catholic priest who represented in Kansas City everything the Roman Catholic Church represented in the world.

The men with whom he mingled, the men he worked with for the common good, the men to whom he had given honors, were also the men with whom he took quick issue if they made a statement or placed an act that militated against the position or the rights of Catholics. And, as in Portland, he won their increased respect by the very firmness of his always courteous but never yielding opposition. They became aware of Catholics as fellow citizens with equal rights—and with a voice that would claim them.

In this southern Midwest of the United States there was a whole socio-religious atmosphere to oppose. It is easy at a distance to make abstract analysis of the rights of man and reach certain conclusions which do not require any substantial change in your own way of life. But it is not easy, even for good men, to free themselves from traditions rooted in the regional culture by which they were formed. This was the region where the title of "American" went only to those who were "free, white and Protestant." It took time for men brought up in this tradition to accept as equals Negroes, Jews, Catholics and members of the Latin races. The fathers of the leading businessmen and industrialists had been pioneer individualists whose philosophy had had no reason to include the working man of the industrial age. They were distrustful of unions.

Bishop O'Hara, without ceasing to love them in charity

or respect their rights as individuals, confronted them in word and in act with the teaching of the Catholic Church on the oneness of all men in the Mystical Body of Christ.

With regard to the Negro, Kansas City still recalled "the Missouri Compromise." There were no Jim Crow streetcars, but segregation was enforced in schools, hospitals, hotels and in a hundred different ways.

Bishop O'Hara made no obstreperous challenging announcement. He quietly let it be known that the Catholic schools would accept every qualified student without regard to color. He saw to it that no color line would be drawn in his Catholic churches and organizations.

The revolutionary move was accepted as quietly as it was made. Only a few individual parents objected. Their protests gained them nothing but a little homily on the Mystical Body. Bishop O'Hara had judged the social temper correctly. People were ready to accept the change though not quite ready to make it. In 1955, when the Kansas City public schools obeyed the Supreme Court decision against segregation, their way was made smooth because Bishop O'Hara had traveled it ahead of them in 1951.

Then he went a step farther and started (of all things!) a maternity hospital in which there would be no segregation. But there was still no accredited general hospital in which Negro surgeons and nurses could practice with full use of adequate facilities. So the bishop decided to extend the maternity hospital into a general one. The result is Queen of the World Hospital which had its formal opening on May 22, 1955.

This hospital, incidentally, shattered another precedent in addition to sweeping away racial barriers. For the first time in the history of the United States, Catholic nuns are practicing surgery in a public hospital. Previously, the eighteen Maryknoll nuns who are graduate M.D.'s were permitted by

Church Law to practice the medical profession only in mission lands.

Bishop O'Hara obtained the unique permission by applying to Rome through the Apostolic Delegate. The arguments he advanced were repeated as reasons for granting the concessive brief which Rome sent the Maryknoll Mother General. They pointed out that only 2 per cent of Kansas City's sixty thousand Negroes were Catholics and the nuns would therefore be working in mission conditions; that practice in a United States hospital would be excellent training for the mission field; that nuns who were doctors ran less risk of becoming servants in their own hospitals and that they could see to the observance of the Catholic moral code by being present on an equal professional footing at doctors' meetings and conferences.

The implications in some of those arguments could possibly spread the permission to other parts of the United States.

Discrimination against the Negro entered also into the labor question. It was at a labor gathering that Bishop O'Hara made one of his most dramatic presentations of the hospital situation. Every year, in conjunction with the Rockhurst College Institute of Social Order, the Bishop celebrated a Labor Day Mass. This was attended by workers of all faiths, black and white.

Sermons on such occasions are usually expected to confine themselves to general statement, to stay on safe ground. At the Mass in 1953, Bishop O'Hara was too full of indignation about a current situation to be anything less than specific and direct:

"Lest you say I am engaged in generalities and platitudes, let me call to your attention the necessity of re-vivifying the social conscience of Kansas City in a matter that concerns the denial of reasonable conditions and compensation for labor in an important sector of our community. . . .

". . . one tenth of our people are selfishly denied proper facilities for the adequate training of the physicians to whom they naturally look for medical advice and care. This is a disgrace for which all of us are responsible. I speak of the now well known fact that there is not in the metropolitan area of Kansas City an accredited and properly equipped general hospital to which a Negro doctor can take a private patient for care."

He went on to tell of a brilliant young Negro doctor who had just returned from postgraduate studies in the University of Pennsylvania School of Medicine. He had come first in a class of sixty-eight picked students. Now he was back in Kansas City. But if he wanted freedom to practice his profession, he would have to move to another community. The bishop went on:

"This is my message to Kansas City on this Labor Day: no longer to deny intelligent Negro doctors the opportunity of employment in their skilled profession. Sacred Scripture bids us honor the labor of the physician. Kansas City must provide without further delay accredited and properly equipped hospital facilities in which competent Negro physicians may work side by side with white members of their profession in promoting the health of this community."

To that audience of Kansas Citians, black and white, employers and employees, those were jolting words. Even in the labor unions it was customary to have "colored" and "white" locals.

But the words had their effect. One of the first substantial donations for Queen of the World Hospital was $12,000 from the interracial Hod Carriers Union. They were apparently pleased that the bishop meant it when he said "without further delay."

In Kansas City, as in activities of national scope, Bishop O'Hara never hesitated to risk powerful criticism by allying himself with unjustly treated minorities.

In the Negro fight for equality, he was a member of the National Association for the Advancement of Colored People, on the Urban League Citizens' Committee, a sponsor of the United Negro College Fund and, in 1941, presided over the interdenominational Clergy Council of the Midwest on Negro welfare.

In 1943, he received a letter of thanks from President Quezon of the Philippine Republic for his interest in Filipinos in Kansas City. He had founded a Filipino-American Catholic club at his cathedral.

His interest in Mexicans had been continuous since his first visit to their country in the persecution days of 1928. As assistant chairman of the NCWC social action committee, he had taken an active part in the fight of American Catholics to prevent passage of the Borah resolutions. In Kansas City, he organized Guadalupe Center which Sister Celine, S.O.S.S., studied as a model of work for Mexicans in the United States as her M.A. thesis at St. Louis University.

When the war against Japan brought hysterical action against Americans of Japanese origin, Bishop O'Hara became a sponsor of the Japanese-American Citizens' League, and in 1949 received their official thanks (along with a carton of Utah celery) for the real aid he had given them through their difficult days.

In 1944 Bishop O'Hara joined the Committee of Catholics for Human Rights. In 1945, his name was at the top of a list of names which included Reinhold Niebuhr, Max Eastman, Thornton Wilder, Louis Bromfield and John Dewey, on a petition sent to the President by the National Committee on Conscientious Objectors of the American Civil Liberties Union. The petition asked that three thousand conscientious objectors in prison and six thousand at CO jobs be released at the end of the war.

In 1947, he was vice-chairman of the National Committee for Equality in Naturalization.

Support of such causes was not calculated to endear him to the powerful majority. But he was acting according to his principles as an individual and setting an example as a bishop. That was all that mattered.

Interfaith matters in Kansas City were handled by Bishop O'Hara with the skill of a veteran diplomat. On the one hand, his apostolate of goodwill toward non-Catholics and his belief in the value of Catholic participation in community activities were motives for joining in them wherever possible. On the other, his episcopal guardianship of the unicity of the Catholic Church kept him assiduously on guard against any impression that Catholicism was merely one of several equally good religions.

Thus, the bishop was a long-time cooperator with the National Conference of Christians and Jews. When a Jewish group in Kansas City announced an institute on "the Principles of Judaism" and "Jewish Worship," the bishop not only allowed his priests to attend the lectures at the Temple of the Congregation B'nai Jehudah, but went himself, acted as chairman at one of the sessions and gave the invocation.

Several things lay behind this decision. One of them went back to his Portland days when he had heard Rabbi Wise establish that the Jewish religion was nothing more nor less than respect for Jewish history and observance of Jewish tradition. A second was his interest in the Jewish apostolate of the Sisters of Sion who conduct one of the most universally respected convent schools in the diocese. Another was his desire to unite himself with the Pope in expressing Catholic brotherhood with the Jews who were at that time, 1943, suffering in Nazi Europe. He had previously put himself on public record about this last in a message addressed to the president of the National Conference of Christians and Jews:

"Please convey to Dr. Israel Goldstein, president of the Synagogue Council, on my behalf the following message for the forthcoming fast of Tisha bov:

" 'Our profound sympathy goes out to the Jewish people for the terrible slaughter of so many thousands of their race by the savagery of the Nazis.

" 'The blood of these innocent victims cries to Our Father in Heaven against the perpetrators of these outrages against human brotherhood and brands them with the brand of Cain. In these tragic days of grief and mourning of the Jewish people may we all understand that we are our brothers' keepers; may all who profess the Christian faith especially understand the declaration of Pope Pius XI that all Christians are spiritually Semites.' "

Publication of this message in newspapers and national-circulation media like *Time* magazine brought Bishop O'Hara some scathing letters from the noisy minority of anti-Semitic Catholics. It also left him, however, in a strong position to object against any apparent Jewish interference with Christian belief or practice, as when a New York group of rabbis moved to ban the singing of Christmas carols in public schools.

The bishop's participation in community efforts brought him as a matter of course into frequent collaboration with representatives of the Protestant majority. Nor did he hesitate to accept an invitation to address six hundred men of the Associated Men's Bible Classes. He took for his topic "Peace in Harmony."

But he was equally quick to enter the lists against them whether over a political measure infringing upon Catholic rights or a public misrepresentation of Catholic belief.

He had not forgotten his old Portland technique of using the newspapers to see that his positive statement of the Catholic position received at least as wide an audience as the erroneous attack. A notable instance was his neat turning of the tables on press reports of a Kansas City lecture by the notoriously anti-Catholic Bishop Bromley Oxnam.

The Methodist bishop of New York spoke in the Municipal

Auditorium on October 31, 1948. The following day's morning newspaper carried a report of his talk and the afternoon paper printed a letter from Bishop O'Hara which said in part: "The spirit of mutual respect among the various religious groups in Kansas City has been one of the most happy as well as one of the most characteristic aspects of our community life.

"As a Catholic bishop I have been frequently invited to address Protestant men's Bible classes, Jewish assemblies and many smaller groups. In every case we shared the expressed belief in the primacy of the spiritual in human affairs and a full recognition of the claims of conscience.

"For myself, I have rejoiced in every evidence of deepening spirituality in all groups, whether Catholic or non-Catholic. In this crisis of world civilization which America faces, all of our spiritual resources will be tried to the utmost.

"The inflammatory address of Bishop Oxnam here yesterday must not be allowed to set Protestants and Catholics at each other's throats in hatred and discord. . . .

"I shall have no part in controversy that stirs the embers of hatred and distrust among American citizens. Washington in his Farewell Address and Lincoln in his Letters repudiated the Oxnams of their day. Our fellow citizens of today have been witnesses of the intelligent and devoted fidelity of the Catholic Church in America, as exemplified both in its bishops and its patriotic people, to the principles of democracy.

"In conclusion, I accept the gratifyingly friendly and emphatic assurances which have come to me unsolicited that many loyal Protestant clergy have viewed with regret and disapproval the attempt of Bishop Oxnam to sow religious discord in our community."

There were times when Bishop O'Hara's promptness and authority in replying to Kansas City newspaper reports on anti-Catholic statements gave his words national circulation as the Catholic answer.

When, in 1944, the Soviet newspaper *Izvestia* accused Pope Pius XII of supporting the Fascist-Nazi side in World War II, there seemed to be a suggestion of glee in the prominent way so many American newspapers played up the story. The bishop's reply in Kansas City was so prompt and to the point that it went out to the newspapers and radio stations of the nation in the following United Press dispatch:

> Kansas City, Mo., Feb. 2 (U.P.)—The charge made by *Izvestia* that Pope Pius XII favors Fascism is "totally false," Bishop Edwin V. O'Hara, of the Kansas City diocese, said.
>
> "Pius XII has expressed himself and his attitude towards fascism adequately in an encyclical 'Darkness Over the Earth,' issued October 20, 1939," Bishop O'Hara said. "In this encyclical he says:
>
> " '*Whoever considers the state to be the end towards which all is directed and all must bow is of necessity an enemy and an obstacle to all true and lasting progress among the nations.*'
>
> "I believe this is an adequate answer to those who charge the Vatican with pro-Fascist sympathy.
>
> "My personal view is that there is an unfortunate tendency on the part of Fascists to call all who oppose them 'Communist' and for Communists to call all who oppose them 'Fascist.'
>
> "This is just another example of such name-calling."

Throughout his apostolic life Bishop O'Hara, who was never anything but a busy man, took the time and trouble to make public correction of such public misstatements wherever they occurred in an area where he was a representative of the Catholic Church. Sometimes these were short, blunt statements reaching mass audiences like the one above. At others they were carefully worded reprimands to quarters where the circulation of the misstatement might be small but the influence of the man who made it, and the people who read it, great. The importance of these corrections, especially coming from a voice that has earned respect, go far beyond the incident that calls them forth. They sow the seeds of a change of attitude toward Catholicism. This change of attitude is inevitably reflected in the writing and thinking of the man who has once been called to order. It therefore affects all his readers, all his hearers, all his pupils. The simple correction of one published error thus becomes an effective weapon in forming the mind of America. It reaches beyond the readership of Catholic publications and gains Catholic truth a hearing where it is most needed.

But it must be done both intelligently and in charity. It must be part of the Apostolate of Goodwill. Bishop O'Hara's use of the weapon has always exemplified this.

During his first summer in Portland he made a significant remark after hearing James Field Spaulding speak on Tennyson, Browning and Matthew Arnold. He said, "One lesson I have learned from Arnold is that persuasion is the best method, not argument or scorn." He lived by that.

The tributes from Bishop O'Hara's fellow citizens quoted earlier, and those that will follow later, are proof that the same approach as used in Portland brought the same results in Kansas City.

In 1951, Bishop O'Hara was the subject of a full-length biographical article beginning on the front page of the Kansas City *Star* under the heading, "Leaders in Our Town." After the article appeared, Frank Bruce, of the Catholic publishing firm, wrote to the bishop: "The story in the Kansas City *Star* is far more significant than is suggested on the surface of things.

"Not so many years ago Catholic priests were insulted on the streets of Kansas City. Not so many years ago, the prejudice against Catholics in Kansas City was one of our American blights. There are a great many who still must learn that the Church has terrific responsibility on public relations."

There had indeed been change since the days of which Mr. Bruce wrote. In 1941 the city could be the scene of public Catholic events like the First Diocesan Eucharistic Congress. It could allow the base of its towering war memorial to be turned into an outdoor altar, watch the Blessed Sacrament carried reverently in public procession and look on edified as twenty thousand Catholics stood through a pouring rain and proclaimed their faith. It had nothing but favorable comment when a similar crowd thronged the Municipal Stadium for the Family Rosary Crusade during the celebration of Archbishop O'Hara's Golden Jubilee in 1955.

CHAPTER XXI

Latin America

ARCHBISHOP O'HARA'S INTEREST in Latin America went back to his Oregon days though it became most active during his years in Kansas City. While working on his book *The Church and the Country Community*, he had wanted to add a study of Latin American conditions to his survey of Catholic rural life in Europe. An American who had become a leading cattle raiser and business executive around Buenos Aires, Mr. Francis O'Grady, visited him in Eugene with an invitation that he extend his Catholic rural life interest to the Argentine. But he had been unable to make the journey at that time.

His first trip south of our border was made to Mexico in 1928. His reason was not so much rural life (though he did make inquiries about that) as an American priest's interest in the concentrated campaign against the teaching of Christian doctrine that was going on right at this nation's doorstep.

At that time, Mexico's religious persecution was in full cry. As the only Catholic in an organized tour of eighty Americans (led by a Congregationalist minister and counting sixteen other Protestant clergymen) he listened to Mexican government representatives explaining their policy, was able to learn from Mexican Catholics the true situation as opposed to the prevailing view in the United States, saw at first hand the official American collaboration with the anti-religious government forces, and was able to present in the seminars held by the group some facts about the persecution of Catholics.

He was in Mexico at the time of the assassination of President-elect Obregon and saw the triumph of Calles. He heard public blame for the assassination placed on Catholics and listened to agrarian leaders repudiating these charges and putting the crime squarely on Morones and his radical labor group.

He had prepared himself for the journey by study of recent Mexican history. While in the country he was able to get in touch with men who brought him evidence, in the form of previously published books and statements, that the Catholic Church for the past twenty years had been far from reactionary. He learned of its progressive work with the poor and the disinherited, its activity on behalf of distribution of land to small owners, its establishment of Raffeisen credit unions, its application of *Rerum Novarum* principles to contemporary problems of the living wage, hours of labor, housing, agrarian reform, industrial accident insurance and usury.

He embodied the results of his studies and observations in a series of seven articles for the press service of the NCWC, later reprinted as a pamphlet, *Letters from Mexico.*

By the time he came to Kansas City, he had a number of reasons for making his postponed journey to the continent of South America. He had come to feel strongly that confraternity organization and training of the laity for the teaching of Christian doctrine would be of great help to the priest-poor dioceses of South America. With this in mind, he founded in 1943, an Inter-American Institute of the CCD with headquarters in Kansas City. Its general purpose was to further, in any way possible, the greater collaboration of the

Catholics of the United States with their South American brothers.

As things worked out, the principal function of this institute was to act as a medium for providing scholarships enabling Latin American priests to pursue social studies in the United States.

The scholarships came into Bishop O'Hara's bestowing through a fellow prelate who shared most of his own views, Archbishop Robert E. Lucey, of San Antonio, Tex. They were based on gifts from a New York convert friend of the Wall Street Catholic apologist, John Moody.

Mrs. A. M. Tilney had been received into the Church by Bishop O'Hara's old teacher at St. Thomas College, Alexis Carrel's friend, Father Cornelius Clifford. She took a strong personal interest in the work done through the scholarships but left all decisions and arrangements in Bishop O'Hara's hands.

An invitation from Archbishop, later Cardinal, Mota, to give an address at an exposition of North American Catholic Educational and Charitable Institutions at Sao Paolo, Brazil, in April 1945, was the occasion for making the long-postponed South American journey.

There were three purposes, in addition to the scheduled talk, in Bishop O'Hara's mind when he left Kansas City on March 13, 1945. He would study Catholic rural life in the South American countries, speak of the Confraternity of Christian Doctrine, and interview candidates for the Inter-American Institute scholarships.

A fourth interest would be satisfied through Father John Friedl, S.J., of the Rockhurst College Institute of Social Order, who accompanied him as secretary. For Father Friedl would be studying the South American scene from the viewpoint of his own specialty, labor-management relations.

In Washington, D. C., came the first indications that this visit of a United States bishop to Catholic South America was to be something of a progress-in-state as well as a study trip. It was the era of President Roosevelt's Good Neighbor Policy toward South America. Our State officials had become exceedingly conscious that the Catholic Church provided a strong common bond between the two continents.

Bishop O'Hara's Missouri neighbor and friend, Vice-President Harry S. Truman, invited him to his office and did all he could to expedite his journey. He arranged for the bishop to say the prayer at the opening of the Senate that day and had him visit the Pentagon Building for discussions with several civil and military South American experts.

One incident of his visit to Mr. Truman's office stayed in the bishop's mind. While he was there, the Belgium ambassador came to present his credentials to the Vice-President in the absence of Mr. Roosevelt, who was ill. After the ambassador had spoken of conditions in his country (saying that in this war it had not been the German army that had followed a policy of oppression in Belgium, but the Gestapo), Mr. Truman replied that he intended to bend every effort during the coming months toward world peace. At the time, Bishop O'Hara thought this an unusual statement from a Vice-President. He was to recall it a month later when Mr. Roosevelt's unexpected death made Mr. Truman President of the United States.

In the Caribbean countries, in Brazil, Uruguay, Argentine, Chile, Peru, Ecuador, Colombia, Panama, Costa Rica, Guatemala and Mexico, the bishop found himself greeted and entertained almost as much by the American embassy as by the chancery office. In the public press he was saluted as a spokesman for the United States as well as a representative of the North American hierarchy.

This became most evident when the announcement of President Roosevelt's death reached him in Buenos Aires. In that city his host was the patriarchal Cardinal Copella. But the man to whom he felt closest was Bishop de Andrea who was greatly loved by the people but too outspoken to be in favor with the men in power.

When special editions of the newspapers brought the news of President Roosevelt's death, the general sadness of the Argentinians was obvious. Some of them came to Bishop O'Hara and asked if he would celebrate a memorial Mass. He checked with the chancery office and the Cardinal gave permission—on condition that the Mass was not advertised. Bishop de Andrea invited him to say the Mass at his church of San Miguel. In accordance with the wishes of the chancery office, there was no public announcement. But the word got around. When Bishop O'Hara came forward to read his statement on the President's death, he found himself facing a crowded and distinguished congregation. Not only was the papal nuncio present but also about a hundred representatives, civil, military and naval, of the diplomatic corps in Argentina from many nations.

If there was no publicity before Mass, there was plenty after it. It was a leading story in all the newspapers. *La Nación* carried the bishop's statement in full in column one of its front page. *La Prensa* had the same full account with pictures of the large congregation swarming out of the church. There were pictures of Bishop O'Hara reading his statement. The stories did not fail to note that the diplomats remained in their pews after the Mass and waited upon Bishop O'Hara to offer their condolences.

The two-month schedule allowed sufficiently long stops at each major city for Bishop O'Hara's capacity for winning friends to assert itself. He was able to gain insight into the Latin American situation from several different levels. Church leaders brought him around their dioceses to see at first hand the ecclesiastical problems and how they were met. Ministers of agriculture, education and public welfare explained the problems of their departments in various countries. Catholic lay leaders came to him and discussed their organizations and their aims.

He met some of the most famous contemporary Catholic writers living in Latin America. George Bernanos came to see him and talked interestingly in rapid French. When Bishop O'Hara asked M. Bernanos about the attacks on Catholics in his books, the author of *The Diary of a Country Priest* was quick to justify himself. "When I was a boy in school," he said, "I would doze over my lessons. The teacher used to come along and rap my knuckles and I would wake up and study. In my books I am trying to wake up a sleeping body of Christians."

In the succession of prelates Bishop O'Hara met on this trip there were several with whom he formed especially close ties on the basis of common interests.

But it was not Bishop O'Hara's way to see a country only through the eyes of its officials, civil or ecclesiastic. His known interest in the lay apostolate led to many fruitful talks with people from every walk of life. He also managed to get off by himself occasionally and exercise his Spanish by meeting the man in the street. On one such occasion, he had gone shopping only to find the stores closed at 2:00 P.M. He dropped into a lunchroom . . . and was served by a man who had lived in Ohio for twenty years.

One of his best guides in Argentina was Mr. Francis O'Grady, the American who had visited him in Eugene seventeen years before.

In São Paulo, the bishop visited the Convent of Sion and was greeted by Mother Therese Emmanuel who told him she was Alice Bandry from Great Falls and that a talk he had given there on the House of Sion in Jerusalem had started her on the road to Sion.

He even met people from Minnesota who had relatives in Lanesboro.

When the bishop returned to Kansas City in May he had

very good reason to be satisfied with the results of his journey. As he had interpreted the Catholic United States to Latin America, so now he used his first-hand knowledge to preach inter-American cooperation to the United States.

He lost no time in strengthening bonds among the nations in his own particular fields of activity. Before the year was over, he had sent Miss Miriam Marks and Miss Blanche Vignos over the route he had followed to explain American confraternity organization and methods. Arrangements were completed for six Latin American priests to follow studies at the Catholic University of America. These priests, whom he first invited to Kansas City to live in parishes there and become familiar with English, were influential apostles typical of the men who were to follow them in succeeding years. Father Herrera of Costa Rica, for example, had been one of two priests caring for a parish of twelve thousand souls. The catechetical program he conducted had forty teachers and four thousand children. He had taught religion and ethics at the local college and had spent the last year and a half organizing laborers and young Catholic Actionists. His diocese had 130 priests for 700,000 Catholics. Father Sendoya, from Colombia, had spent the five years of his priesthood teaching Church history in a major seminary. After he had been in the United States some months, he was to sum up one of the important effects of the scholarship program in something he told one of his fellow students at Catholic University:

"I remember well reading of the condemnation of 'Americanism' made by Pope Leo XII in his letter *Testem Benevolentiae*. There it was in the manuals so I spoke of it to my classes. Many people in my country think it is still very much alive. There are many prejudices at home. I laugh at them now, but some things I believed myself. It will not come to an end until many of our priests see how very Catholic is the life of the Church here; they are the ones to tell the people."

Fifteen months later, in July and August, 1946, an invitation to accompany Dr. and Mrs. Charles A. Breitung, of Oklahoma, on the same grand tour of South America permitted Bishop O'Hara to see some of the first fruits of his 1945 visit. The scholarship priests who had not stayed for further study in the United States greeted him along the way and proved that they were already putting their new knowledge of Catholicism in North America to good use. Translations and adaptations of CCD literature and of the revised catechism were in use or under way. South American biblical scholars were universally interested in the work their United States confreres were doing on the Bible.

Friendships were renewed and the bishop was able to congratulate five of the Latin American prelates on their elevation to the Sacred College of Cardinals: Archbishop Mota, of São Paulo; Archbishop Caro, of Santiago; Archbishop Jaime de Barros Cammara, of Rio de Janeiro; Archbishop Guavera, of Lima; and Bishop Caggiano, of Rosario, Argentina.

It seemed as if the bishop of Kansas City had anticipated Rome by a few months in paying special attention to South America.

By the time Bishop O'Hara made his third circle of the Latin American countries in 1953, he felt as much at home in cities like Lima, Santiago, Buenos Aires, Montevideo, São Paulo, and Rio de Janeiro as he did in many cities of the United States. This time he had gone to attend the Latin American Rural Life Conference at Manizales, Colombia. He had traveled down the east coast and up the west, reversing his itinerary of previous years. Everywhere he went he was received not only with the respect due his office but also with the warmth reserved for a friend.

The eight years since his first visit had seen much coming and going between Catholics of the two continents. Prelates, clergy and lay people had been up to the United States in increasing numbers to attend CCD congresses, conventions of the National Council of Catholic Women and various other groups. Spanish and Portuguese translations of literature from the CCD central office were becoming more common. Lines of liaison had multiplied.

Cardinal Mota had been his guest in Kansas City and that city saw all the Americas united in a Marian celebration when the Cardinal took part in two ceremonies welcoming Canada's national madonna, Our Lady of the Cape, to Kansas City in 1947.

The number of "his priests" back at work in their own countries had increased to fourteen. They all looked upon the bishop with filial affection and were eager to repay the hospitality he had shown them. They did repay him well with the one reward he wanted. He found them time after time in posts of influence informing their fellow citizens about the Catholic vitality of the United States and putting to work the techniques they had learned. One, Father Hurtado, S.J., was the outstanding priest of the workers in Chile. Another, Father Munoz, had been at the Manizales Conference as head of rural Catholic Action for the same country. In fact, no fewer than four of the fourteen priests had been sent by their nations as representatives to that Latin American Catholic Rural Life Conference. Another was professor of scripture in a major seminary and several others were doing notable work in education, catechetics and various fields of sociology. The bishop was well satisfied that Mrs. Tilney's scholarships had been put to good use.

CHAPTER XXII

Apostle of St. Pius X

WHEN BISHOP O'HARA first visited Rome, in company with his sister, Mrs. Anna Daniels, in the summer of 1910, the Head of the Church who crowned his pilgrimage by receiving him in audience was Pope Pius X. Although he was later to be received—and honored—by Popes Pius XI and Pius XII, it was the first Pope he met, the future canonized saint, who remained in his mind and heart as an ideal of all the papacy stands for to every Catholic.

He had been impressed by the simplicity and holiness of the man. He had seen in his painstaking concern for the good government of the Church in essential matters a pattern and a set of directives for his own pastoral life. As the years went on, Bishop O'Hara's principal duties became more and more concerned with the execution in the United States of mandates issued by Pope Pius X. One is tempted to see a dispensation of Providence rather than mere coincidence in the fact that the encyclical *Acerbo Nimis*, on the teaching of Christian doctrine, was issued in the year of Bishop O'Hara's ordination, and every anniversary of the one calls for a celebration of the other.

By the time he came to Kansas City, Bishop O'Hara had become known throughout the country for his constant reference to the teachings of the Pope of the new Canon Law, the

Pope of Frequent Communion, the Pope of the Confraternity, the Pope who had given the modern lay apostolate its *mot d'ordre* in his command "to restore all things in Christ."

As he penetrated more deeply into the mind and work of Pope Pius X he became more thoroughly imbued with a sense of how comprehensively "this saintly pope" had embraced the threefold function of the Catholic pastor: to teach, to govern and to sanctify. His paternal concern over doctrine, law and the means of grace were epitomized in *Acerbo Nimis*, in the new code of canon law and in the decrees on early and frequent Communion. Bishop O'Hara became fond of pointing out that no Pope in the history of the Church had had more direct influence on the lives of more people. From the time of Pope Pius X, every individual in the Universal Church has been affected by the new code and by his decrees on frequent reception of the Eucharist.

When in 1943, the first official steps were taken toward the canonization of Pope Pius X, Bishop O'Hara was naturally a leader among promoters of the cause in the United States. In 1931, he had been present at Rome as representative of the Social Action Department of the NCWC when Pope Pius XII commemorated Pope Leo XIII's *Rerum Novarum* in his encyclical *Quadragesimo Anno*. In 1945, he made his Epiphany Pastoral to the diocese of Kansas City his own *Quadragesimo Anno* in commemoration of the fortieth year of *Acerbo Nimis*. The pastoral began: "Forty years ago the Servant of God, Pope Pius X, addressed an inspiring letter to the Catholic world on the teaching of religion." It went on to announce a catechetical congress to be held in Kansas City that year with "the double purpose of rallying us to the work of the Confraternity of Christian Doctrine and to prayer for the beatification and eventual canonization of Pope Pius X, its modern founder."

The congress was built around a symposium on Pope Pius X in which twelve United States scholars, under the direction of Bishop O'Hara, presented studies of different aspects of the pontiff's life and work. These studies, with a preface by the Apostolic Delegate, Archbishop Cicognani, and a chapter by Bishop O'Hara on "Pius X—Servant of God," were published in book form as *A Symposium on the Life and Work of Pope Pius X* (Confraternity of Christian Doctrine, 1946). The book was a principal source for the sermons, articles and popular volumes which spread knowledge of the Pope and devotion to him through the United States in the years immediately preceding his canonization.

Each one of Bishop O'Hara's four pilgrimages to Rome as bishop of Kansas City had a direct connection with the cause of Pope Pius X. The war in Europe had prevented the usual quinquennial visits of the bishops of the United States *ad limina apostolorum* which should have taken place in 1944. Bishop O'Hara anticipated his 1949 visit by accompanying the national pilgrimage of the Confraternity of Christian Doctrine to Rome in 1948. This pilgrimage, led by Archbishop Richard Cushing of Boston, was impressive both by its numbers and by the evidence it brought of America's fervent interest in the beatification of Pope Pius X. It bore with it the nation's petition that the Pope of the confraternity be raised to the honors of the altar. The petition was presented to Pope Pius XII with the millions of spiritual offerings made during a "Crusade of Prayer for the Beatification of Pope Pius X" conducted by the confraternity with the cooperation of the ordinaries of many dioceses. This solid manifestation at Rome of the national organization he had brought into being must have been a cause of deep spiritual satisfaction to Bishop O'Hara.

He had even more cause for justifiable pride when he returned to the Holy City in 1950. This time he led a confraternity pilgrimage to the tomb and to the birthplace of Pope Pius X. He also represented the United States, as head of a delegation of sixty, at the International Catechetical Congress held at Rome that year. His paper, delivered in Latin on "The Parish Confraternity of Christian Doctrine in the United States of North America," warmed the heart of Cardinal Pizzardo, prefect of the Sacred Congregation of Seminaries and Universities and secretary of the Supreme Sacred Congregation of the Holy Office. It was the only report, from all the nations present, showing a national organization of parish confraternities erected in literal conformity with the requirements of canon law.

A subsequent letter of Christmas greetings from the Cardinal to the bishop of Kansas City departed from the customary formal salutation to begin: "Your Excellency, and Dear Friend." It spoke of the Cardinal's gratitude for all the blessings of the Holy Year and added, "Amongst all these benefits and blessings, the memory of what Your Excellency has done for me, your unfailing generosity and faithfulness of heart, fills me with gratitude."

The letter specifically mentioned material aid the bishop had brought for the pontifical seminaries under the Cardinal's charge. But the two prelates were also united in common interest in the teaching of Christian doctrine, the cause of Pope Pius X and in Catholic Action. On his visits to Rome, the bishop had a personal friend as well as an eminent sponsor in Cardinal Pizzardo.

The 1950 pilgrimage to Riese was an unusually satisfying experience both for Pio Sarto's home town and for the Americans who visited it. Riese was an unspoiled little Italian town off the usual tourist-pilgrim beat. The arrival of the group from the United States was a festive occasion in which all the inhabitants took part. Bishop O'Hara took to the town at once and he was not long in winning the hearts of the priests and people. He found that the poverty of the place had prevented them from doing any work on the parish church, which had fallen into a rather sad state of disrepair since the day Giuseppe Sarto was baptized in it.

Bishop O'Hara asked the pastor, Monsignor Valentino Gallo, to have an estimate made of what it would cost to have the church restored to what it had been one hundred years before, when the future pope attended it. He promised to seek the aid of his colleagues on the episcopal committee of the Confraternity of Christian Doctrine in raising a fund for the restoration. On his return to the United States, he learned that the cost would be approximately five million lire, or $8,000.

By February, 1951, the generosity of his fellow prelates had enabled him to send a check for $5,000 to Cardinal Canali, of the Instituto Per Le Opera Di Religione, for forwarding to the pastor of Riese. The balance of the $8,000 was in Monsignor Gallo's hands before the beatification ceremonies of that summer.

When Bishop O'Hara returned to Riese at the time of the beatification ceremonies of June 3, 1951, he was welcomed as an adopted father, the *patrono* responsible for bringing their old church back to its former glory in time for the celebrations surrounding the beatification of its most famous parishioner.

The Americans who accompanied him on a third pilgrimage to Riese at the time of the 1954 canonization were treated to a spontaneous demonstration of the fact that the bishop of Kansas City had become something more than a mere visitor to the town. They descended from their buses with the trepidation, the feeling of intruding on someone's privacy, common to sensitive people in a strange place. But they were taken completely by surprise at the reaction of the villagers in the square when the bishop made his appearance. Heads turned quickly in his direction. Eyes lifted for a second look. Then wide smiles appeared, a handful of shouting children came tumbling to grab his coat, and old people stepped forward laughing and chattering their welcome as they knelt to kiss his ring. It looked more like a well-loved parish priest coming home after a long absence than anything else.

On June 2, 1951, Bishop O'Hara was present when the incorrupt body of Pius X, which had not been embalmed after the Pope's death in 1914, was placed in its new casket. On Sunday morning, June 3, the day of the beatification, he saw the body of Blessed Pius X placed above a temporary altar before the great altar of St. Peter's. He joined in the first prayers addressed by the Church *to* Blessed Pius instead of *for* him.

He took his pilgrimage of forty people that year, not only to the tomb and the birthplace of the new beatus but also to St. Mark's, the church from which Archbishop Sarto had ruled as Patriarch of Venice. In that city, the future Pope had engaged in several works, like the organization of catechetical instruction, the federation of Catholic Action organizations and the promoting of Catholic publications, which paralleled the similar activities fostered by the bishop of Great Falls and Kansas City. This visit increased the feeling of spiritual kinship with which Bishop O'Hara stood by, as assistant to the Pontifical Throne (an honor he had been granted by Pope Pius XII in 1949), while the reigning pontiff pronounced the solemn eulogy of his blessed predecessor.

That same pilgrimage to Rome brought Bishop O'Hara another honor—a worldwide acclamation of the Catholic rural life work he had begun single-handed in Oregon thirty years before. He attended the First International Catholic Rural Life Conference and was elected by the representatives of twenty nations the first president of the new international organization.

In 1954, Bishop O'Hara led another American pilgrimage to Rome for the canonization of St. Pius X, the man who had meant so much in his life, the saint he had worked so hard to make better known in the United States. It was a day of triumph, of fulfillment. He shared it with his patron and ideal in the Mass he celebrated at the tomb of the newly canonized Pope. He felt its echoes in the warm reception he received from the little people of Riese. And he brought it back with him to Kansas City, to his continuing work in the spirit of Pope St. Pius X.

CHAPTER XXIII

Honors, a Golden Jubilee
and More Activity

BEFORE THAT SAME YEAR, 1954, was over, Pope Pius XII showed Rome's appreciation of Father O'Hara's apostolic labors by raising him to the dignity of archbishop *ad personam*. The decree was dated and signed by the papal Secretary of State, Cardinal Montini.

Messages of congratulation came from people who had known Archbishop O'Hara, worked with him, served under him, through the forty-nine years of his priesthood and before. They covered a wide range of appreciation and praise. But the words that stood out from all the rest were spoken by Cardinal Samuel Stritch, on September 23, 1954, at the Immaculate Conception Cathedral in Kansas City. He was speaking before a crowded congregation and in the presence of archbishops and bishops from all over the United States gathered to pay tribute to the recipient of this new papal honor. The proclamation from Rome had just been read. It had recounted the principal accomplishments of the Bishop's life and announced his elevation to the new rank. When Cardinal Stritch rose to speak, many in the congregation were wondering what he would single out as the new archbishop's most distinctive achievement. He answered their thoughts by summing up his eulogy in these words: "We could say many things in congratulating him this morning but we think that we say it all when we say to him that under the inspiration of St. Pius X he has been and is the great catechist in the Church in the United States."

The reference to St. Pius X, the title "the great catechist in the Church in the United States," could not have been more nicely calculated to make Archbishop O'Hara feel that all his years of working had remained true to their inward goal.

The nature of this latest papal honor bestowed on Edwin Vincent O'Hara made it a singularly apt recognition of his achievements. Normally, the title of archbishop goes with the place rather than with the man; he wears it by virtue of heading an archdiocese. But the unusual distinction "archbishop *ad personam*" means just what it says. It is given to the person for reasons of personal worth. There is something of this idea of service to the Church-at-large in a passage from one of the congratulatory messages that came to Archbishop O'Hara on this occasion. A letter from Great Falls told of Cardinal Stritch speaking at the 1954 Golden Jubilee celebrations of the diocese. The Cardinal recalled that the diocese had been erected by St. Pius X and added ". . . and then you had Bishop Edwin O'Hara . . . whom you know we all feel belongs to the whole world."

A quick glance through the pile of messages that came to the new archbishop gives support to the Cardinal's words. It also has the effect of a series of flashbacks over the archbishop's priestly career. The pleasant note of informality it reveals in many of the letters from lay people speaks volumes for the warm personality of the dignitary addressed. And it affords glimpses of activities that have not been touched upon in this selection of events from a busy career.

One is struck by the variety of media through which the news reached the archbishop's host of friends. The letters often say "I read it in" . . . the Washington *Post*, the Philadelphia *Inquirer*, *The New York Times*, the Chicago *Tribune* and so on right across the country. It seems as if every major newspaper in the nation had considered this appointment important news.

The messages recalled friendships from Lanesboro to Kansas City. A layman, Thomas J. Geary, wrote from Chicago: "This humble individual knows the story of a young man and cleric who learned early to climb heights, like the hill to St. Patrick's church at Lanesboro."

Another layman, Thomas A. Woods, brought back the days when they were classmates at St. Thomas College: "there comes to mind a couplet I often heard you quote in the old days at St. Thomas.

> *'Ah well! For us all some sweet hope lies*
> *Far deeply hidden from human eyes.'* "

The Portland messages included one from a non-Catholic, Dr. Ralph A. Fenton, recalling AEF days in France of World War I: ". . . when you enlightened me on the great service of the little Cure of Ars at dinner in your convent garden."

A Eugene letter from another layman, George Campbell, was as amusing as to the point when it spoke of receiving ". . . a word photo of you from Kansas City, perfect without retouching, and one that those who know you can enjoy—'Bishop O'Hara has us holding our breath most of the time wondering what next . . . but he is a wonder worker.' "

The rural life movement was represented by some of its greatest names. Monsignor George J. Hildner wrote from Villa Ridge, Mo.: ". . . in the long story of your many services in the Church of America not the least should be your title as 'the founding father of the Catholic Rural Life Movement in the United States.' It was a happy day for our Catholic Rural Church when the Conference was born of your zeal and inspiration."

Monsignor Ligutti wired: "To our founder and honorary President we extend heartiest congratulations. If any one in the world deserves great honors it is you because of your work, vision, tenacity and leadership."

The confraternity and its works was the theme of many messages. In an obviously heartfelt greeting from Fort Wayne, Ind., Archbishop John F. Noll said: ". . . and I want you to know that having followed your career from the days of the American Federation of Catholic Societies, I have been edified by your zeal which through the blessing of God has wrought untold good to millions of American children who, otherwise, would not be receiving systematic religious instruction."

The warm tone in the congratulations from fellow members of the hierarchy conveyed the admiration which Bishop Stephen S. Woznicki, of Saginaw, Mich., summed up by saying: ". . . there are very few in the hierarchy that can claim equal achievements and surely none that can surpass them. . . ."

Cardinals Spellman and Mooney spoke of "well merited recognition of your great service to the Church" and "appropriate recognition of the noteworthy work you have done not only in your own diocese but across the country. . . ."

Archbishop Edwin V. Byrne, of Sante Fe, struck apt phrases in praising "your resourceful zeal and ability of organization."

From Rome, the Superior General of the Holy Cross Fathers, the Very Reverend Christopher O'Toole, referred to one of the many good works the archbishop had encouraged: ". . . I remember especially the great encouragement which you gave to Father Pat Peyton as he was starting on his rosary work."

Father Peyton himself wrote from Dublin: ". . . to thank you for all that you have done to help me and the Family Rosary Crusade ever since the very beginning."

A telegram from "Carlton and Evelyn Hayes" brought memories of the Christendom series of historical texts which the archbishop had projected under the editorship of the former ambassador to Spain and the work of Mrs. Hayes at the beginning of the parent-educator campaign.

When Sister Madeleva wrote from her president's office at St. Mary's College her message, like so many of the others, was as much a personal letter as a note of congratulations. It, too, referred to the archbishop's influence on good initiative: "We are all profoundly and justly proud . . . you kept your secret well during our recent visit . . . again let us share with you in the purple splendor of your way . . . at this moment we have registered for our School of Sacred Theology for the coming year, ten sisters of other communities and six laywomen, all excellent students so far as we know. This is a part of the fruit of your hands."

A number of the lay people who had been closely associated with the archbishop got a light touch into their congratulations. Mary Jane Sullivan and Catherine Bauer wanted to know: ". . . does this make you More Most Reverend— or is it Mostest Reverend?" An old friend in Kansas City, Mr. Louis Bressent, asked: "Do you remember the old rhyme

> *'Todjy, Todjy,*
> *I'm glad I knowed ye!'* "

Even the more formal official messages had a note of personal warmth in them. Cardinal Pizzardo, writing in his capacity as "Secretary of the Supreme S. Congregation of the Holy Office; Prefect of the S. Congregation of Seminaries and Universities," was evidently speaking as much as a friend as an official when he began his letter, "I read with great joy, in last evening's *Osservatore Romano*, that His Holiness has conferred on you the personal title of Archbishop, and I wish to be amongst the first to congratulate you and wish you *'ad multos annos.'* "

The Cardinal went on to express his pleasure "that the Holy Father so fittingly chose this year of the glorious canonization of St. Pius X to confer the title of Archbishop on you, as a recognition of all Your Grace has accomplished with tireless activity. . . ."

Taken all together, the messages speak for themselves. They tell of a respected prelate, an honored citizen, a beloved priest and a well-liked man.

Within a year, these tributes were to be repeated in a still wider range and in an even more formal manner. In October, 1955, the archbishop celebrated his Golden Jubilee as a priest and his Silver Jubilee as a bishop. He joined the two dates with that of the Diamond Jubilee of the diocese of Kansas City, put them into the month of the Rosary and centered them around Father Patrick Peyton's Family Crusade, the worldwide movement which he had helped start on its way.

The Jubilee messages and speeches would make a fair-size book which would be in itself a sufficient proof of Archbishop O'Hara's achievements in fifty years of priesthood. Most precious of the messages was a letter from the Vatican signed by His Holiness Pope Pius XII. The delicate lines of the autograph reminded the archbishop that he already had in his possession another letter addressed to himself and signed by the same hand—but in a different name. It was the last communication to arrive in the United States bearing the signature "Eugenio Pacelli, Secretary of State."

The Vatican's representative in the United States, Archbishop Cicognani, came to Kansas City to attest to Rome's appreciation of the jubilarian in person and in public. His two addresses revealed an intimate familiarity with the Archbishop's work. At the Jubilee Mass on October 28, he reviewed the history and importance of one aspect of that work, saying: "The two jubilees, sacerdotal and episcopal, of your beloved shepherd, Archbishop Edwin V. O'Hara, are echoed throughout the land because vast is the good that has been accomplished and notable are his merits. I select only one of them now, one that is of general interest in the Church, the project of the new translation of Sacred Scripture; to the Archbishop it was confided and he has directed and inspired it with indefatigable zeal." At the luncheon the same day, he chose an outline of the catechism and confraternity work to justify the conclusion, "His catechetical work has been vast, widely beneficial and magnificent."

The spokesman for his fellow prelates of the American episcopate was the Most Reverend Edward D. Howard, archbishop of Portland in Oregon. Archbishop Howard had been the jubilarian's classmate in the seminary at St. Paul, his archbishop during a decade of his Oregon pastorate, had consecrated him to the episcopacy in St. Mary's Cathedral, Portland, on that same feast of Saints Simon and Jude twenty-five years previously and was to have the sad duty of pronouncing his funeral sermon before another year could pass. His words at the Jubilee Mass were therefore based on a long and intimate knowledge of the man they eulogized.

In a sermon which linked Archbishop O'Hara's name with those of Cardinal Suhard in France and Cardinal Lercaro in Italy, he went beneath the surface to define some of the qualities that lay behind the pioneering accomplishments: ". . . I wish only to show how well he has sensed the needs of our day. I wish to bring out how fearlessly he has chosen new methods, how he has analyzed our problems, prayed and sought for their solution, and then proceeded to act."

He spoke of the archbishop's early encouragement of the lay apostolate over opposition from "the usual fears on the part of die-hards." He said that Archbishop O'Hara "was well aware of the teaching office of the priesthood, but he knew the layman could be the Church's champion once he had learned to speak."

Near the end of his sermon his former classmate, who was as well informed as anyone about the direction the archbishop's plans were taking, brought up "another project of Archbishop O'Hara's which we ought to consider this morning. It is not his exclusively, but his role in it has been outstanding. This does not surprise us, for it is a project that seeks to bring the Church closer to the world, and the world closer to the Church. I speak of the movement in recent years to put certain portions of the ritual into the language of the people. . . . We may thank Archbishop O'Hara that now the non-Catholic will know the Church better, even as the Catholic loves it more."

The actual anniversary was but the high point in a full year of jubilee celebrations and honors. The impressive mass of intelligent tribute to solid objective achievement must have been satisfying to the Archbishop. But it was far from making him feel that his work was finished. The Jubilee was not even a pause in his planning for further pioneer steps. On the contrary, the celebrations were so many occasions for a quiet word that would smooth the next trail he intended to break.

There were a number of stimulating items on next year's agenda: a national hymnal that might possibly provide a base for the longed-for reformation of popular church music; a national congress of the CCD which would bring together ten thousand people, including one hundred bishops, for four days of real work on the teaching of Christian doctrine; three world congresses—Rural Life scheduled for Santiago, Lay Apostolate to be planned for 1958 and, most important of all, an International Congress of Pastoral Liturgy at Assisi and Rome.

And running through all of them the reasonable hope of again being the sort of revolutionary St. Pius X had been and bringing about a further cautious advance in the matter of the laity and the liturgy.

So it was with the heart and zeal of an apostolic young priest that the seventy-four-year-old archbishop packed away his jubilee souvenirs and looked forward to the year 1956.

CHAPTER XXIV

Active to the End

DURING THE LAST MONTHS of Archbishop O'Hara's life, the matters he was working on were such as to project his name into the future. But circumstances arranged that he should, in a rather extraordinary resemblance to a farewell voyage, revisit the scenes of much of his early life.

The funeral of an old friend, Father Vincent Flynn, Rector of St. Thomas College, brought him back to the places he had known as a child and as a student. With his sister, Mrs. Anna Daniels, and his nephew, Father Robert O'Hara, he took the occasion to revisit Amherst township. He saw the old farm and the schoolhouse his father had built. He said Mass in Lanesboro, at St. Patrick's where he had been baptized and first offered the Holy Sacrifice. He walked again through the halls of St. Thomas and mingled with the seminarians at St. Paul's where Archbishop Ireland had ordained him priest.

An invitation to preach at Archbishop Howard's jubilee brought him to Portland. He offered Mass again in the cathedral where he had spent his first years as a priest, where he had been consecrated bishop. He renewed acquaintance with Sister Miriam Theresa, former Governor Oswald West and other colleagues in the fight for a minimum wage. He went to Eugene and said Mass in the church he had built. He traveled the roads of Lane County with some of the nuns who had taught his first religious vacation schools.

In other fields, however, his last months were linked to the past by continued activity rather than reminiscence. He was with them because he had never left them.

In Catholic rural life, for example, he contributed a foreword for *The Rural Life Prayer Book*, he answered a writer's request for help in a study of "Catholic Culture and Rural Life," he was engaged in correspondence about a new edition of his book *The Catholic Church and the Country Community*, he was delighted to learn of a vigorous revival of the devotion to St. Isidore he had planted in the early years, he was scheduled to give a talk on the opening day of the World Catholic Rural Life Conference in Santiago, Chile, and was looking forward to that occasion as a reunion with "his priests" in Latin America.

The catechism was still a present issue as he wrote to the publishers to ensure that a re-run of the revised Baltimore would have the correct additions on the new regulations on fasting, advised Miss Ellamay Horan on problems connected with her current catechetical writings, or exchanged letters on the teaching of Christian doctrine to the elementary grades with another old colleague, Father Aloysius Heeg, S.J.

His shepherding of the Bible translation brought him letters from Cardinal Fumasoni-Biondi praising Volume Three of the Old Testament and from Archbishop G. B. Montini inquiring from Milan about the progress of the work. It also kept him in constant touch with Fathers Louis Hartmann, C.SS.R. and Stephen Hardtegen, O.F.M., whose Catholic University headquarters is the coordinating center for the work of translation.

Another of the archbishop's lifelong interests, encouragement of the lay apostolate, also ran like a thread through the activities of this final year of his life. He went to New Orleans for the convention of Serra International which elected one of his Kansas City men, Mr. Norman Gordon, to its presidency, and spoke at the banquet on June 23. The Serra Club movement among Catholic laymen had held his admiration from the time he was first introduced to it by the Catholic publisher Mr. Frank Bruce. He was very pleased to have it in his diocese and placed great reliance on the solid type of men who were in it. He was especially pleased that the work of encouraging vocations was such an essential part of the organization that it became the only lay group aggregated to *The Pontifical Society for Priestly Vocations* with canonical status and a Cardinal Protector. He was also in correspondence during this time with at least four of the young people who had won his protection in their attempt to make the Kansas City *Sun Herald* a functioning Catholic daily. He was planning for American participation in the projected second world congress of the Lay Apostolate. He instituted the Pius X Medal as an award for laymen with a sustained record of outstanding work in the confraternity.

In Kansas City itself, he was carrying on with accustomed distinction his dual role of priest and citizen. At a gathering addressed by former President Harry S. Truman, he was awarded the Brotherhood Citation of the National Conference of Christians and Jews for "outstanding service in human relations."

His work as an educator was also recognized by an award in those last months. Brother Augustine Philip, president of Manhattan College, New York, announced on May 15 that Archbishop O'Hara would be the recipient of the de la Salle Medal, a distinction granted only rarely by the Christian Brothers "to recognize men who have made noteworthy contributions to education." The announcement of the award traced the archbishop's "long interest in and contribution to education" back to "his earliest assignment as superintendent of schools for the Archdiocese of Portland in Oregon." The formal presentation of the medal was to have taken place at the CCD congress in Buffalo.

That congress, held September 26-30, was one of two events around which Archbishop O'Hara was centering much of his planning and labor during his last months. The other was the International Congress of Pastoral Liturgy, held at Assisi and Rome, September 18-22.

He had leading parts to take in both and he spent months in detailed preparation for them. He saw in those two great gatherings following one upon the other an unparalleled opportunity for carrying certain suggestions to Rome and then returning to seek a mandate for taking practical steps towards implementing the suggestions in the United States.

His vision was as always protected by a prudent reticence about his specific plans. Even the men who shared some part of that vision, the men whose ideas he would shepherd into acceptance, could for the most part only guess at how much or how little of their enthusiasms he would find presently practical. But it is possible to find in the report he was taking to the Assisi-Rome congress some indication of the direction his thought was taking.

President of the congress was His Eminence, Caeteno Cardinal Cicognani, prefect of the Sacred Congregation of Rites, a prelate who had come to know Archbishop O'Hara very well through his brother, the Apostolic Delegate to the United States. The occasion was considered of such importance that it had been decided to have five cardinals as vice-presidents representing as many large divisions of the Catholic world. His Eminence, Edward Cardinal Mooney, archbishop of Detroit, was named vice-president for the English-speaking peoples. To Archbishop O'Hara was assigned the task of making a survey and report on the observance of the new Holy Week ceremonies in the United States in 1956.

Conducting such surveys in such a way that the reports turned into programs for future action was, as we have seen, something of a habit with Edwin O'Hara. This one started off much the same as the others and was apparently headed in a similar direction.

It began with a letter and memorandum going to all the ordinaries of the United States over Archbishop O'Hara's signature on the authority of Cardinal Cicognani and Cardinal Mooney. The memorandum asked for a report covering three phases of the subject: a) the steps taken to carry out the directions of the Sacred Congregation of Rites concerning the instruction of clergy and faithful in the proper use of the new *Ordo* and a fruitful participation in the ceremonies; b) the success enjoyed or difficulties encountered; c) suggestions and comments regarding possible changes in rubrics with a view to greater effectiveness of the Holy Week ceremonies in the *cura animarum*.

The first two phases had between them over a score of subdivisions to encourage sufficiently particularized reply. The third was an obvious invitation to any prelate who thought the liturgy should be "popularized" still more.

The response was prompt and very good. The memorandum went out at the end of April and before the end of June Archbishop O'Hara was able to report to Cardinal Mooney that the replies of ninety ordinaries had been collated by a special committee of two of the country's leading liturgists, Father Godfrey Diekmann, O.S.B., editor of *Worship*, and Father Michael A. Mathis, C.S.C., director of Liturgy Program, University of Notre Dame.

The reports left no doubt that the leaders of the Church in America were overwhelmingly in favor of the changes and the great increase they had brought in lay participation in the Holy Week ceremonies. There were, however, a few who would have preferred the Holy See to make the whole *Ordo Instauratus* permissive rather than mandatory. But the majority indicated that they would like even further changes in the same direction.

This is clearly seen in the list of "Chief Recommendations in Reports of Holy Week Services Sent by Ordinaries" which Archbishop O'Hara finally carried with him to present to the congress as a fruit of his consultations with Cardinal Mooney and others on the study analysis made by Fathers Diekmann and Mathis.

After some specific suggestions for each of the three Great Days, two recommendations were listed under the heading "Vernacular":

"All extended responses calling for the participation of the people should be in the vernacular. This suggestion includes: the Palm Sunday Processional hymn, the Litanies, the Pater Noster on Good Friday, the *Improperia* and the Lessons at the Vigil to which the people are expected to listen. If the Exultet, which is very long, and the blessing of the water were in the vernacular, it would serve to make the Vigil service seem shorter.

"Renewal of baptismal vows in the vernacular has had the startling effect of showing the desirability of more participation for the people with vernacular responses in the liturgy. People lose contact with the ceremonies in long readings in Latin. The mother tongue during the renewal of baptismal vows transforms the congregation from spectators to participants. Language difficulties make the participation of the faithful in responses and chants mediocre."

The final recommendation, under the heading "Missionary Needs," probably sounded to many the most radical of all. But it asked no more than a return to early Christian practice:

"The inspiring Liturgy of Holy Week should be adaptable not merely to well established parishes but also to the thousands of towns and villages in our rural areas where there may not be even a chapel. 'The Church at Prayer' through the Liturgy should bear witness to Christ in every village through the restored 'ministry of the Diaconate,' combining the functions of catechist and prayer leader."

As it was with the suggested catechism changes—which were also made by competent persons acting under authority of the bishops and out of their advice—we find a strong resemblance between these recommendations and Archbishop O'Hara's own thinking.

And there are indications in other correspondence of those same months that the archbishop had hopes, and definite ideas, for working through the confraternity toward greater participation by the laity in the liturgy.

This correspondence had to do with preparing for the Buffalo congress of the CCD. Although the complex work of arranging the program was done out of the National Office in Washington, the archbishop took more than a merely supervising part in it. In addition to helping design the overall plan, he frequently offered specific suggestions—even including discussion outlines and suggested readings—for work groups in which he was particularly interested at the moment.

For one of these work groups, headed by a fellow bishop, he suggested a study of canon law with regard to lay participation in liturgical functions. When the national office submitted the agenda for another group, he appended two pages of "Supplemental Suggestions" to his reply which also said, "I would like to have some special consideration given the function of the liturgy in catechetics and also the place of kerygmatics in the catechetical process."

Interest in the laity and the liturgy was also behind his hope that the congress would bring to publication stage the work on a national hymnal he had started on its way in 1951. At that time, he had appointed Father John C. Selner, S.S., president of the St. Gregory Society, and Dr. Clifford A. Bennett, director of the Gregorian Institute, co-chairmen of a temporary hymnal committee. Three years later, four surveys of music and texts had been completed and a permanent hymnal committee set up in three main divisions: music, literary and general. These committees included people like Monsignor Thomas Quigley, superintendent of schools for the Chicago archdiocese, Father Richard Ginder, F.A.G.O., editor of *The Priest,* Mr. Paul Hume, music critic of *The Washington Post,* Sister M. Madeleva, C.S.C., president of St. Mary's College, and the English Jesuit, Father Clifford Howell.

The direction of this work was in some ways as difficult and as delicate as that of the catechism. But it was approaching acceptable completion, though as late as the day before his departure for Europe the archbishop was writing to invite yet another expert to join in the discussions at Buffalo. One of the suggestions Archbishop O'Hara made to this committee had to do with singing the Mass in the vernacular.

When the archbishop left Kansas City on September 6 (his seventy-fifth birthday), his head was full of plans and his heart brimming with quiet confidence that some of them would come to maturity.

He was leaving behind him a number of "beginnings" right in his own city and diocese. New Year's Day had seen the formal opening of the renovated cathedral. The renovation had been undertaken, in order to retain a building which was an historic landmark in the city, against the advice of those who said it was impossible to repair and modernize such an unsuitable structure. Now it had been completed with the help of Miss Charlton Fortune whose splendid mozaic of Mary Immaculate dominated a tasteful, well-lighted, fireproof, airy and still devotional interior. A Pius X chapel behind the main altar, also designed by the founder of the Monterey Guild, was formally dedicated on July 1 with the first awards of the newly created Pius X Medal to lay people who had been outstanding for at least five years in confraternity work.

One of the last things the archbishop did in Kansas City was make arrangements for another St. Pius X oratory. It was to be a crypt under the chapel of the Benedictine Sisters of the Perpetual Adoration, a modest little shrine to the canonized pope after whom he had patterned his life. And he pointed to the place at one side of the bare little basement room where he wanted his own remains to be placed when that time should come.

On August 29, another change on which the archbishop had been in consultation with his Metropolitan, Archbishop Ritter, took effect. The Apostolic Delegate announced that Pope Pius XII had decreed a new territorial division of the ecclesiastical province of St. Louis. The change created two new dioceses and joined part of the former diocese of St. Joseph to part of the former diocese of Kansas City under the title Kansas City-St. Joseph. Archbishop O'Hara became Ordinary of Kansas City-St. Joseph and the former Apostolic Administrator of St. Joseph, the Most Reverend John P. Cody, S.T.D., was named as his coadjutor bishop, with right of succession. His former auxiliary bishop in Kansas City, the Most Reverend Joseph M. Marling, who had come in 1947 from his office as provincial of the Precious Blood Fathers to take much of the burden of administering the diocese from his shoulders, was appointed first bishop of Jefferson City.

So it was in an atmosphere of change that Archbishop O'Hara stepped on the plane for New York. He was met there by his old friend, Father John Forest, O.F.M., of St. Anthony's Guild. He celebrated his birthday evening with a combination of reminiscence and planning for the future at the Franciscan farm Umbria in New Jersey. When he boarded the plane next day en route for Old Umbria with his secretary, Monsignor Thomas J. Crowell of Kansas City, he had all his preparations behind him and his plans for the big days ahead clear-cut in his mind.

He would stay with the Fathers of Sion in Paris. Then on to Milan, the birthplace of the confraternity, for a talk with Archbishop Montini. Then Rome and six days of meetings and conversations, discussion and planning with friends like Cardinals Cicognani and Pizzardo, the scholars at the Pontifical Biblical Institute and others.

All that he hoped for from those talks will never be known.

We do know that he planned full participation in the Congress of Pastoral Liturgy, then an immediate return to New York and straight on the same day to Buffalo where he would have two days of preparation for the opening of the CCD congress.

But death interrupted the schedule at Milan. The archbishop was taken suddenly by a heart attack on the morning of Tuesday, September 11, the day he was to have seen Archbishop Montini. He had received absolution twice from Monsignor Crowell and a priest from the nearest parish was in the room within minutes of his death to administer Extreme Unction. Archbishop Montini came immediately to the hotel with his auxiliary bishop and secretary.

The archbishop of Milan, successor to St. Charles Borromeo, sang the Requiem Mass for another apostle of Christian doctrine. The flowers heaped on the coffin that lay before the altar included a large bouquet from America's ambassadress to Italy, Mrs. Clare Boothe Luce, a personal friend of Archbishop O'Hara's and a member of his first national lay committee of the CCD.

The body was flown back to Kansas City for solemn funeral services and burial in the so recently selected crypt which now had to be rushed to completion.

The funeral was a final and fitting testimony to the esteem Edwin O'Hara's life had won from his family, his friends, his fellow citizens of all faiths and his Church.

The official flag of Kansas City was flown at half-mast, the first time that tribute had been paid any man other than a president of the United States. His friend Harry S. Truman wrote, "He was one of the finest men I have ever known." Thirty-three members of the American episcopate—an extraordinary number for a funeral since appointments have to be cancelled and schedules disrupted without due notice—came to show their respect for their colleague even to the grave. The messages of condolence that came to Mrs. Daniels and to Bishop Cody were sorrowing repetitions of the congratulations that had been jubilantly poured out such a short time ago. They came from the Holy Father himself, from the Apostolic Delegate, from prelates, priests and the laity of three continents. Perhaps Monsignor Ligutti's wire to Mrs. Daniels best summed up the burden of all: ". . . our beloved brother, our friend, our founder. A great churchman because he was a great man."

Many masses were said in the cathedral and in the adjoining St. Pius X chapel while the body lay in state. One of them was more moving than the rest. It was a simple Mass, a quiet Mass, a family Mass. It was offered by Archbishop O'Hara's nephew, Father Robert O'Hara, a son of that brother James who had stayed on the old homestead after the mother's death. The servers were Father Robert's brothers, Michael and James. Attending were their sister Sister Edwin Marie, S.N.J.M., the archbishop's sister and companion for so many years, Mrs. Anna Daniels, and two daughters of the archbishop's brother Robert. Preparing in the sacristy for his part in the funeral ceremonies was James O'Hara's son, Father Robert's nephew Edwin, a seminarian of the third generation from Owen O'Hara. The Mass was an unspoken promise that the tradition Owen O'Hara and Margaret Nugent had brought to that farm in Amherst township, the tradition Archbishop O'Hara had exemplified so splendidly, would be carried on.

Archbishop Howard's funeral sermon was as fine and as sincere a compliment as could have been devised. It was as daring as it was simple and direct. As it developed, the congregation was overwhelmed at the majesty of the tribute it implied. The archbishop of Portland simply recited the promises the Church exacts of candidates for the office of bishop in the rite of consecration and then showed how the words might have been shaped to describe exactly what Archbishop O'Hara had done with his life.

". . . will you, by word and example, teach the people for whom you were ordained, all that you know of the divine Scriptures? . . ." As the promises followed each other, one almost gasped at the realization that this amounted to a public examination of conscience. Over how many people could parallel words be spoken? What greater tribute could one pay the dead?

On the day of the archbishop's funeral, the International Congress of Pastoral Liturgy opened in Assisi. Liturgists from all over the Catholic world listened as the report Archbishop O'Hara had worked upon so diligently was read for him by Auxiliary Bishop Leo F. Dworschak of Fargo, N. D.

At the Buffalo congress the following week he was present, not only in the tributes paid him, in the memorial Mass said for him, but even more in the very existence of the big, enthusiastic and eminently successful congress itself.

It was true there were many profound and revealing tributes. The profound ones elaborated on a theme Bishop Joseph A. Burke of Buffalo stated with simple grandeur in his welcoming address: "Archbishop O'Hara built the Confraternity. It is his masterpiece." The revealing ones told something of the archbishop's early struggle to convince others that such an organization was both desirable and feasible. The Most Reverend John M. Gannon, Archbishop-Bishop of Erie, gave first-hand evidence of this when he presided over a session on "Lay Participation in the Confraternity Instruction Program." He admitted frankly that he had gone to that meeting of the bishops which saw the appointment of an episcopal committee for the confraternity as a member of the opposition. Even when he had heard Bishop O'Hara describe his vision of an organization such as they had now rising where there then was nothing, he did not believe it was possible. "But I so much wanted to believe that it could happen," he added, "that I was all in favor of letting Bishop O'Hara go ahead and try."

A walk through the Hotel Statler during those four days proved how well Bishop O'Hara had gone ahead and tried. And what one saw there was the real tribute the Buffalo congress paid to the memory of Archbishop Edwin O'Hara, the real sense in which he continued to be present among them.

In one room, the best of North America's Catholic biblical scholars were discussing the Dead Sea Scrolls and their possible significance to the work of translation. In another Sister N. Angelica, S.C., was talking on "Newer Tools and Approaches in Religious Instruction of the Blind Child." A number of rooms were given over to lay training courses in which veteran lay teachers experienced in confraternity work, from university professors to kindergarten teachers, were teaching other lay teachers how to go out and teach still other laymen how to teach religion. There were twice a day sessions of work groups on topics such as: the Apostolate of Good Will, Radio Apostolate, Television Apostolate, the Parish High School, Use of Released Time, Parent-Educator Program, Popularizing Bible Reading, Religious Discussion Clubs, Religious Education of Mentally Retarded Children, the Blind, the Deaf, and Migrant Workers. There were separate Spanish and English work groups on inter-American relations. The new hymnal was taking shape in one room and a program for Catholics at secular universities in another.

Active confraternity workers from every state in the union and from a dozen other countries were exchanging information and catching each other's enthusiasm about experiences in the same worthwhile work.

All of them were obviously in earnest. They were really working at this duty, this privilege of imbuing themselves with the principles and practices of their faith in order that they might make the impact of that faith felt all through the world in which they lived.

This was Archbishop Edwin O'Hara's monument. And it may well be that this picture of men at work because he had set them to work is the best way to leave the story of Edwin Vincent O'Hara, a story in which death is an incident, not the end.

CARMELITE MONASTERY
Beckley Hill
Barre, Vt., 05641

DATE BORROWED

————————————————————
————————————————————
————————————————————
————————————————————
————————————————————
————————————————————
————————————————————
————————————————————
————————————————————
————————————————————
————————————————————
————————————————————
————————————————————
————————————————————
————————————————————
————————————————————
————————————————————
————————————————————